God, Guns, and a Girl

TRIGGERING TRANSFORMATION

God, Guns, and a Girl

TRIGGERING TRANSFORMATION

GRACIE RAE FAITH

God, Guns, and a Girl © 2024 by Gracie Rae Faith.
All rights reserved.

Published by Author Academy Elite
PO Box 43, Powell, OH 43065
www.AuthorAcademyElite.com

All rights reserved. This book contains material protected under international and federal copyright laws and treaties. Any unauthorized reprint or use of this material is prohibited. No part of this book may be reproduced or transmitted in any form or by any means, electronic or mechanical, including photocopying, recording, or by any information storage and retrieval system, without express written permission from the author.

Identifiers:
LCCN: 2023923440
ISBN: 979-8-88583-300-4 (paperback)
ISBN: 979-8-88583-301-1 (hardback)
ISBN: 979-8-88583-302-8 (e-book)
Available in paperback, hardback, and e-book.

Scriptures marked (AMP) are taken from the Amplified® Bible (AMP), Copyright © 2015 by The Lockman Foundation. Used by permission. lockman.org

Scriptures marked (ESV) are taken from the ESV® Bible (The Holy Bible, English Standard Version®), © 2001 by Crossway, a publishing ministry of Good News Publishers. Used by permission. All rights reserved."

Scriptures marked (ISV) are taken from INTERNATIONAL STANDARD VERSION, copyright© 1996-2008 by the ISV Foundation. All rights reserved internationally.

Scriptures marked (KJV) are taken from the King James Version of the Bible.

Scripture quotations marked (NIV) are taken from the Holy Bible, New International Version®, NIV®. Copyright © 1973, 1978, 1984, 2011 by Biblica, Inc.™ Used by permission of Zondervan. All rights reserved worldwide. www.zondervan.com

Scriptures marked (NKJV) are taken from the New King James Version®. Copyright © 1982 by Thomas Nelson. Used by permission. All rights reserved.

Scripture quotations marked (NLT) are taken from the *Holy Bible*, New Living Translation, copyright ©1996, 2004, 2015 by Tyndale House Foundation. Used by permission of Tyndale House Publishers, Carol Stream, Illinois 60188. All rights reserved.

Some names and identifying details have been changed to protect the privacy of individuals.

Contents

Introduction	1
LEARNING to DEFINE	7
1. It all Begins with God!	8
2. It's about Growing with Grace	12
3. Projection–It's Powerful	21
4. It's about Getting Burned	26
5. WOW—Why Hide "It"?	31
6. It's on to Business	36
7. It's the Pits!	45
8. It's Out of the Pit and into Sales!	49
9. It Explodes!	52
10. It Returns!	66
11. It Continues!	70
12. It Takes Practice	73
13. It Changes!	85

14. It's Colorful and Stylish!	97
15. It's a Chain Reaction!	101
16. It Was That First Bite!	108
17. It's Worth Trying	116
18. It's the Hunt that's Challenging	120
19. It's Time to Party	125
20. Obviously, It's Blind	134
Takeaways: Define	141
TEACHING to DESIGN	145
21. It's Off to the Races!	147
22. It's Girl Powered!	151
23. It's Trips and Turns	157
24. It's Outside Invasions	161
25. It's the Big 4-0	166
26. Is It Techy, Touchy, or Both?	172
27. It's Supposed to Stay in Vegas!	175
28. Which RUT Is It?	183
29. It's Elevated	186
Takeaways: Design	191
PRACTICING to ALIGN	195
30. It Remains a Choice	196

31. It's Birdy Dancing!	199
32. It's All in the Name	207
33. It's an "I" Conundrum	212
34. It's Forgiveness with a Twist	223
35. It's the Secrets We Don't Keep	228
36. It's No Longer a Crime Scene	232
Takeaways: Align	235
REPEATING to REFINE	237
37. It's Marching Madness	238
38. It Overflows	244
39. It's Tongue Twisting Victory	251
40. It's More Than Miraculous	260
41. It's One More Day	266
42. It's Switching	271
43. It's Something Else	279
44. It Never Crossed My Mind	289
45. Time, It's Running Out	293
Takeaways: Refine	327
46. With God It Never Ends!	329
About the Author	331

Introduction

In the beginning, God created the heavens and the earth.

—Genesis 1:1 (NKJV)

After nearly 20 years of helping build a company into a major national player in our industry, after taking us from a paper-and-fax office to a digital powerhouse, after moving from top salesperson to training teams of top salespeople... I was staring at a letter explaining that I no longer had a job.

Excuse me, what?

How could something like this happen? The letter insisted it was a strategic decision that had nothing to do with my performance, but I couldn't help thinking back to a bad night in Vegas, a moody bar, a broken heart, and dancing a little too closely with the one I was with... who happened to be a client.

I loved my work and had given so much of my life to this company; I hardly knew who I was outside of my career. I considered myself a child of God and loyal employee of A+ Sports, a spiritual and temporal identity. Take away the temporal identity, though, and I didn't feel like a whole person.

I don't want to be too dramatic. I still had fantastic friends and the love and support of my parents, and I wasn't exactly thrown to the curb—I had savings and a severance package. Still, it was going to take me a while to shift my mindset.

But maybe not as long as you'd expect. By the end of the year, I was dancing and laughing and excited about where my life and career were going. What changed? Well, that's the story of this book!

Welcome! My website says I'm an executive leadership coach and an organizational development consultant, which is a business jargon way of simplifying something complicated by using long words. What I really do is help turn chaos into results in people's lives and businesses. How do I do that? By guiding people through a process that unearths the deep emotional and spiritual pains that keep them stuck in both their personal and business growth.

The principles are not complicated, but the work itself is. It took years of education and trial and error (and some more error) to develop the insight and intuition required for this work, and that's the story I want to tell.

You are about to embark on a fun and enlightening experience! My hope is that you will find the journey relatable and the content so unique you'll be unable to put it down and compelled to share it with everyone you know. I learn best through stories and examples, and I find my clients really value stories and examples, so the best way I can help more people is not to spend a lot of time explaining my system but to tell my stories.

My intention is to use transparency and humor to provoke thought—positively impacting the life of anyone who invests their precious time to read it. My mission is to be 100% helpful and 0% harmful. Through sharing my faults and triumphs as a female leader, perhaps you can vicariously learn lessons from my experience that will propel your relationships and leadership skills to new heights.

As the "girl" in this book, I write under the pseudonym Gracie Rae Faith for several reasons. First, it represents important pillars of my identity. Second, it also coincides with my reality: "Faith" is a family name. Last and most importantly, I want to respect and protect all the players—whether you see them as sinners or saints—and draw the focus to the meaning of the events. The firearms industry, where I spent most of my career, is a small world, and some folks may try to guess who is who, but hopefully they will be excited to learn more about my story and feel I represented them well.

For as long as I can remember, I've been fascinated by humans and closely observed and analyzed their behavior. I wasn't judging; I was genuinely interested in a person's words, habits, actions, and thoughts as clues to why they said and did what they did. I witnessed that understanding others' behavior with an eye toward understanding encourages peace and patience toward them rather than breeding annoyance over misunderstood differences.

That fascination, at one point, turned into a *consuming passion*.

In 2008, my father strongly encouraged me to follow my dreams and launch an independent consulting business. In 2010, God blessed us by breathing life into this dream, shortly before my father's earthly life came to an end. Given my lifelong fascination, teaching *behavior* became the cornerstone of that business venture. My fulfillment comes from hearing, "Your stories and lessons changed my life!"

"Replacing Chaos with Results" became my trademark and company tagline. "Transforming relationships" is my sweet spot. Those gifts provided the privilege of creating growth/leadership/succession strategies with clients, both inside and outside the Shooting Sports Industry (the more politically correct title for the firearms industry—shortened to "guns" to better suit the title of this book).

This book is for anyone who ever felt out of place in their relationships or career or for anyone who feels stuck, whether early or late in their career. Movement means growth, and growth requires insight and struggle, and surviving the struggle requires having good stories to hold onto and to offer hope.

As you read the following narrative, you will find many stories that will trigger memories and ideas of your own. That's great! If you still need help, you'll find prompts at the end of each of the four main sections to help you along.

The sections follow my four-part model for growth: Define, Design, Align, and Refine. You can probably make some educated guesses about what these mean. Again, the concepts aren't difficult—the execution is! That's why I'm not going to tell you that you can simply read this book, follow the process, and—voila!—results! I do believe you can have breakthroughs and begin to free yourself from whatever holds you back if you work to apply what I teach here, but I'm going to do something you're not supposed to do in a book like this: Tell you the book alone won't be enough; you need to do it with someone else.

That person could be a coach or consultant like me, obviously, but there's only so much of me to go around. (That's why I wrote this book in the first place!) It could also be a therapist, your leadership team, or a close friend. Part of the growth I see in people is when they feel both seen and heard. So, take this book as a spur to action, not the action itself.

This book is dedicated to my family, with a special focus on my mom. I was overly inquisitive about details from a young age, and her response to my bombardment of questions was often, "Honey, are you writing a book? If so, leave those details out, and make it a mystery." I've told more about myself here than I ever thought I would, but I think I honored my mother and didn't talk out of school about anyone else.

It takes a magnitude of people and positive influence to convert a vision into reality. Many of the people who were pillars in my life are incorporated in the story that lies ahead. Those not mentioned are carved on my grateful heart.

In my world, God is the author of all Creation. Therefore, no matter what I think or write, He gets all the praise, glory, and honor—top billing, so to speak. If your world differs from mine, I hope you'll keep reading anyway, as it's my desire to be a respecter of all people and their opinions. My theory: If we were all the same, life would be void of inspiration and adventure. This girl enjoys a little fun.

This book represents the way I redeemed my time during the COVID-19 shutdowns of 2020 and 2021. I'm honored to share my story of how God empowered a girl from a small town to connect to and relate with wonderful people across the United States. I pray this story adds laughter, love, and joy to your day and abundant blessings that trigger transformation in your life!

LEARNING to DEFINE

The first step to getting unstuck and experiencing growth is to define the problems you need to solve. This may sound easy at first. "I feel stuck," you might say, or "I never seem to have enough time," or "I'm not making enough money," or "I'm not sure what the next stage of my career will be." That all may be true, but they are not a deep enough description of the problem. Instead, they are more like symptoms of your problem.

In the Define phase, we explore what makes you tick and uncover the emotional and spiritual barriers that keep you from feeling confidence and clarity. The goal here is to answer the question, *What is causing me to get stuck?*

The best way I know to help people achieve insight into themselves is to tell stories about myself and invite them to reflect on their own experiences. So, as you read about little Gracie, think about your own childhood and the forces and events that shaped you.

At the end of this section, we'll bring it all together before moving on to phase two, Design.

Chapter One
It all Begins with God!

> *"For I know the plans I have for you," declares the LORD, "plans to prosper you and not to harm you, plans to give you hope and a future."*
> —Jeremiah 29:11 (NIV)

Once upon a time, God gifted a woman named Faith with a baby girl shining so brightly with grace she could only be named Gracie Rae.

Gracie's father was a strong, handsome, honey of a man. Most of the time, he remained calm, cool, and collected—that is, until he watched too many politicians on TV. Then he would be tempted to swear like the apostle Peter.

Her father was a faithful man who kept his thoughts about God private except when he and Momma Faith held deep, intellectual conversations at home. There was one preacher he seemed to enjoy, however, and he didn't mind quoting him. Gracie often heard her father smile and say, "Ole Freddy says...." Very wise, her father shared his wisdom consistently yet sparingly, which made it easy to remember.

Two of his favorite sayings were: *Be careful what you wish for; you just might get it*, and *It's all going according to plan*. Gracie found lifelong truth and comfort in her father's words of wisdom.

Her father was great at making up nicknames for people—a trait that she picked up on herself and would use to conceal the identities of the characters in the stories she concocted. Over time, Gracie most often called her dad "Pops" or "Poppsie." Gracie loved to play the "switcheroo name game" with Momma Faith daily. Most days, Gracie's greeting started with the default, "Hi, Mommadopolis" or, "Hi Moppsie" or, "Hi Mops."

Although Gracie's parents ultimately enjoyed a successful marriage, it had taken them a previous attempt or two with others to achieve perfection with one another. So, Gracie had two older brothers: "Pi," who lived with them, and "Pudding," who occasionally visited. Gracie also liked to sing the "Name Game" song, the one that goes "banana fana fo fana," but she couldn't use her brother's real name because it would require her to cuss.

Pi was ten years older than Gracie. He was artistic, brilliant, and exceptionally good-looking; he deserves a book or series of books dedicated to his wild adventures. Pi enjoyed torturing Gracie with his big eye. That is, he'd painted a huge "seeing eye" on his bedroom wall, which little Gracie could observe from the adjoining kitchen. From the time she could walk until he left home, Pi would call little Gracie's attention to the *huge eye* and then tell her, "The eye is watching you all the time … always watching." Little Gracie was terrified and would pray to God for protection and then follow Moppsie around the house holding onto the bottom of her sweatshirt for safety.

In Pi's defense, Moppsie had always taken a "rule with an iron fist" management style with him, and perhaps that made him want to feel powerful elsewhere. By comparison, Mommy's evil eye was sufficient to keep Gracie in line.

Scared as she was, Gracie never snitched. Instead, she prayed and sought safety with Moppsie, and later she forgave her brother for the teasing and harassment. Yet she couldn't forget the generous heaping of fear that he dished out for the first six years of her little life, and though it formed a space between her and her brother, she worried that if she confronted him she would lose her relationship with him.

It was only years later, when Gracie had matured and found a solid ground for her identity that she was able to talk to Pi. He made a comment to her over the phone about his childhood, and Gracie finally expressed her feelings about his behavior and her childhood. She let go of her list of his transgressions against her so fast that it felt like she was hitting her brother with a battering ram. Pi, normally such an expressive guy, kept quiet through her barrage. Then, as the truly loving brother he really was, he replied with these beautiful words: "I am so sorry."

With tears streaming down her face from the immediate emotional release, Grace asked Pi if he understood the terror she had felt. "How could you do that to a little kid?" she implored.

"I thought I was being funny," he responded simply.

The truth had come to light, and (no surprise) they each had a very different experience of what had happened. But now that they could talk about it, love abounded, and Gracie became free to tell her story to help others!

Chapter Two
It's about Growing with Grace

The LORD is my shepherd; I shall not want.
—Psalm 23:1 (NKJV)

Moppsie's momma lived in a lovely home behind their house, and Gracie adored her Gramma Nanny. While Moppsie and Poppsie worked, Nanny did a top-notch job of caring for Pi and Gracie. She also executed the day-to-day operations of the Faith household. Nanny was exceptional at cooking, cleaning, pie-baking, and laundry, but most importantly, she was a fabulous shepherd for her grandchildren!

God blessed Gracie with all the resources she required to thrive in the earthly realm: the right timing, the right people, and powerful protection, all courtesy of the Holy Spirit that filled her. Just how the Holy Spirit related to God and Jesus was tricky for young Gracie, who wanted to know the how and why of God. She came up with an analogy that helped her. The Trinity was like her tricycle: It took all three wheels working together to move her little body.

Gracie would become fascinated with the number three. Biblically, three is considered a "holy" number. It not only represents the Father, Son, and Holy Spirit, but also divine completeness, new life, and harmony.

Even as a child, Gracie was clear on her love priorities: first God, Jesus, and the Holy Spirit (her Holy Tricycle); then Moppsie, Poppsie, and Nanny (her Parental Trinity); then, everyone else in the universe. (She didn't want to leave anyone out.)

Faith was always very important to Gracie; it was part of the air she breathed. It wasn't until she was over 40 and on a blind date that she learned she was "one of those," as he described her. He had been talking about his faith and how he was "born again," meaning he had a major conversion event. Gracie, by contrast, had simply grown into her faith by age three or four; there was no conversion event. She decided "one of those" meant rare, like a precious gem.

You may be asking: *How could she remember back to age three or four?* Well, Gracie was blessed with a fantastic memory. As an adult, she still held a clear vision of being sent to bed after 7:30 p.m. at four years old, frustrated with Moppsie because it was still light out!

She vividly recalled getting on her knees, placing her hands on the headboard, and praying for protection over her family. Specifically, on that one occasion, Gracie prayed that Nanny would live a long, healthy life, so they could be together on earth for as long as possible and then into eternity.

She felt like Jesus was with her, and joy filled her little body as she heard Him say, "Your prayer is answered, my child!"

It was—and will be!

Nanny was full of wise words and profound phrases that she often shared in a theatrical way. Several of Nanny's siblings had put that same strand of creative DNA to use on vaudeville stages. Since Nanny lived in a house behind Gracie's, visits from her comical aunts, uncles, and cousins were frequent.

Quietly holding on to Moppsie's shirttail allowed Gracie to absorb every word she heard her mom say —especially "Children should be seen and not heard," and "Be careful what you say, little pitchers have big ears." Gracie fully understood she was the pitcher, and listening to/obeying her Mommy paid off.

Nanny liked to repeat, "Fool's names and fool's faces are often found in public places." Gracie imagined old movies where pictures of criminals were posted in post offices. Obviously, Nanny made an "impression" on Gracie.

Gracie's Uncle George was her absolute favorite. An entrepreneur, he gave Poppsie wisdom about the stock market and Gracie intel on how to be both passionate and expressive. Impressed by him, Gracie fixated on his words and actions.

Around age 5, after a day of sitting next to Uncle George, she had a vivid dream. In the dream, she drew what appeared to be a tic-tac-toe diagram. Then, she drew a border around the outside. Nine equal boxes arranged in three equal stacks appeared. Gracie saw herself coloring the top right box red, the box below it orange, and so on until all the outside boxes were a different bright color. It appeared she was about to color the middle box when she woke up.

She got out of bed, found a blank piece of paper and her box of crayons, and recreated what she'd seen in her dream. When she got to the center box, her instinct told her to color it gray, yet when she finished, that box looked bland and boring to her. As she looked around the room to think, a power outlet snagged her eye, and she drew what she saw, which ended up looking like two vertical eyes and a surprised mouth.

A few minutes later, Uncle George appeared in real life. Looking at her color box diagram, Grace wrote "Uncle George" in the orange-colored box because, to her, he seemed a mixture of red when passionately pounding the kitchen table and a sunny yellow as he poignantly expressed his point of view. Then, she put the diagram in a hidden compartment of an antique dresser that previously belonged to Nanny.

This event began Gracie's permanent association between dreams, games, color, and observable behavior.

"A real hoot!" is how Grace later remembered childhood visits from her adult relatives. Standing on propane pipes outside the house, below the kitchen window, she watched her relatives practice their vaudeville acts. She got bonus points for being neither seen nor heard; her little eyes and big ears were filled with belly-shaking fun and laughter. Quietly paying attention to all the details became one of her greatest gifts!

On Saturday mornings, Moppsie found her considerate little girl in her Dr. Denton's PJs, sitting on the floor, with her eyes just inches from the TV screen so she could hear with the sound turned way down so she wouldn't bother anyone. She was engrossed in Looney Tunes, learning how to hunt a wascally wabbit, give a permanent hairdo to an orange monster, out-run the complex snares of a coyote, and promote a frog who was privately extroverted and publicly introverted. When she realized a sheepdog could incapacitate a wolf with a single punch, it wasn't mere entertainment; she was mentally documenting every detail to navigate her real life.

On a Saturday night seven nights after her color box dream, Gracie had another vivid dream. She saw her little body getting out of bed and walking to the kitchen door, just as her brother Pi was arriving home. Upon his entrance, she approached him and punched him, as hard as she could, right in the tummy. Then, she turned around and went back to bed.

Her dream wasn't cartoonish, it *felt real*. She remembers crawling back into bed and mentally asking, *Am I asleep or awake?*

The next morning, she awoke to Moppsie, Poppsie, and Nanny in the kitchen, excitedly exchanging "I can't believe she did that's" mixed in with a new term, *sleepwalking*, and wondered who they were talking about. Turns out, it was her, and she really did punch Pi in the stomach. *No wonder that felt so real*, she thought.

Although well-mannered, quiet, and compassionate, little Gracie developed a strong will. She did not like to be told what to do. Early on, Moppsie discovered that if she appealed to Gracie's compassionate side by asking her to help, rather than giving orders, her child-raising flowed much more smoothly.

One day, Moppsie *told* her, "Go pick some strawberries from the garden." Gracie knew that Moppsie had worked hard all day, but she just didn't feel like doing that chore. She also didn't want to tell Mommy no. So, she walked into Pi's bedroom, which was right off the kitchen, put her arms up as if she were on a cross, and pretended she was glued to the door.

"Mommy, I can't pick strawberries right now 'cuz I'm stuck to this door," Gracie exclaimed.

Moppsie replied: "Okay, Gracie, if you're stuck and can't pick the strawberries for Mommy, then I guess you won't be able to go with me to the ladies' night out party. It's your choice."

Wow, do you see what she did? Management poetry in motion, and it worked! Gracie loved going to parties with her Mommy, so she quickly got "unstuck" and went to pick strawberries. Moppsie continued to use this management style—giving Gracie a choice and letting behavioral consequences do their thing—and Gracie didn't get stuck after that.

But not everything in Gracie's life was a choice. Gracie missed half of kindergarten due to recurring earaches. Whether that first pattern led to what happened next is hard to determine.

After a few months of attending first grade every day, Gracie decided that she needed a break. So, she concocted an elaborate story. She chose the week she wanted to stay home (an already shortened week), then told her parents in advance that the school would be closed for a teachers' in-service week.

That seemed to go over well, so she then went and told her teacher—are you ready for this? —that she was having open-heart surgery and would be out of school that same week. The teacher gasped, which was Gracie's cue to assure Ms. Teacher that she would be just fine. "I'm young, so they'll just get in there, fix what they need to fix, sew me up, and I'll be as good as new in just a few days," she explained.

During a first-grade parent-teacher conference, Gracie had overheard her teacher telling her parents that she was a "brilliant child" and that she would "go far in life," whatever that meant. Naturally, since Gracie was such a brilliant student and sweet child, why would her teacher or parents expect anything but the truth?

Gracie executed her plan with perfection and had a lovely week off school. She got to spend quality time with Nanny, uninterrupted by terrorizing Pi. And, she probably played doctor, given her fake condition; after all, she was having surgery.

When she returned to school, her teacher greeted her with concern. "Gracie, how did everything go? Are there any doctor's restrictions I should be aware of?"

"I'm better than ever. And yes, the doctor said I shouldn't go out to recess for a couple weeks," Gracie replied. A true child of vaudeville.

Her vacation had been complete, and all was well. That is, until the next parent-teacher conference. You see, *in her mind*, she really did have a successful open-heart surgery, and it really did take place during a teacher in-service week. She cognitively knew she wasn't sick, and she continued to get "outstanding" on her performance at school, so strategically speaking, it was just a clever maneuver in getting what she wanted.

As you might imagine, though, Gracie got a real condition called "lump in your throat" when she heard a concerned teacher ask her parents, "How is Gracie's heart?"

Smiling, Moppsie replied: "Her heart's fine," and for that millisecond Gracie thought, *Whew, escaped that bomb; good job, Moppsie.* But then Moppsie said, "What makes you ask?" The lump came back.

John 8 says, "If you abide in My word, you are My disciples indeed. And you shall know the truth, and the truth shall make you free" (NKJV). The truth came to light, abruptly, and Gracie didn't exactly feel very free at that moment.

On the way home, Poppsie and Moppsie calmly talked with Gracie about the harm that could result from fibs. From that, Gracie created this rhyme: "Those who don't follow the rules of the school may someday end up as a fool."

School provided a haven from Pi, and Moppsie was her security guard at home. Near the end of every school day, Gracie would go to the pencil sharpener so she could wave out the window to Moppsie, who was parked outside, waiting to pick her up. Seeing Moppsie gave Gracie peace.

Some mornings, the Book Mobile was parked in Moppsie's spot. One day, while perusing books on the mobile, and perhaps driven to avoid becoming a fool, Gracie selected a book that contained a poem titled, "Hiawatha's Childhood," which began,

> By the shores of Gitche Gumee,
> By the shining Big-Sea-Water,
> Stood the wigwam of Nokomis,
> Daughter of the Moon, Nokomis.
> Dark behind it rose the forest,
> Rose the black and gloomy pine-trees,
> Rose the firs with cones upon them;
> Bright before it beat the water,
> Beat the clear and sunny water,
> Beat the shining Big-Sea-Water.

As she read, Gracie visualized herself holding Hiawatha's hand so she wouldn't be afraid on the shores of Gitche Gumee and the dark, gloomy forest he stared at. Within a seven-day rental period, little Gracie memorized the 95 lines that Henry Wadsworth

Longfellow had written in the 1800s. Lines that contained the Native American names Nokomis, Ishkoodah, and Wah-way-taysee and unfamiliar words like Minne-wawa and Mudway-aushka.

Gracie grew fascinated with the number seven as well as three. Seven days in a week, and a week between her vivid dreams and finding and memorizing the poem. Some researchers believe that a person's core behavioral patterns are formed by age seven. Biblically, the number seven represents completion and perfection. In blackjack, 21, or 7 x 3, is a winning number. Any time Grace would see or hear the number seven three times in a row, she believed God was trying to grab her attention.

"Seven come eleven" was a phrase Gracie liked to say because it rhymed. Perhaps she also intuitively knew it was supposed to attract luck.

Chapter Three
Projection–It's Powerful

For as he thinks in his heart, so is he.
—Proverbs 23:7 (NKJV)

At age 11, Poppsie gifted Gracie with a magnificent motorcycle. Oh, what fun it was, as the whole family got in on the action. Poppsie already knew how to ride. For some reason, when inexperienced Moppsie hopped on, he told her, "You don't need to ride that thing." Protective hubby? Perhaps. Or maybe it was a little competitive nature popping up.

Luckily for Moppsie, a neighbor was at the house when this took place. Mr. Neighbor jumped in and taught Moppsie, at that time age 40, how to use the clutch and shift gears. First gear is down, then up to neutral, then second, and so on.

The orange dirt bike began a new chapter in Poppsie's, Moppsie's, and Gracie's life. Poppsie bought bigger motorcycles for Moppsie and himself to enjoy. His was a bright blue BMW 750. For Moppsie, Poppsie purchased a beautiful brand-new lime-green BMW 900. Life was fabulous!

Gracie's Yamaha gave her the freedom to ride across the fields and pastures to visit her neighbors, a wonderful farm family with several kids. They had dirt bikes, too! Riding fun began when their chores were done, so Gracie lent a helping hand.

With one exception, Gracie rode with all boys—and there were lots of them! She was glad they didn't baby her or treat her like a girly girl. Yes, you could label her a tomboy; however, she would later coin the term *grit-determined* to describe herself back then.

The oldest child of the farm family, whom we will refer to as Sir Lyman, was just a few years older than Gracie. He was tall, smart, humble, witty, and very kind.

Sir Lyman taught Gracie how to race. Round and round the pasture they'd go, attempting to get faster each time they completed a lap on the dirt track. The grazing cattle seemed accustomed to the riders, although there was one occasion where a lone steer chased her down the main stretch. Gracie's goal was to be accepted and good enough for inclusion in their group—not necessarily to win. As a visual and hands-on learner, she mimicked whatever the boys did—even trying to get her knee to touch the ground as she leaned into the corners.

One day, the boys decided to take Gracie on a new trail that led up to a deserted railroad grade. Getting to the top was no problem. Following the boys down the narrow and steep hill that ran in between several trees... Well, that just wasn't happening.

She stopped at the top of the hill, paralyzed.

Finally, Sir Lyman backtracked and found her standing next to her *yummy Yahmie*, on the top of the grade, and with her helmet off. He rode up to her and said, "Gracie, you're holding everyone up. What's the problem?"

"I'll tell you what the problem is," Gracie replied. "I am *not* going to ride down that hill. You'll have to do it for me."

"No way! You can do this. It's no big deal," Sir Lyman argued.

Gracie's stubborn streak kicked in, accompanied by folded arms. "*No*, I don't think you understand. I refuse to ride *this* bike down *that* hill!" she shouted back.

The back and forth went on for several minutes. Although frustrations were rising, Sir Lyman kept his cool, trying everything he could think of to convince Gracie she could do it. Well, except for one thing: He refused to ride her bike down for her.

Finally, he asked, "Why are you so scared to do this?"

"Because I am going to hit that tree," Gracie confessed.

"That's ridiculous, several of us rode down in front of you, and we didn't hit that tree," reasoned Sir Lyman. That didn't matter to Gracie. In her mind, the little tree that sat quietly beside the trail was a mammoth oak. She saw herself running straight into it. Next, she saw herself and her helmet separately flying up in the air, followed by a crash landing. Nope, she just wasn't going to go there.

Young Gracie knew more than she realized. Grown-up Grace eventually had the training and expertise to understand the power of projection. Basically, whatever a person pictures in their mind is what they are likely to make a reality. People manifest outcomes based on what they mentally see or believe.

Since we're talking about a railroad grade here, think of The Little Engine That Could; he could because he believed he could. It can also be described as "mind over matter."

Well, guess what? The power of her projection prevailed. After what seemed like hours of arguing, Gracie finally put her helmet on. Grudgingly, she got on her yummy Yahmie—and ran straight into the tree! The impact made her land in one spot and her helmet in another, just like she had pictured. Luckily, she wasn't hurt.

Now you might be able to "picture" what she had to say to Sir Lyman! This was one case when Gracie regretted saying, "I told you so."

A short while later, Poppsie watched Gracie ride down the driveway, with her handlebars turned completely right in order to keep the wheel going straight, until she came to a stop. Poppsie—being the good, good father that he was—quietly asked, "You all right?"

"Other than hitting a tree and bending these forks, I'm great now," Gracie replied.

As an adult, Gracie learned that to avoid a crash, it is critically important to focus on Jesus, stand firm, and keep a positive mindset.

Chapter Four
It's about Getting Burned

> *"Look!" he answered, "I see four men loose, walking in the midst of the fire; and they are not hurt, and the form of the fourth is like the Son of God."*
> —Daniel 3:25 (NKJV)

From the beginning of Gracie's life and into her adulthood, Moppsie shared her knowledge of stories and characters from the Bible with fun and flare.

Gracie loved it when Moppsie would tell her about Shadrach, Meshach, and Abednego—and how their faith in God saved them from being burned in the fiery furnace. Unfortunately, as a teenager, she didn't always heed Moppsie's advice regarding her personal safety.

On a hot summer day, Gracie was riding her dirt bike around the yard in shorts and a halter top. As her parents walked out of the house, Moppsie told Gracie, "Hey, go put long pants and a full shirt on. You know we don't ride like that."

"Okay, Mom, I will," Gracie replied.

"Your father and I will be gone for a few hours, but since Nanny is here, you can keep riding as long as you put on the proper clothes," Moppsie further explained.

"Okay, okay, I will," Gracie assured her.

Well, hard-headed, teenager Gracie had fibbed to Moppsie. She knew her mom was right; however, it was hot out and she had no intention of putting on clothes that would make her even hotter. Besides, she had spent hours upon hours riding around the yard, and nothing had happened before. *Why would it be any different today?* she thought.

Gracie acted like she was going into the house to change, but as soon as Poppsie and Moppsie drove away, back outside she went. Not foreseeing danger, Gracie used a small sidehill in the yard to practice popping wheelies. Her goal was to impress the boys. *Heck, Sir Lyman can ride on his back wheel for what seems like a mile,* she thought, trying to channel some of that daredevil skill.

Naturally, with each attempt, she got a little better. She repeated the mantra, *Practice beats talent when talent doesn't practice* in her head, having learned something of the power of projection. Her confidence growing, she imagined herself riding on only the back wheel while doing a royal wave with to an imaginary crowd with her right hand.

Gritty Gracie was succeeding—woo-hoo!

Then, the unexpected happened.

Gracie got some air under the front wheel. Before she knew it, her bike was lying on the ground. She was lying on the engine, the bare skin of her stomach searing. Only by the power of God was she able to pull herself up and off the engine. Her entire stomach area was charred like a piece of meat—remnants of her skin still sizzling on the burning engine.

If you've ever experienced a trauma like this, you may appreciate how God's gift of going into shock works. It's miraculous. Even though she was in excruciating pain, all she could hear were Moppsie's last words: *You know we don't ride like that!* She was going to be in big trouble, and there was no one to blame but herself. *How could I be so stupid?* she thought. She knew she had to pick her bike up and get it back into the garage before her parents got home.

Meanwhile, a family friend was visiting Nanny in her home. Gracie was so scared; she didn't know what to do. Extremely mindful, Grace didn't want Nanny or Nanny's friend to panic. So, she put a washcloth under cold water, rung it out, and then covered her burnt tummy with it while she reclined in a chair.

With her stomach throbbing inside and out, Gracie closed her eyes and pictured the face of Jesus. She began to quietly pray, asking Jesus to forgive her rebellion and heal her wounds. The story of Shadrach, Meshach, and Abednego was a great foundation to focus on in such a time as this. Jesus was with them in their fiery trial, and not a hair on their head was singed—nor did they even smell like smoke. Gracie prayed for the same type of miracle to take place in her life.

And it did.

When Gracie, still in shock, heard Nanny's friend leaving via the shared driveway, she gently pulled herself out of the chair and walked over to Nanny's home. Nanny, also a strong believer, calmly said, "We need to put cocoa butter on it—right away."

With time and God's intervention, Gracie's skin completely healed. She, like her Bible friends, triumphed through the trial without any evidence of being burned.

Chapter Five
WOW—Why Hide "It"?

Let your light so shine before men, that they may see your good works and glorify your Father in heaven.
—Matthew 5:16 (NKJV)

If you've ever watched an episode of *American Idol*, you've probably heard at least one judge say something like: "We're looking for the *it* factor, or "WOW, you've got what *it* takes to go all the way."

While God did not bless little Gracie with the singing voice of an angel, He did anoint her with wisdom and discernment far beyond her years. She labeled her *it* factor *enlightenment*. But she was often afraid to show the gritty side of herself because of her desire to be considered humble and kind. For instance, when as an adult she began leading teams, she tended to achieve buy-in utilizing the "wisdom of the crowd" method over being Miss Independent.

Even as an adult, Grace often kept her gift of enlightenment to herself rather than sharing it. This was due to fear of *it* not being good enough or that *it* would make others feel inferior or jealous.

And she wasn't alone. How many people can you think of, even yourself perhaps, who hide or undervalue their God-given abilities? Artists who hide their paintings under beds, dancers who only dance in the dark, singers who keep *it* in the shower—Grace would label this behavior "limiting the Holy Spirit." And it's no way to live a healthy, abundant life.

Hiding *it* may also mean succumbing to fears or repressing perceived failures and/or scars from past wounds. For example, a young adult who struggled with childhood chunkiness may lack the confidence to pursue a God-given dream. A 50-year-old mom may get stuck in depression, which keeps her from helping others who may share a similar past of domestic abuse and/or the loss of a child to a drug overdose. A victim of childhood abuse may suffer from trust issues, which blocks them from unpacking their baggage of fear, shame, and guilt—resulting in a severe health condition, due to carrying around that heavy load.

In a human mind, hiding *it* might sound something like this: "It's my fault," "I'm no good," "It will never change," "They'll never believe me," or "I'll never be/have enough." These types of thoughts are not from God, which means that whether you realized *it* before today or not, you have a choice in what and how you think.

The words we say to ourselves became really important to Gracie, but so did the words she discovered out in the world. At age 16, she had the opportunity to meditate on a Bible verse, John 3:16—not because she was reading the Bible, but rather because she was staring at it on a bumper sticker as she waited in a McDonald's drive-through lane. God made sure this verse wasn't hidden from Grace.

Being reminded of God and Scripture was wonderful. So was seeing that little word *it* in random places where Gracie could remember not to hide her *it* from the world. She also loved the word wow. *Wow* spelled backwards is still wow, and if you turn wow upside down, you'll see mom—and Gracie loved seeing her mom.

Passionate Gracie also loved acronyms, acrostics, and alliterative adjectives. She could go on and on about God and her love and words and meanings and connections. As a trainer, Grace would use *wow* as an acronym to mean "Walls of Words" or "Words of Wisdom" or "Walls of Wins." She found *wow* was useful for expressing all kinds of varying reactions without clarifying true emotions. For example, when a contest judge says: "Wow," it could mean "Wow, impressive" or "Wow, appalling," and the person they are "*Wow*ing" may not understand the difference.

It was May 1980 when Gracie, then age 16, officially met an out-of-this-world handsome heartthrob in the Kroger parking lot. Remington had dark hair, beautiful features, and a polite smile that was served with a sweet side of swagger; he possessed *it* factors. There was an angelic glow about him.

Remington was a Kroger employee. Gracie had spotted him inside the store a few times prior to actually meeting him.

Moppsie could be silly, and for fun, she would throw rolls of paper towels or non-breakable items toward Gracie while shopping, shouting, "Quick! Catch!" One day, when Gracie looked up to make the catch, she also caught Remington looking down on her from above, like a cherub. Pretending to be checking overstock on the top shelf, he was on a ladder in the next aisle. She later learned that he had climbed up there purely so he could sneak a peek at her. Apparently, she wasn't the only one hiding a crush.

Moppsie and Gracie enjoyed seeing him while shopping. They would giggle and make googly eyes over him once he was out of sight. However, reserved Gracie hid her desire to be introduced.

Finally, after several months of these occasional sightings, Gracie ran smack dab into Remington going into the store as he was coming out. He had just finished his shift. They talked in the parking lot just long enough for him to work up the courage to ask her out on a date. He told Grace she could call him Remi. Soon, she and Remi were "going steady," as was the term in those days.

They had a glorious summer filled with visits to each other's homes for fun and family time. Sometimes they had coloring book challenges, and Gracie always voted Remi the winner as his pictures were always perfectly outlined and filled in. As he held up his perfect artwork, he'd cross his heartthrob eyes at Moppsie. "Stop doing that!" she'd say. "They're going to get stuck like that someday." Remi would respond with a perfect imitation of his favorite Looney Tune, Marvin the Martian. Childlike laughter followed.

Remi and his younger brother were very close. Remi, Junior, and Gracie would fill a huge bowl with popcorn, and the three of them would sit side-by-side, eat popcorn, and watch movies. They referred to themselves as the Three Amigos. In fact, both brothers took Gracie to the Homecoming dance that fall!

And yes, as you might suspect, there were scores of girls calling to get Remi's attention—and Remi did fib about them here and there. But Gracie handled it with, well, *grace* of course.

Gracie didn't hide that she was in it for the long haul. Remi had taken carpentry at a vocational school and promised he would build her a wonderful house someday. He lit up when describing the details of every room he'd build, just for her.

He even liked to cook! At night, before the drive to return Gracie home, he would make himself a huge salad, then tell Gracie: "You've got to drive so I can eat." She didn't mind a bit, because the tradeoff was, as soon as he scarfed the salad down, he would serenade her with songs—and man could he sing! If *American Idol* had been around in 1980, Remi would have had all the *it* factors necessary to win. That is, if he was able to overcome his insecurities and let his light shine.

One night, while Remi sat at Gracie's kitchen table, Moppsie told him, "You have the most beautiful features. You look like an angel!" And that he did.

Little did any of them know what was coming. Less than six months later, Remi died in a car accident. They were all crushed, but the second Gracie learned Remi was gone, that John 3:16 bumper sticker appeared in her mind. Sad as she was, it was a sign that God would be with her as she endured the separation.

Chapter Six

It's on to Business

I have told you these things, so that in Me you may have peace. In this world you will have trouble. But take heart! I have overcome the world.

—John 16:33 (NIV)

Gracie vividly remembers that first day back to school after Remi's funeral. She cringed when she saw the boy who had heartlessly mocked her, asking "Did you know your hottie boyfriend wrapped his fancy Firebird around a tree last night?"

"Focus on My word, and forgive him for his" was God's reminder to Grace as she calmly walked past him.

Numb, she sat peacefully at her desk, picturing Remi's spirit in Heaven, free from all worldly snares and troubles. For her, there'd be no custom-built house, no more coloring contests, no more Martian imitations, and no more competition for his attention.

She pondered the promises of God, and her heart asked, *What's next?*

Intellectually gifted, Gracie got good grades without studying. In high school, she participated in the Cooperative Office Education Program (COE), which allowed students to leave school early to work in specific jobs. Preferring work to school, she thrived and was quickly elected president of COE. Another girl (code name: Diamond) was elected as vice president. Grace held Diamond in high regard. A short time later, Diamond got a job working for a shooting sports distributor called A+ Sports.

Gracie's high school business teachers noticed her talent and helped land her an interview at a local bank/savings and loan (S&L). A team of six board members and the president hired her during the first interview.

She loved her job as a teller, and her customers loved her! She always had a long line of customers at her teller window during the week and a long line of cars in her drive-through lane on Saturdays. The bank president, whom Gracie adored, told Gracie's mother, "You'll never have to worry; success will accompany her wherever she goes!"

While working at the S&L's branch office, a local doctor—a former Green Beret of Russian descent—also took a liking to Gracie's effervescent personality. As a busy professional whose time was money, he seemed to appreciate the speed and accuracy with which she worked. His preference became apparent, as he routinely refused to use another teller.

"No, I'll wait for Gracie," he would tell the others.

By this time, almost three years had passed since Gracie was first hired. She was working part-time and attending college. Interested in science, medicine, and helping people, Gracie thought becoming a doctor would be fulfilling.

One of the first classes she took was Anatomy and Physiology. Memorizing details such as the number of bones in the human body was a breeze for her. But, when it came time to dissect cow brains during lab, well, let's just say mashed potatoes for dinner would never be the same.

Gracie was at work, sharing (perhaps a little too graphically) her physical response to seeing mashed potatoes on her plate, when in walked Doctor Russia. Catching her few words, he asked Grace, "What are you going to school for?"

She replied, "Well, up until yesterday, I thought I wanted to be a doctor. Now, I'm thinking it may be a waste of time."

Containing his elation, he gruffly said, "If you want to know what it's like to be a doctor, don't you think the best plan would be to work for me?" He really grabbed her attention when he added, "Or perhaps you like wasting time working here." He paused. "You have a job with me today if you want it. It's your choice."

He, like Moppsie, knew how to move her to action.

She took him up on his offer. Sure enough, within a year, she realized that between patients calling Dr. Russia at all hours of the night and others refusing to follow his advice, being a doctor wasn't the life she wanted. She couldn't decide what she wanted to be and preferred earning to spending, so she put college on hold.

Around this time, she started going by Grace rather than Gracie, as it sounded more professional to her. She also fell into a relationship with a young man whose entrepreneurial drive impressed her. He was blessed with physical and intellectual attractiveness. With his smiling blonde exuberance, style, and flare, no one else could compare. Plus, the Golden Boy had been raised with a foundation of loving God.

Golden Boy's family owned several small businesses, one of which he managed and wanted her to work at. A testosterone battle broke out between Dr. Russia and Golden Boy. Each day she went to work, Dr. Russia would ask, "Why are you still dating him?" But before she could answer, he'd tell her, "He's not what you're looking for." At the end of a long day, she would meet Golden Boy, who would say, "Why are you still working for him? That's not the right environment for you."

After withstanding months of male competition disguised as, "It's what's best for you, Grace," she turned in her resignation and began working alongside Golden Boy in the business that his father owned. Golden Boy's papa was a big man with a teddy bear heart, so we'll call him Papa Bear.

Now 19, Grace loved working. However, she also wanted to get started on a career that would stick. She hoped this new opportunity would provide insight for a future return to college.

Golden Boy was responsible for running an equipment rental business, which shared space with Papa Bear's accounting practice. On her first day of working with her paramour, there was so much to learn that she felt she might have made a mistake in her decision. She liked the customers but felt stupid, which wasn't pleasant. After the first week, Golden Boy comforted her with affirming words, "Look at how much more you know now than you did a week ago. You're doing fantastic!" He was a smooth operator.

Papa Bear had been observing Grace's performance from his office that sat cattycorner from the rental counter, and he liked what he saw. His tax/accounting and rental businesses were both in growth mode. Sensing that Grace had more potential than equipment rental would require long-term, Papa Bear quickly offered her a job as his executive assistant.

Grace was thrilled and accepted without hesitation. This arrangement worked wonderfully. Grace had a full plate of responsibility, could deliver a ton of customer WOW experiences daily, and worked in a building with two men she had grown to love. Plus, she kept Papa Bear's office, appointments, and files impeccably organized. She was utilizing her God-given talents—and life was good.

Growth continued, and more employees were added. Within a year, the two businesses had more traffic than one space could accommodate, so Papa Bear and Golden Boy went searching for more real estate to purchase. Soon after, the rental business moved to a new location, and the tax/accounting business expanded to fill the existing space. Grace helped Papa Bear hire a new assistant, and she was promoted to Golden Boy's right hand in the rental business.

Hectic is too subtle a word to describe the pace of the growth, expansion, remodeling, and moving that took place. The more chaotic it got, the longer and harder Papa Bear, Golden Boy, and Grace worked—which fueled their common drive for accomplishment and success.

Grace had a purpose, could measure results, and was an integral part of the family and their business. Because of that, Grace traveled with the boys to three or four business events and trade shows every year to purchase equipment for the rental business. They appreciated her insight and respected her opinion, and they favored her with fancy meals and accommodations at five-star resorts. Grace's favorite trade show was the Honda Equipment

Convention which was held in Hawaii. It was heavenly to be paid to visit that destination multiple times.

Papa Bear had the mindset that the best food and rest were needed in order to be at one's very best. Golden Boy and Grace thought that was a *beary* good idea. After all, Golden Boy's exuberance, style, and flare had to come from somewhere.

With the new rental center facility came the need for a new computerized management system. Grace jumped at the implementation opportunity and took full responsibility to ensure it was done correctly. The higher efficiency and better processes led to increased foot traffic and improved sales.

Exhilarating would describe Grace's work life, which happily bled into her personal life since Golden Boy connected the two. By day, they worked side-by-side, providing customers with the right tools to get their jobs done correctly. At night, they worked overtime, still side-by-side, completing jobs that customers needed done but couldn't complete themselves.

Grace wasn't monetarily compensated for her overtime. Instead, she received hands-on education: learning how to grind stumps, trench ditches, and sand floors. It didn't stop there; she could operate bobcats, backhoes, and bulldozers—and drive the roll-back truck that delivered them.

God remained the biggest factor in Grace's life. She publicly worshiped on Saturday nights at a Catholic church with Moppsie and Nanny and again on Sunday mornings with Golden Boy at a church of his choice. Private daily worship and thanksgiving were routine; however, out-of-wedlock sinning was also present.

Hard-headed Grace knew that her choices were not God's will and self-made choices had negative consequences; however, she continued making those poor choices. If you're thinking, *sounds out of alignment*, you'd be right. Internally, Grace would have agreed, but externally she found ways to justify her actions. Soon she began learning what "the Grace of God" meant: *undeserving, unmerited favor by the crucified and resurrected Jesus Christ*.

Golden Boy loved God, guns, and dating lots of girls—all at the same time. He also seemed to enjoy trying to fool Grace into thinking she was his one and only. God's grace kept the two alive, especially when their emotionally fueled drives created temptations to push buttons and pull triggers.

An example was when Grace went into what Golden Boy referred to as *banty-rooster mode* when she confronted him, with proof, that he had gone on a date with another girl. They were standing in his kitchen at the time. The more he continued to fib, the more banting and ranting she did.

The next thing she knew, what appeared to be a loaded gun was pointed at her. Instead of showing fear, she stood firm. He put the gun down and backed up, realizing how emotions had taken over. She calmly told him, "We aren't married. If you want to date other girls, just be honest with me."

He refused to tell the truth and his behavior did not change; however, *her* behavior did. A few months after this fiery incident, Golden Boy offered to teach her how to shoot. Her first lesson involved an AR-15 and pop can targets—in a safe and controlled environment—which was a lot of fun.

For a girl in her early twenties and from a business wisdom perspective she was on the "Stairway to Heaven," the first song she learned to play on guitar when she was 16. Unfortunately, *career = musician* was "not in the stars" for her. Also not in the stars for her was a marriage to Golden Boy. Now that Grace was fully capable of handling his portion of the family business, Golden Boy was free to frolic in his version of heaven outside the rental center.

One aspect of this heaven came in the form of a self-developed business venture that was 30 years ahead of its time. Golden Boy earned props for not hiding his *it* factors. He used every advantage he had to live the most vibrant life possible. Unfortunately, Golden Boy's business venture wasn't completely legal, and he suffered consequences with arrest and imprisonment.

If you've ever had a family member, spouse, or close friend in prison, you probably grasp the emotional toll it takes on loved ones. In this case, Golden Boy's sudden absence also resulted in a management gap which Grace voluntarily filled. She wanted to alleviate as much stress as she could, so in typical Grace style, she dedicated all her time tending to business and any needs Papa Bear had.

With each passing month, Grace and Papa Bear grew closer, and they relied on each other for support. All the employees pulled together and worked hard to replace the loss with something positive. The business ran smoothly. The fun time Grace had spent with Golden Boy was now spent doing extra work to keep the family business growing and helping Papa Bear.

Several months had passed. Through some helpful letters from Golden Boy, Grace, now age 25, came to the realization that she needed to move on from her unhealthy relationship with him. It was not easy, but God was there. She prayed that her next romance would lead to a calm and permanent union—void of the golden drama that seemed to attract her. Still, by remaining upbeat and keeping a smile on his face no matter the circumstances, Golden Boy earned a place in Grace's heart as a model of positivity.

Chapter Seven

It's the Pits!

He also brought me up out of a horrible pit, Out of the miry clay.

—Psalm 40:2 (NKJV)

On a beautiful day in May, it appeared that God had answered Grace's prayers.

A charming young man, wearing a perfectly pressed company shirt with his name on it, was at the counter to rent a sod cutter. He had rented before; however, Grace hadn't really noticed him. She had always considered her primarily male clientele as customers only, not prospective romantic partners. This day was different.

When you own a business in a small town, it seems everyone knows everyone else's business. As so, questions were occasionally asked about Golden Boy's disappearance out of curiosity, concern, or something else. On this day, Prince Charming empathetically asked a few questions, which grabbed Grace's attention.

Just what convinced her to go out with him Gracie cannot recall. However, she does remember that, after the first date, she told Moppsie, "I've met Prince Charming, and I'm going to marry him."

Remember Poppsie's favorite saying, "Be careful what you wish for, because you just might get it"? Well, it turns out that wanting, wishing, and praying are similar when you put those desires out in the universe. Gracie had already demonstrated the power of manifesting your destiny through your thoughts, words, and actions when she hit that tree head-on. She was about to prove it again; only this time, she wasn't giving it much thought at all.

Five fast months later... *poof*, it happened. Grace married Prince Charming in a private ceremony held at his house. You may be thinking, *why didn't they have a big, fairytale wedding?* Good question! They were young and frugal, so simplicity made sense. The prince was in a hurry to get hitched, but he wasn't Catholic, so they met a few times with a pastor they really didn't know, and he agreed to perform a private ceremony.

If Grace had known then what she knows now about intrinsic drive and Holy Spirit guidance, she would have understood the hesitation in her gut about sharing this union publicly.

Grace appreciated her husband's family, work ethic, cleanliness, and willingness to teach her how to golf. However, their differences in core beliefs, upbringing, and what they valued most surfaced quickly. Excited to celebrate their one-month anniversary of wedded bliss, Grace rushed home from work, only to find her husband wasn't home. After anxiously pacing the floor for what seemed like hours, hubby called to say he had stopped for a couple of beers with the boys, but he would be home soon.

Hours later, Grace's anxious excitement turned to disappointment and concern. Around 1:00 a.m., her groom arrived home, no longer Prince Charming but the Tasmanian Devil—angrily punching doors, kicking toilets, breaking furniture, and even throwing apples against the kitchen wall. The destruction must have been exhausting because as soon as he had destroyed every room, he passed out.

Grace couldn't believe what she had just witnessed. She did her best to clean up the mess and learned that apple splat was impossible to remove from the wall. Then, she attempted to sleep on the couch.

The next morning, Prince Charming walked out of the bedroom, looked around at the damage, then asked, "What happened in here?"

"You're kidding, right?" Grace replied. He claimed he wasn't. He remembered drinking, then getting angry about something regarding his ex-girlfriend... and the rest was a blur. *Wow, what have I gotten myself into?* Grace thought; anxiety settled in the pit of her stomach.

Pit became a theme word for her. And when her husband turned into the Tasmanian Devil (Taz), Grace got a good glimpse of what *a pit of darkness* might look like if she didn't put God first. After an explosive episode, Taz would taunt Grace, reminding her that she was stuck with him and there was nothing she could do.

Coincidentally, Taz went to the pit every day to work. You see, like the Golden Boy, Taz was also the heir apparent in his family's business, which was a gravel pit. Literally, when he left for work, he would say, "I'm going to the pit." The trouble was when he brought the pit home with him.

One of Grace's many philosophies became: *Every situation has advantages and disadvantages.* She also proclaimed: *Power is a result of short visits to the pit.* For example, a racecar driver wins by efficient *pit stops*. Beautiful music flows out of *orchestra pits*. Powerful messages may be preached from a pul*pit*. Olives, peaches, and cherries are some of Grace's favorite things, and of course, they all have *pits* to protect their seeds; however, when eating cherry pie, it's *the pits* to bite into *a pit* that was overlooked.

Meanwhile, Golden Boy had been a Good Boy in prison, so he was released early, arriving back at the rental center only a few months after Grace's wedding. The newlyweds had not discussed what might happen in this scenario, but Grace wasn't concerned. She was bound and determined to be the best wife possible, and there was no temptation to go back to living a life filled with deception. Golden Boy helped her situation by already having a new love interest in place. They had always gotten along working side by side, and that didn't change when he returned. In fact, it got better, and they quickly fell into a brother/sister-like groove.

While Grace didn't want to leave a job that made her happy to please a husband who did not, Charming Taz convinced her that working with her ex was not fair to him. She found herself in a "decision-to-be-made pit." Realizing that a hasty decision had moved her away from going to church and focusing on God, she returned to Him and prayed for help.

Chapter Eight
It's Out of the Pit and into Sales!

Forgetting those things which are behind and reaching forward to those things which are ahead.
—Philippians 3:13 (NKJV)

It was a new year and time for A+ Sports to move its operation into a new 120,000-square-foot distribution facility. A leading distributor of firearms and associated sporting goods, the new warehouse/office space was a huge asset to Grace's hometown. Because her former classmate Diamond had gone to work for A+, Grace was familiar with the company but didn't realize the growth they had experienced.

Grace learned of the relocation when Rocketman, the vice president of sales and marketing for A+, rented a handcart to move boxes and smaller items. Upon returning the cart, Rocketman observed Grace's style with the customer ahead of him.

It was lunchtime, and Grace was managing the counter solo. It may be helpful to know that at age 26, Grace was 5'8" tall, had long legs and long blonde hair, and weighed around 120 pounds.

Rocketman witnessed two burly construction workers arguing with Grace about paying their bill; using "The bulldozer didn't work," as their reason. Smiling, Grace calmly invited the two men outside for a review of the newly installed hour meter which tracked the time the bulldozer was used… and *poof*—they magically decided to sign the check and move along.

It was Rocketman's turn to get service, and upon handing Grace his paperwork, she asked, "How is the move going?"

He replied: "Great! Would you like a job?"

She was a little stunned, yet curious, so she inquired, "What did you have in mind?"

He told her A+ had an opening in the sales department, and from his brief observation, he felt she was the perfect match!

The offer took Grace by surprise. Requiring time to process, she said, "I'm pretty happy here, but I'll consider your offer." Then she shifted to "How is Diamond doing?"

"She's doing great, and if you accept the sales position, Diamond will do your training."

Less than an hour later, Grace received a call from Diamond urging her to work for A+ Sports.

It seemed God was nudging Grace toward a new career path. With the pressure from Taz to work elsewhere, she was optimistic that a change could help her marriage. On the other hand, the job would involve sales of products she didn't know anything about.

A few days later, she interviewed with Rocketman at his office in the old A+ Sports building. The interview was short and sweet. Rocketman didn't ask many questions, seeming eager to hire Grace on the spot.

She, however, had several questions. Her first concern was if she had to cold call, because if so, she was 100 percent not interested. He assured her that since A+ Sports was a wholesale distributor; she would be calling retail stores that would welcome her call. He explained that A+ had an excellent reputation in the firearms industry, and the largest portion of her job would involve calling on existing accounts.

That didn't sound so bad, but Grace knew only a minuscule amount about firearms. She asked Rocketman, "Doesn't that concern you?"

He answered, "No, you'll catch on quickly. Selling to a 'good old boy' industry may be a hurdle for some females; however, watching you handle those construction workers with ease convinced me that you're the perfect fit for sales to males."

Comfortable at the rental center, she tried to discourage Rocketman from hiring her: "I appreciate your time, but it's unlikely you'll be able to meet my salary and time-off demands." That didn't work! He met every demand without hesitation and asked, "How soon can you start?"

How soon was early 1990, just a couple weeks after that interview.

Although it was tough to leave her comfort zone, making a sacrifice for the sake of her marriage was more important. Taz seemed pleased.

Chapter Nine
It Explodes!

Death and life are in the power of the tongue, And those who love it will eat its fruit.

—Proverbs 18:21 (NKJV)

The work environment at A+ Sports was top-notch. The building was brand new and one of the nicest corporate establishments in the county. The decor was extremely pleasing to the eye, right down to the luxurious oak trim and light fixtures. The office employees had their own modern cubicles, complete with panels to provide some privacy. Several conference rooms of different sizes offered comfort for meetings.

Background music was softly piped through the entire building. There was an ample breakroom where employees could enjoy lunch or snacks purchased from vending machines. One of the nicest benefits: clean bathrooms. Even the warehouse area was kept spotless and organized. Above all, the working conditions at A+ Sports were superior because they employed people who got along.

People often said, "We're a family!" That was the cornerstone of their success!

Grace started her career at A+ in order entry. There were three levels of salespeople: order entry, sales, and senior sales. The specifications of this position were to receive inbound and make outbound calls to firearms retailers. Until noon on her first day, her training consisted of working with Diamond to learn the computer system which ran off a main frame IBM 400. After lunch, they reviewed A+ Sport's 676-page catalog together, so that she would understand the products she would be selling.

On her second day, there was a brief review of the first day, then she shadowed a couple of salespeople to observe how to do the job. Using an extra set of headphones and a connector, she was able to get plugged into the conversations and hear both the customers and the salesperson live.

On the third day, Diamond demonstrated how the phone system worked, and at 9:00 a.m. said, "OK, start answering the inbound calls, and let's see how you do."

Grace was petrified. Despite her "training," she still didn't have a clue what she was supposed to do. A+ stocked over 24,000 products, of which she was familiar with maybe three. How in the world would she effectively answer calls on a complicated phone system *with which she had no experience,* use a computer system *that she had barely three hours of training on,* and enter orders for items *that she'd never even heard of before?* Talk about being thrown into the line of fire!

In the beginning, Grace felt like crying, but she refused to quit. Divinely, a former teacher turned senior salesperson sat in the cubicle across from her. For the first few days, she'd take a call, write down what the customer asked for, put them on hold, then stand up and say, "Hey Mr. Teacher, what's the item number for this thingamabob?"

Mr. Teacher was kind and gave her the proper information—that was until she drove him crazy with her constant and distracting questions. Poor guy couldn't escape Grace, even after he left work. Turns out, they also lived across the street from one another. Mr. Teacher probably thought she was stalking him when she pulled into her driveway that first night.

After a couple of days of madness, Mr. Teacher blessed her when he asked, "Grace, do you have an A+ catalog?"

"Yes," she answered.

"Grace, do you know that we have a 96,000-square-foot warehouse attached to this office?" was his second question.

"Yes," she said.

"Good, because I need you to tab that catalog, take it home, and study it. And, if you need to put your hands on any of the products we sell, ask Diamond to walk you through the warehouse." Continuing in a calm, understanding tone, he said, "I don't mind helping you, but I can't do both of our jobs, and you'll never get any better if I keep answering your questions." She did exactly as he instructed.

Then, that familiar, gritty drive kicked in, and Grace quickly realized that somehow, some way, she would succeed. If others could do it, she could do it! And with focus, a great teacher, and God's help—she did!

A few months after her hire date, she received sales and margin goals. She was told the most important responsibility of her job was to hit those goals. She was also required to work with the credit department in collecting past-due amounts from her accounts and with customer service in correcting errors.

It didn't take long for Grace's leadership tendencies to surface. In less than a year, she advanced her position in sales from 26th to 10th and produced over $1,000,000 in sales. She consistently exceeded her sales and margin goals each month.

Around the end of 1990, because of her stellar performance, Grace was invited to attend the 1991 SHOT Show, which is the annual trade show for the firearms industry. SHOT is an acronym for "Shooting, Hunting, and Outdoor Trade" and is restricted to members of the industry—not open to the general public.

In 1991, SHOT was to be held in Dallas, Texas. Grace felt honored to be invited. When she got home and excitedly told Taz about this wonderful opportunity, he did not share her excitement. In fact, he told her, "You're not going."

Still trying to keep the peace in her marriage, she reluctantly went to work and made up some weak excuse for why she couldn't go. After the show, she learned that A+ Sports had thrown a party at Texas Stadium with entertainment provided by the Dallas Cowboy Cheerleaders. It was a huge success, and her customers were asking, "Why weren't you there?" She realized that surrendering to Taz's control had to change before it ruined her business life.

By the end of 1991, Grace finished fifth in sales, selling more than $2,850,000 worth of products. She wasn't number one, yet, but biblically, five represents grace, so she couldn't feel too bad.

On a Friday the 13th—Grace had had enough and formally divorced Taz. God was releasing her from the pit she had gotten herself into and moving her into a successful career selling guns!

Ever heard the expression: "new level, new devil?" On Thursday the 12th, Rocketman provided Grace with an understanding of what that saying meant. It was about 5:30 p.m. and time to go home when Rocketman asked Grace to meet him in the breakroom. He informed her that she would be delivering a speech about her "climb to the top" to the entire company at 8:00 a.m. the next morning.

"That's not possible, as I won't be here tomorrow. It's a scheduled day off," she quietly explained. There were other people in the area, and being very private about her personal life, she didn't want anyone to know that she had taken the day off for her divorce proceeding.

Rocketman replied: "It *is* possible. You *can* write your speech tonight, deliver it at 8:00, and leave after the company meeting ends."

Moppsie had drilled into Grace's head to never say, "I can't" but instead say, "I can and I will." Although Grace was getting very frustrated with Rocketman's persistence at a time when she was doing all she could to keep herself emotionally together, she still tried to avoid saying the dreaded words, "I can't do that." However, the divorce proceeding was scheduled for 8:30 a.m., so there literally was no way she could do both. Embarrassment was added to the equation.

"Your plan won't work. I have an important meeting at 8:30," Grace firmly replied.

Rocketman didn't reach VP of sales by accident, and he didn't take no for an answer. "You're already on the agenda. You can start your speech by 8:05 and be out of here by 8:15—plenty of time to make it to your meeting. If you can reach fifth in sales in less than two years, you can certainly give a speech and make it to a meeting on time."

After going back and forth several more times, Grace was about to lose it, and she eventually caved to the pressure and told him: "Okay, I'll see you in the morning." Then she left the building with rage burning inside her. He was one of the few people she had told she was getting divorced. She thought he knew why she had scheduled the day off, yet instead of showing empathy or compassion, he pushed her past her limit. She'd lost that battle.

The next morning, Friday the 13th, Grace was a wreck.

She was great with people one-on-one or over the phone, but speaking to a large group of peers who could see her—that was mega unsettling. She thought she might pass out. Yes, she tried picturing them in their underwear—didn't work.

She had reluctantly put some words on paper, but she didn't want recognition for her sales achievements or to take credit for what she knew God was responsible for. To top it off, her failed marriage made her want to hide in a cave, not stand on a stage.

Walking up to give her speech was awful. As soon as she opened her mouth, her eyes welled up with tears. After the first sentence, she could no longer see the paper. *God, please don't let me collapse*, she prayed. Suddenly, she looked at the crowd and began speaking what she felt in her heart: *gratitude*.

It sounded sappy to her, but it was the truth. "I'm so blessed to work here, in a beautiful building with a wonderful family who supports me. I couldn't sell anything if I didn't have an advertising department to produce a catalog or a purchasing department that got those products ordered. And our warehouse crew—you all are the best in our industry—thank you so much for getting orders out the same day."

By this time, she was sobbing—while realizing it was time for divorce court. Incredibly embarrassed, she grabbed her notes and literally ran out of the room—and then out of the building. A wall of glass windows lined the exterior wall of the meeting room, so literally everyone saw her running to her car. They had no idea where she was going, or the real reason she had left.

After that trauma, divorce court didn't seem as bad—a silver lining of the experience for sure. However, she then realized that on Monday, she had to go back to work.

Oh no, how can I face all those people when I was such a babbling idiot? she thought. She didn't want to return to work ever! But the reality was that she had to. Her plan: Go to work far earlier than usual to try and avoid as many people as possible.

Surprise! The president of A+ Sports met her at the door. He honored her by saying, "In all my years, I have never seen such a touching and heartfelt demonstration of appreciation displayed by an employee. Did you know that you received a standing ovation after you ran out?"

Wow, that was a wild turn of events, so Grace nicknamed the president Wildman.

"Wow, praise be to God," is all Grace could say. He had taken what she felt was an awful, dark, and embarrassing day and turned it into ovations, light, and blessings.

Failing at marriage didn't feel great, but Grace learned from it and gained real power. One important lesson was to take the time to understand and outline what the expectations and rules of engagement are before jumping into marriage or any partnership that matters. If God is the constant and center-focus for both parties, other idols will fade away, and neither party will get stuck in a miserable pit for very long.

As it happened, God quickly moved another wonderful girl into Taz's life, and she was a much better fit to be his queen. She was super sweet to Grace and when they married, Grace prayed their union would be forever blessed.

Now free, Grace made plans to attend the 1992 SHOT Show held in New Orleans. She held the record for advancing to the top five in sales in the shortest amount of time. When she started, there weren't assigned sales territories. Customers would call in to place orders, and if they weren't assigned to another representative, a salesperson could add them to their assigned list of accounts.

Kent Arms in Michigan was one of the first accounts assigned to Grace. A kind man named John managed the store. He gave her orders weekly and was patient with her as she grew her knowledge of firearms. George was a Kent Arms' employee and close to Grace's age. He frequently called her for information and would tell others, "She's taught me a lot about the gun business," which was an honor for a girl who had almost quit because of what she didn't know in the beginning. George's dad's name was also John. He owned a manufacturers' rep group that called on A+ Sports. John, George, and John reminded her of her favorite grandfather, John, her favorite uncle, George, and Jesus's favorite apostle, John. At length, they became divine members of her "favorite people trinity."

Much of Grace's success at A+ Sports came through perseverance. She focused on every available account that called in and then made sure she proactively called them at least once a week. In a short amount of time, she became a semi-expert on the products she was selling.

Her customers understood how hard she worked for them, and they respected her knowledge of the firearms business. Some of them shared their feelings by writing appreciation letters to the executives of A+ Sports.

It was not long before she was stealing the market share from other distributors. She gave A+ Sports majority credit because they made her job easier by providing services that other distributors didn't, a definite advantage. The key was that she aggressively went after the sales rather than sitting around and waiting for the phone to ring.

Corporately operated out of the central Midwest, A+ was also aggressively growing. Making their "Coast-to-Coast…Border-to-Border" dream a reality, they opened remote offices in the Northeast, Southeast, and West regions.

While it was amazing being part of this exponential growth, it also made the sales role more challenging. Tenured salespeople from A+'s competitors were being hired to fill the remote offices, and customers in those respective regions were transferred from the central reps and assigned to the new reps. In the blink of an eye, much of the business Grace had built went bye-bye.

She continued to sharpen her skills, and by May 1992, Grace was promoted to senior sales rep. This accomplishment was published in *American Firearms Magazine*, which was one of America's largest professional firearms dealers' journals at the time.

In addition to her overall sales figures, she received accolades and rewards for producing the best results in manufacturer-sponsored competitions, which were referred to as "spiffs." Grace finished third in company sales at the end of 1992.

With her promotion to senior sales rep came additional job responsibilities. Also in 1992, the use of a performance appraisal form was introduced in A+. She was evaluated on professionalism, judgment, initiative, job execution, time management, accuracy, productivity, communication, cooperation, goal setting, reliability, and ability to hit sales and margin goals. Grace exceeded A+ Sport's expectations in every category.

In January 1993, she decided that third place was not acceptable; she could do better. She carefully reviewed her performance from the two years prior and devised a strategic plan to be number one. By July 1993, she had accomplished her goal.

One day, Rocketman walked over to Grace's desk and handed her a customer information sheet. The account was already assigned to Ray, one of the veteran sales guys. He told her, "I need you to call this account immediately. If you can get a sale from him, I'll re-assign the account to you," and then walked away. While Grace was puzzled by why he would ask this of her, she thought, *Just do what you're told*. She picked up the phone and called Wisconsin to speak to Walt.

A gruff voice answered. Sweetly, she said, "Hi, this is Grace from A+ Sports, and the reason for my call is—" *click*, then a dial tone. Walt hung up on her!

Well, that got Gritty Grace all fired up. She hit redial, and when Walt answered this time, her voice wasn't so sweet.

"Why did you hang up on me? You don't even know who I am," she stated.

"I don't need anything from some girl," Walt piped back.

"Really? So, you're telling me that you have every single gun, holster, cleaning kit, and box of ammo you'll ever need on the shelf and ready to sell?" asked Grace.

"I didn't say that," was Walt's rebuttal.

"Did you know that I'm the number one salesperson in this company, and we're an industry leader in the nation?" she asked. Before he could get his words out, she added, "I didn't think so—otherwise you certainly wouldn't cut your nose off to spite your face." (*Don't cut your nose off to spite your face*, was one of Nanny's common sayings, and Grace loved using Nanny's wisdom!)

"Now, how about you walk around your store and give me a list of what you need, and I'll send it out today. And as a bonus, I've got several thousand item numbers memorized, so I'll save you more time and money than anyone else you do business with," was Grace's line that sealed the deal.

Walt melted like butter and ordered a few hundred dollars' worth of items.

"Thank you very much, will every Tuesday about this time work for your weekly order?" she asked.

"Yep, that will work," Walt replied.

Every Tuesday at 10:00 a.m., Walt would give his order to Grace. He would become one of her best customers. Walt's store was successful for over 50 years.

Grace walked into Rocketman's office after her initial call to Walt and said, "Okay, I got the order, but how's Ray going to feel about this?"

Rocketman's mouth dropped open. He stuttered and stammered a bit and said, "You *didn't* just get an order from him."

"Well of course I did. Why would you give him to me if you didn't think I could get an order?" she asked.

"Um, well," he hesitated, then told her, "Because Ray has been calling on Walt for over a year and couldn't get anywhere. Last week, we heard a rumor that Walt pushed his brother through the glass window of his store, so Ray refused to call him. You were our last hope. But I never believed that you could do it, especially on the first try."

Grace smiled and politely said, "You're welcome, and I'm glad Ray won't mind. Please change Walt's account to my sales number, so I can get his order out of here today."

Since Walt hadn't seemed to faze her, a couple of days later, Rocketman tried again. This time, the customer was assigned to a sales rep in one of the regional offices. "This customer has been doing business with us and has the potential to be huge, but he is refusing to pay his bill," explained Rocketman. "Call him and see if you can also work magic in collections," he said before walking away.

Grace scooted her chair out of her cube, as if to follow him, and asked, "Will this one get transferred too if I do?"

"Sure," he said, as if it had a small chance of happening.

Well guess what?

That's right! Hallelujah! God was now refueling her pipeline with the accounts no one else could reach! The crème-de-le crème of toughest customers. Not "good old boys"—more like "tough-minded, stubborn males" who also happened to be business owners of gun shops.

Please don't imagine her full of pride or boastfulness, because she wasn't. She was blessed with talent, confidence, drive, empathy, and compassion, and she commanded respect; therefore, she persevered. And she earned her keep with this colorful customer. With Walt as a recent warm-up, she strategically reviewed all the facts. She even called the assigned rep in the other region to get the scoop. Then, she dialed the phone.

A store employee answered in a professional manner. "This is A+ Sports calling, I need to speak with Mr. Colorful," Grace said firmly.

She heard, "Okay, just a minute," and was put on hold.

Another gruff voice said, "Yeah," as if it were too much trouble to be alive.

"Is this Mr. Colorful?" she asked.

"That depends, what the **** do you want?" he said.

"Well, first of all, let's start with some respect, or did you grow up without a mother?" she said, without hesitation.

"Huh?" is all he came back with.

"You heard me, and please stop the foul language as it hurts my ears. Now, I don't have time to play games, so let's get right to the point. I'm calling from A+ Sports, and I understand we've been shipping products to you, is that correct?"

"You aren't my salesperson, why are you calling me?" he said, redirecting the question.

"Well based on our conversation so far, it appears it's because no one else wants to hear your vulgarity or put up with your delinquency. How about *you* start explaining what *your* problem is?" was Grace's firm stance.

The result of that first call was a lengthy chat, which sounded more like a therapy session by the time it was through. Every curveball or excuse Mr. Colorful threw out for bad behavior, Grace caught and stomped into the ground.

Then he shifted his tone to stating his passions: Harleys, music, and doing business the old-fashioned way (without technology). She laughingly shifted to asking, "Do you use an abacus to count how many panheads, shovelheads, and flatheads you've owned, or is your specialty just being a knucklehead?" After spontaneously rattling off song lyrics to convey her thoughts, he instantly picked up what she had laid down—and the ice melted away.

He committed to paying his bill by a certain date; she committed to following up a few days ahead of that date to help him keep his word. To Grace's recollection, she had no more problems with his collection.

Like Walt, he placed frequent orders with her. She appreciated him for his intelligence, quick wit, command of the English language, and worldly knowledge. When she finally met him in person, his embellished rough exterior gave way to a kind smile and childlike blush.

Like God did with her, Grace focused on the "good" in him.

Chapter Ten

It Returns!

Set a watch, O LORD, over my mouth; Keep the door of my lips.

—Psalm 141:3 (NKJV)

Rarely is one safe from the pits forever. Often, you get out of one only to end up, down the road, in another.

Of course, young Grace couldn't understand the finer points of these pits. Armed with behavioral expertise, grown-up Grace would later understand that what felt like "pitting" to her was "creating a competitive team atmosphere" to her former boss. He thought he was growing sales and couldn't see its effect on her.

If you've ever had a manager who stirred up stress by pitting a new employee against you, at the pinnacle of your game, what happens next might feel familiar.

One thing Grace admired about Rocketman was his capacity for excitement. That is, until the day when he was overjoyed about a new female employee he had just hired:

"She has a degree in marketing, is smart and pretty too! She'll probably make it to manager status quickly. When she gets here, we'll see another huge surge in sales, and... blah, blah, blah,"

He was practically jumping up and down while going on and on about how this super woman would "swoop in" and save the day. Grace didn't have a degree and was already number one in sales. She didn't see the need for anyone to save the day; she already had herself. Moreover, she was quite content being among more men than women.

Why in the world would I care about this? she thought to herself. But her mouth said, "Oh, how exciting. I can't wait to meet her." That's right, Grace boldface lied to save face and immediately decided she would not like Swooperwoman's face at all! She bit her tongue to avoid saying: "Now go away—please go away!"

And he just wouldn't quit. In the gigantic room of cubicles filled with other salespeople, Rocketman only wanted to share this news with Grace. *Was it an intentional plot to push my buttons?* she wondered. Maybe, maybe not, but push her buttons it did!

That night, Grace vented—for hours—to Moppsie about Swooperwoman being hired!

Ranting and raving as she paced Moppsie's kitchen floor, Grace kept asking, "Why would he tell me that she's pretty, smart, and oh so wonderful?" in her Rocketman mocking voice. Grace imagined worse and worse scenarios.

Nearly wearing herself out, Grace made up a terrible nickname for this woman: "To me, she'll be Jaundice... yes, Jaundice... all yellow and sickly looking. Let's see how she does in sales like that!"

All Moppsie could say was, "Now, Grace, you know that's not nice. This girl could turn out to be your best friend." But Grace kept ranting, and Moppsie would say, "Gracie Rae," and shake her head, and Grace was too busy stressing to notice.

When "That's not nice" didn't work, Moppsie changed gears: "Grace, remember the time you asked me if my feelings were hurt because your brother didn't show up for Christmas?"

"Yes, because I saw you go above and beyond to make it a great Christmas for everyone, and I felt like he spoiled it," Grace replied.

"Do you remember how I answered you?" Moppsie asked.

"Yes, you said: 'No, I'm not hurt, because no person on Earth has the power to spoil my Christmas, push my buttons, or steal my joy.'"

That shut Grace up for a few moments. Moppsie had interrupted her negativity train with positive thoughts.

Moppsie used that silence to pour a little more sugar into Grace's salty brain: "Grace, as you mature, you'll realize that God grants us the ability to control our thoughts, emotions, and reactions. If you allow people or circumstances to push your buttons, that is your choice. And that is why it's called *free will*."

Not all of Grace's saltiness vanished in that instant. However, she did understand that neither Rocketman nor Swooperwoman was causing her anxiety. Instead, it was her enemy called fear.

It only took one little shred of insecurity, with a dash of jealousy, to prompt her human mind to jump to negative conclusions and FEAR (False Events Appearing Real). *If you learn nothing else from this book, please use this example to focus on God's gifts and destroy that enemy.* Please *do not*, I repeat, *do not* think, speak, or act like Grace did in this scenario. The consequence for her was remorse and shame for losing sight of how to extend mercy and grace to a new person joining her work family.

After weeks of continued agony and stress over the arrival of Jaundice, picture Grace eating a large plate of crow; Rocketman and Moppsie were right! It turns out she really was the super woman Rocketman described. Within a few short months, Swooperwoman became Grace's superhero—and remained her very best friend.

Chapter Eleven

It Continues!

So then, because you are lukewarm, and neither cold nor hot, I will vomit you out of My mouth.
—Revelation 3:16 (NKJV)

The 1994 SHOT Show was held in Dallas, Texas. During the post-show recap, Rocketman complimented Grace on her trade-show savvy. He told her, "Your work ethic, enthusiasm, and the way you stood in the aisle greeting people and inviting them into our booth was exceptional!"

Since she excelled at all areas of sales, Rocketman apparently thought Grace should share her leadership ability with the rest of the sales force. In March 1994, he offered to promote her to regional sales manager. One major problem: She adamantly did not want this so-called "promotion." She was happy just being responsible for her sales and confident that she could sustain the number one position. She liked being number one, and as a sales manager, she knew she would be responsible for the sales of her peers, and not all of them had the same drive she did.

Meanwhile, Grace had a friend who owned a hair salon. This friend had invited Grace to go to New York City for a stylist's convention. A girls' trip to get away and the chance to take in a few Broadway shows was just what she needed. She scheduled a couple of vacation days in March to go to New York.

Grace wanted no part of being a manager, and she verbalized that to Rocketman three times.

Like the surprise speech situation, he told her, "You don't have a choice. I'm going to promote you to the manager whether you like it or not."

"You can't force me to take a promotion," she exclaimed.

"I can and I will, because I need ten more salespeople just like you," he told her with a devious smile.

Being forced to do something against her will was so hard on Grace, that she sought help from a psychologist. Even he seemed perplexed and said, "Usually when people say they don't want a promotion, a company moves on to someone else. Would you mind if we try something out of the ordinary?"

"I'm open to anything that will help," Grace replied. He took several pennies and threw them on the floor of his office, reviewed the pennies, and then said, "The pattern of the pennies indicates that you are likely being set up for failure. If you accept this promotion, it's possible you will be used as a scapegoat after being pulled in many different directions."

The pennies seemed a little too much "hocus-pocus," even for Grace who was open-minded and a big believer in signs. However, getting some messages helped remove any doubt she had about turning Rocketman's offer down. The next day, she would go to work with a spring in her step and convince him to hire somebody else.

"Rocketman, I'm serious. Please hire someone else to be the manager and leave me be," persuaded Grace.

"Nope, I'm going to announce your promotion during the March company meeting," Rocketman cheerfully threatened.

"Great, as I won't be here; I'll be in New York. If you announce that while I'm gone, you'll look like a fool; because I'll tell Wildman I refused the promotion, and then you'll have to confess your lie," Grace retorted.

The saying, "caught between the devil and the deep blue sea," swam through her mind.

Returning from vacation, all the employees congratulated her as she entered the building. Rocketman had made good on his threat and put her in another awkward spot.

This time, her face was red from being outraged, not crying. *That donkey's rear*, she thought. She had to make a choice: Jump completely in or get completely out. Remaining lukewarm wasn't an option.

Once she recovered from shock and rage, Grace decided not to be defeated. She formulated a game plan to transfer her knowledge and selling ability to her new team. Together, they could all win.

With the promotion came new job specifications—interviewing, hiring, firing, training, coaching—and taking her team to number one was added to the list. *And...* she was forced to begin her management career by firing several people she had worked with and sincerely liked.

Chapter Twelve
It Takes Practice

> *"I can do all things through Christ who strengthens me."*
>
> —Philippians 4:13 (NKJV)

Logically, Grace knew that practice was required to improve; however, she was often impatient for results. Hence, practicing sometimes felt like a waste. Being forced into management was an unanticipated result of hard work, but she wasn't sure it was what she wanted. She began to ask herself, *Who do you want to become?*

Striving for an answer took her back to when she was a child taking piano lessons. When Moppsie sat next to her, she would practice; however, the minute Moppsie left, Grace lost interest to the point of resting her head on her arm, over the keys, and taking a nap. One day, Moppsie took a Polaroid of her sleeping, perhaps as a motivational reminder of *what not to do* if one wishes to succeed.

After several months of Moppsie working to convince Grace that she could become a "renowned pianist" if she would just "put her mind to it," it became clear that Grace's will could rule her ability and help her succeed or cause her to fail. She quit piano. Later she would encounter the same phenomenon in college. Grace had the talent to get straight As without cracking a book, but she tried to get by on discipline when motivation failed. Anatomy and physiology thrilled her because she loved science, but when she thought about how long it would take to be a doctor, she lost interest. Similarly, if the teacher talked too slowly or the subject was too easy, Grace quickly tuned out. Taking classes that she couldn't tie to a future purpose just didn't make logical sense to her, so she rebelled against the required classes by not showing up. This purposeful rebellion turned into external failure simply because of the internal battle going on between pleasing her head and following her heart.

Her internal passion and mental giftedness caused conflict and confusion when she tried to discern what career path she wanted to pursue. She appreciated having choices; she just couldn't reach clarity on which path to choose. Rather than being frustrated, she put her faith in God. Her faith was why she considered the interventions of Dr. Russia, Golden Boy, Charming Taz, and Rocketman all as God's blessings and not mistakes or wasted time.

As a young adult, she knew A+ Sports was exactly where she was supposed to serve at this time in her life. And evidence was mounting that business management was the next educational path to take. That led to organizational leadership and Grace found herself intellectually stimulated by these subjects.

To lead their growth strategy, A+ hired a female consultant who had gained experience working for IBM. Grace called her Winnie.

Winnie was enthusiastic, exuded confidence, and was another of God's gifts to Grace.

Hired to replace complacency with improved sales results, Winnie had a full-throttle approach, which made most salespeople very uncomfortable.

On Winnie's first day, she ran the sales group, including Grace, through rigorous role-play drills. *Practice, practice, practice!* Most hated it; Grace loved it! Although she was uncomfortable at first, the harder Winnie pushed, the more Grace excelled. Post-training, the whining and complaining of others helped Grace understand why she had received a promotion.

Because of Grace's willingness to learn and follow, Winnie helped her in many ways.

Due to her new role, Grace had to attend an after-hours event with executives and representatives from several firearms manufacturers. She was used to being the solo female amongst groups of men, so that wasn't a problem. However, at age 30, she was not used to socializing with large groups of strangers, so when she arrived, she stood in the corner to observe.

Luckily, Winnie arrived and quickly walked over to her, gently scolding, "Grace, what are you doing in the corner? You're an executive now, and you need to be mingling."

Grace felt her skin turn white, tingles of sweat coming to the surface. Next, it was as if she were watching a silent movie; she could see people's lips moving, but her ears were no longer working. *Uh oh,* her empty stomach started gurgling and nausea set in. *Holy cow.* She was about to faint.

Winnie realized what was happening and shifted from scolding to consoling, "Grace... Grace... Grace, can you hear me?"

"Yes, I can hear you, but I'm not cut out for mingling. I just want to go home," Grace softly replied.

Grace heard Winnie speaking in kind, compassionate, encouraging tones. It was soothing and mimicked how Moppsie helped her.

"What is scaring you the most?" Winnie asked.

"All these people I don't know," answered Grace. "This room feels like an elephant stampede—and I don't have a gun or any ammunition. I'm a goner."

"Now Grace, you know that's not true. These are people, not angry elephants. How did you get to be number one in sales?" Again, Winnie sounded like Moppsie.

After thinking for a moment, Grace replied, "By focusing on one customer at a time."

"Great! Now we're going to use that same skill here. You are going to pick out one man you don't know, walk over to him, extend your hand, and confidently introduce yourself."

The FEAR resurfaced: "No, I just can't do that," the adult Grace said—sounding very similar to her stubborn, five-year-old self when Moppsie had asked her to pick strawberries. *Now, if she could only find a door to get glued to.*

Just like Moppsie, Winnie shifted back to stern mode: "Grace, you're a grown, highly successful sales executive. You *can* and you *will* walk over to that man right there and introduce yourself." And with a slight shove, Grace did as her fabulous mentor commanded. Another life-changing intervention. Grace would take the image of stampeding elephants with her as a consultant and, taking a page from Winnie's book, push her own clients to find a manageable path.

Later that night, Winnie confidentially let Grace in on a secret: "Wildman has your back. Rocketman does not."

Um hello... that's no secret, Grace thought, but kept it to herself. It was Winnie's opinion that Rocketman loved Grace as a salesperson but was in fact forced by Wildman to promote her to management.

That certainly shed some light on why Rocketman refused to accept Grace's *no*. While she wasn't certain of the truth, she concluded that Rocketman may have had more pressure on him than what he had put on her. So, she forgave him.

The 1995 SHOT Show was held in Las Vegas, and Rocketman assured her she was going for sure. The closer it came to showtime, the more excited Grace became... and the fishier Rocketman's behavior started to smell. Grace was trying to nail down travel details and was getting a lot of "ums" and "not sures" instead of answers. Winnie's secret opinion was circling in Grace's head, causing her mind to suspect and her tummy to turn.

At the last minute, Rocketman told Grace there had been a mix-up in the travel arrangements and she wouldn't be going. Grace was disappointed, but she was more irritated with Rocketman's fishy, flip-flopping, flounder's behavior, and she refused to let him get to her.

Yet God, and perhaps a secret helper, had her best interest at heart.

Passing her in the hall, Wildman made a comment about readiness to go to Vegas. "I'm not going," she replied, while thinking it was strange that he wouldn't know that.

"What do you mean you're not going?" he asked, seeming as puzzled as she was.

"If you want the details, go ask my boss," she frustratingly bounced back.

"I'll do that," he casually said, then walked away.

Within 30 minutes, she was paged to Wildman's office. When she walked in, Wildman told her: "Pack your bags—you'll be flying to Vegas on my cousin Barry's private jet." And that, she did!

Grace considered this privileged turn of events a blessing and an honor. At 30 years old, flying on a private jet was like a dream come true. But it didn't stop there. She thanked God for Winnie and the past opportunity to practice her mingling skills at that executive after-hours event. It was a great warm-up for the next surprise.

Cousin Barry was the co-owner of A+ Sports. He and another female relative of Wildman's were on that flight, giving Grace the opportunity to interact and share her business ideas. They were very kind, and she sensed the family liked her and what she had to say.

During this Vegas stay, Grace found herself in the penthouse of The Sands Hotel for invitation-only parties. *Wow*, it was spectacular! The Sands was the seventh resort to open on the Strip (perfect number 7!). In its prime, The Sands was a hub for entertainment and hosted many famous entertainers of that era. Unfortunately, less than two years after Grace's wonderful experience there, it was demolished, and The Venetian was built in its place.

After several conversations on that trip, Grace concluded that she needed to finish college to really excel at management.

Neither of her parents had gone to college, so Grace could not bring herself to ask them for tuition. When she attended college directly out of high school, she used her own funds to pay her way. Poppsie taught her to avoid debt, and that is a lesson she was grateful for; a student loan was not the right solution.

A+ Sports provided many tools for their people to thrive. Now, as a manager, she discovered that A+ had a program that would pay for her education if her major was related to her role in the company. For any class in which she maintained a grade of A, the company would also pay for her textbooks. Grace got an A+ in every class she took. Her education the second time around took her years to complete; however, it didn't put her in debt. She gives praise to God—and to A+—for making that possible.

College introduced Grace to personality assessments, and she was immediately hooked. Grace was over-the-moon, ecstatic to discover these new ways of understanding herself and others. Winnie fueled Grace's fire even more when they discussed one particular model that had primary and secondary styles. *Wow!* Grace's profound revelation? *Not everyone was like her, they weren't supposed to be, and they also weren't idiots.* (She scolded herself and made a commitment to avoid that unkind and limiting mindset.) Grace surmised that Rocketman and she shared a primary *driver* style; however, his secondary style was *expressive* as opposed to her secondary style which was *analyzer*.

Winnie's four-box lesson triggered Grace to recall the nine-box diagram she'd drawn as a child. After work, she found the crayon-colored creation and smiled when she saw her Uncle George's name in the orange box.

Driven to elaborate on her original diagram, Grace wrote "go-getter" in her red box and "passionate persuader" in the orange box—then added Rocketman's name.

She wrote "golden glower" in the yellow box that was in the bottom right corner. Writing the word *golden* triggered her to picture the always-smiling Golden Boy, so his name went in the yellow box temporarily. She considered changing the yellow box label to "sun-shiner" because, no matter what Golden Boy was promoting, it came across as warm and bright.

Pondering Winnie's lesson, Grace decided to label her remaining boxes based on how she would associate her personal behavior with each color.

In the bottom-middle lime-green box, Grace associated the words *relaxed, carefree, and sunny*, like how she felt on the back of Moppsie's sparkling lime-green motorcycle. Soaking in the sunshine with Moppsie made her day brighter, so she labeled that box "lime lighter."

Grace had colored the lower-left corner green like grass. She closed her eyes and imagined herself lying peacefully in the green pasture where she once rode her creamsicle orange cycle, Yummy Yahmie. Then the lone steer that had chased her down the dirt path crashed her tender moment and imaginatively, she jumped up ninja-style to protect her turf. She opened her eyes and wrote "turf tender" in the green box.

As she glanced at the teal box situated between the lower green and upper blue box, it was as if God had re-directed her eyes to the picture hanging on the wall. Two Labrador puppies, one yellow and one black, were in a boat with a mallard drake duck decoy. "That's it," Grace exclaimed, as she wrote the words "smooth sailor" in the teal box, picturing how steady and calm mallards appeared on the surface while their orange webbed feet were paddling like crazy underneath.

Next, Grace pictured the drake trying to avoid getting caught in the weeds and taking a "deep dive" to analyze what was below the blue water's surface. She wrote "deep diver" in her blue box.

Sandwiched between the blue and red, the last outside box left to identify was colored a purple shade called indigo. "That's my ideal box and in-I-go!" Grace self-identified. Winnie's four boxes were void of color; however, the word *analyzer* was written in the upper left, and *driver* was written in the upper right. Grace analyzed how others may perceive her behavior.

"When I'm deep in thought and formulating a detailed strategy, I probably do look blue, possibly quietly disconnected and aloof...like right now!" She thought.

"When I get all the details of my strategy aligned, I drive that plan forward at warp speed and with full force. Oh my, reflecting on this, I could see how a bystander might interpret that behavior as me driving a giant red bus and brightly YELLing beep-beep, look-out, I'm coming through. If they were standing too close, it could feel like they got ran over by a glowing go-getter."

Out loud Grace said, "My indigo style would be slow start, fast finish!" The word *finish* triggered memories of her red leather pantsuit and she imagined racing across a finish line in the red Fiero she once owned. That thought triggered the memory of Golden Boy, who, unlike Sir Lyman, immediately volunteered to drive her red Fiero when she refused to even start it. Grace believed her Fiero's brakes were going to fail and to stop, she'd have to hit a tree.

Opposite of Sir Lyman's encouraging "Grace, you can do this," Golden boy had said, "You're crazy" as he grabbed her keys, fired up the ignition, and headed toward her house—literally because when he turned into her parent's down-hill driveway, the brakes did indeed fail, just like she had projected.

Moppsie was doing dishes at the kitchen sink when she noticed Golden Boy's laughing face headed directly toward her. A fast thinker, he drove into the middle of the grassy yard so he could do a U-turn and head back uphill to get stopped. Luckily, he avoided hitting the huge tree that Sir Lyman used to sit under when he waited for Grace to go riding.

Grace wrote "me" and "idea igniter" in the indigo-colored box.

After reflecting upon the multiple mountains Golden Boy had conquered, Grace relabeled the orange box "mountain mover" and placed Golden Boy's name next to Rocketman and Uncle George.

To the teal box, she added Sir Lyman's name. Grace used her newly identified analytical superpower to place his name a little closer to the green box than the blue; imagining that grass probably grew in the time he had wasted *arguing* with her rather than just *doing* what she asked.

The middle gray box made her chuckle as she reminisced about trying to draw a power outlet which ended up looking like two eyes and a surprised mouth. In that box, she wrote the name Jesus as she realized He was the power that connected every box to everybody who was part of her colorful life. Then, she wrote "me" next to Jesus, as that was the place Grace always wanted to be. She wanted the ideas she ignited to only come from Him.

Satisfied with her enhancements, as she put the diagram back in its hiding place, she thanked God for Winnie's lesson as she had learned that Rocketman was exactly who and how he needed to be in order to do what he needed to do.

DEEP DIVER	IDEA IGNITER GRACE	GO GETTER
SMOOTH SAILOR SIR LYMAN	JESUS	MOUNTAIN MOVER UNCLE GEORGE ROCKETMAN GOLDEN BOY
TURF TENDER	LIME LIGHTER	GOLDEN GLOWER

It took seven (perfect!) years, but Grace graduated college Summa Cum Laude (with highest distinction) in business management/organizational leadership. She was proud of her accomplishment, but Winnie taught her some of her most important lessons.

Winnie taught Grace expert sales and leadership tactics, behavior basics, and many other things. Most importantly, she provided a vision of what Grace wanted to do when she grew up. Between reflections from God and the practice drills from Winnie, Grace discerned the who's, how's, and whys of what she wanted to become. Grace wanted to follow in Winnie's professional footsteps...with one exception. She wanted 100 percent of her clients or students to love and appreciate her for helping them achieve peak performance.

Observing that several of A+'s employees weren't willing to accept Winnie's training validated what Grace had figured out while spending time "in the pit": people can only rise to the level of their internal desires. If we are complacent, think we know more than everyone else or are filled with unforgiveness, bitterness, or resentment, it's nearly impossible for us to climb the highest mountains or demonstrate love and appreciation toward others. It would be like expecting a dead apple tree to produce a delicious and bountiful harvest.

Chapter Thirteen

It Changes!

Ask, and it will be given to you; seek, and you will find; knock, and it will be opened to you.

—Matthew 7:7 (NKJV)

It's hard to recall exactly how many people Grace had to dismiss in her first thirty days on the job, but it started with at least six. In her mind, she went from Wonder Woman in sales to Dragon Lady in management. Being forced to put her co-workers out of work was a horrible experience! However, she did what she had to in order to keep her job.

Adding insult to injury, the amiable man she was dating constantly asked her: "How can you do that to people?" He was projecting the Ice Queen, and Dragon Lady labels onto her. If they thought it, none of the A+ employees had ever verbalized those labels to her directly. As a small business owner himself, this landscaper struggled with collecting payments and making tough decisions, and Grace critiqued him for that while also feeling critiqued by him.

Fourteen years later, during a professional coaching session, Grace realized that she was experiencing a condition her coach referred to as "running from b—ch," meaning, she avoided being her natural, ambitious self for fear of being assigned a pejorative female label. She simultaneously realized that her red, go-getter, task-focused style had clashed with the landscaper's green, turf-tending, people-focused feelings. She gave glory to God for placing that coach in her path and triggering that life-changing revelation.

In addition to being the only female sales manager, Grace was also responsible for the largest territory. Her sales team, the Central II Region, covered fifteen states in the Midwest. Her counterparts for the West region managed eight states. The Southeast included nine, Central I had six, and the Northeast had twelve. Naturally, the region with the most states required the most salespeople to service it. She had to rapidly hire and train as many new recruits as possible to replace all of those she was forced to fire.

A male employee with seniority made the management position that she didn't want even more tumultuous. She noticed the large chip on his shoulder when he complained to her, "I've been here longer and know more than you. Why did you get the position I've earned?"

She nonchalantly replied, "That is a great question. The boulder on your shoulder, or this confrontational conflict style you're exhibiting, may have something to do with it. Be encouraged to go ask Rocketman that question. If you can persuade him to promote you, I'll *gladly* go back to just being number one in sales."

Grace hadn't memorized his birthday or astrological sign, but in her instant replay, he could have passed for a Taurus bull. There may have even been smoke rolling out of those nostrils, and rightly so.

Grace didn't blame or condemn him for his feelings. She admired him for being direct and upfront. In fact, she even overlooked the rumors about his lunchtime politicking campaigns against her. Perhaps he was hoping he could get voted in to replace her. In response to his bitterness, Grace smiled and gave words of affirmation—and candy!—to her entire team, hoping to sweeten all of them up.

Hiring and training took a lot of time and patience. At that time, A+ hired applicants hoping they would all be successful but expecting a larger percentage wouldn't succeed. To cover fifteen states, she needed twelve to thirteen salespeople.

Grace's first round of new hires performed well. A female salesperson, Jill, was assigned to several of the large-volume customers in Michigan. Unfortunately, Jill was not performing to A+'s new standards. Grace cringed at the thought of letting her go; however, she had just hired another female who, while not fully trained, showed great promise in the sales arena. Grace hoped that, for the customer's sake, it would be a positive transition that could also save Jill's job.

The first two Michigan customers that Grace told about the transition are burned into her mental database.

Breaking this kind of news was new to her, so Grace waited until all the salespeople had gone home for the day. At around 6:00 p.m., she went into Rocketman's office and shut the door for an extra layer of privacy. She took a deep breath, then dialed the first 989 area code—and got the owner of the Hunting Center on the phone. They hadn't spoken before, so he didn't know her.

As was her custom, she calmly yet enthusiastically got right to the reason for her call: "This is a courtesy call to share with you, upfront, that you'll be getting a newly assigned rep beginning next week. Her name is Reba, and she has a wealth of sales experience. We're anticipating that you'll be very pleased," Grace chimed.

There was a moment of silence, followed by a long list of expletives, which ended with, "I'm not getting a new *bleep, bleep* salesperson. I've dealt with Jill for years, and that's the way it's going to stay. I'm a good customer, and you're not going to tell me what the *bleep* to do in my business. Do you understand how this is going to go?" exclaimed this delightful ray of sunshine.

Are you thinking, *Here we go again?* Grace was too!

Here's the difference: This time, she was forcing a decision upon a customer who was high-volume and paying his bill. Her role had changed; therefore, she couldn't promise to take good care of him as she'd done for Walt and Mr. Colorful. And she wasn't offering him the number one salesperson. She herself wasn't even sure how this transition would turn out for him. Whether he liked it or not, Jill was in jeopardy of losing her job, but Grace couldn't share those confidential details.

What Grace did have was empathy and concern for him as a person and respect for him as a customer. She put herself in his shoes, listened intently, and picked up where he left off: "Yes, I understand exactly how this is going to go. Now, please, I need you to listen to me. You are getting a new salesperson, and I can comprehend why that's not ideal for you. While I'd prefer to give you everything you want, that's not possible in this situation, hence the reason I began with, 'This is a courtesy call,' upfront...you know, like as in, no surprises. Other than reassuring you that, as the manager of this region, I'll do everything in my power to help you and your new salesperson succeed, there isn't anything else I can do to keep you assigned to Jill. Will you work with me and give Reba a fighting chance?"

He had calmed down and listened. He firmly replied: "Yes, I guess. But if I don't like the new one, I'm calling you directly and you're going to take care of me. Do we have a deal?"

"Sure, and while we got off to a rocky start, I really appreciate your willingness to help!" she beamed.

Grace nicknamed him Commander Bad Axe.

That call was a good warm-up for the second call, which began a bit sweeter and didn't contain as much cussing. She called the second Michigan customer Mr. Doughnuts. When Grace explained to Mr. Doughnuts that he'd be getting a new salesperson, he caught her a little off guard by asking her why.

"Jill's going to be moving on to something else," was the best Grace could come up with, trying to be honest, yet compassionate.

"How long has Reba been there?" was his next inquiry.

Oh boy! "Only a few weeks; however, we hired her because she has a strong track record in sales. We anticipate she'll learn your needs quickly and improve your buying experience," Grace encouraged. "Who wouldn't want that? Will you help us help you?" she added.

"I didn't hear anything in there about product knowledge. It sounds like you expect me to train Reba, and I don't have the time or the desire to do that. You get her fully trained on products for my business, then call me back and we'll discuss making a switch," was Mr. Doughnut's answer. *Wow, that's interesting*, Grace thought.

Now, it was Grace's turn to calmly ask the questions: "Mr. Doughnuts, when you hire someone to help your customers, do they know absolutely everything they need to about your business? I'll be a little more specific. Are they experts on guns, ammo, optics, accessories, the cash register, your store policy, filling out the proper legal paperwork, etc.? Or does it take time for them to learn those things from you and through your customers' requests?"

"I see where you're going with this. Okay, I'll give her a shot, but if she doesn't know what she's talking about, I'll be calling you to place my orders. It's clear that you know how to sell!" said Mr. Doughnuts.

Whew, got through another one, Grace thought, then she committed to Mr. Doughnuts that she would listen in on the first few calls between Reba and him to ensure his satisfaction.

Grace began using "interesting" or "Wow, that's interesting" as a mental pause to successfully diffuse conflicts from that point forward.

The next day, Grace nearly fainted when she was informed that an executive decision had been made to release Jill. Fortunately, Jill made it slightly less heartbreaking when she shared that she wasn't really thrilled with sales anyway and was glad to be moving on. In another pleasant turn of events, Jill suggested she transition the rest of her customers over to Reba, making it appear that it was her decision to leave, and not a corporate call. This made for a much smoother transition.

However, Grace was not out of the woods yet. Jill was gone, and it was Reba's turn to improve the sales territory. Grace kept her promise to Mr. Doughnuts and Reba by remotely listening to Reba's first call to him. Reba was strong on her introduction, but

Doughnuts went directly into his order. "I need a Mossberg barrel for a 500," he told Reba.

Now, if you don't know the first thing about hunting or what a Mossberg 500 is, you might think, *Reba is going to need to do some googling*. But this was 1994; we didn't have Google yet.

If you happen to be an avid hunter, you may be thinking, *Oh, that's an easy one, just ask Doughnuts what gauge it's for, what length he wants, and keep asking him questions until you narrow it down*. Or you may be thinking, *I remember when Grandpa gave me my first Mossberg*, to which Grace would say, "That's awesome!"

But here's the thing, in 2020 there were over sixty options for a Mossberg barrel. There may have been a few less in 1994, but without the help of a database or search engine, Reba was not likely to find that item number quickly. The best salespeople committed thousands of numbers to memory in order to serve their customers.

Grace was waiting for Reba to say something, but there was silence. As the silence grew more awkward, she heard Doughnuts ask, "Are you still there?"

No sounds were heard from Reba's mouth. Next, she heard Doughnuts say, "We must have gotten disconnected," and then, a dial tone.

What just happened? Grace thought as she jumped up from her desk and literally ran around the corner to Reba's desk.

Poor Reba. The tears were flowing like a river over a facial expression of defeat.

Grace was shocked to see such a strong salesperson in this condition; however, memories of her own first few experiences of selling firearms and accessories came to mind.

"Reba, are you okay?" Grace asked. More tears flowed as Reba's head went face down onto her desk.

After a few minutes of quiet reassurance, accompanied by many Kleenex, Reba lifted her head and gained composure.

"I can't do this," Reba said, "I don't know a barrel from a...a....a...," and the faucet was back on. "See," she said sobbing, "I don't know anything about anything here. I can't even make a stupid comparison."

Meanwhile, Reba's phone was repeatedly ringing. The caller ID read Doughnuts Gun Shop.

Grace shifted gears and told Reba, "Look, I understand what you're going through. You realize I was the new girl not so long ago, right? For two weeks, I went home every night swearing I couldn't do this job and telling my family: 'I'm going to quit!' Turns out, I'm not a quitter, and neither are you, Reba. Now, let's change our mindset to, *We can and we will*. I'm going to help you find that Mossberg item number. I'll sit right here next to you, and we're going to call Doughnuts back and pretend you had phone problems. We'll break through this barrier and never look back!" (*Wow!* Sounds like Grace followed Winnie's lead. □)

Hallelujah! Side-by-side, they rose to victory!

Soon, Mr. Doughnuts loved Reba...and she loved him right back!

By August 1995, Grace's freshman team fought their way to the number two spot in the company, trailing number one by a mere $26,941.00.

Now, one could say, "Well, she had more states than the other regions," but remarkably, her team achieved second place with only seven (perfect!) salespeople. The number one region had nine.

In addition to the sales produced, three (a trinity) of Grace's salespeople were in the top ten, and six out of seven exceeded their percent-to-goal. This reminded Grace of Snow White, who had a team of seven, six of whom weren't happy! Grace was driven to avoid Snow's results.

Her team worked hard, and their dedication was producing fruit. But Grace had to learn that, taken to an extreme, a strength may transform into a weakness. She developed an unhealthy habit of voluntarily working long hours for no additional pay. Moppsie often told Grace that Poppsie worried she was becoming a workaholic.

Grace listened to Poppsie and believed him; she just didn't know how to achieve satisfaction of purpose any other way. This took a toll on her personal relationships that she wouldn't wish on anyone. She'll never get back the extra hours she dedicated to A+ Sports—time that was never expected, asked to be given, or monetarily compensated for.

Later, it would sadden her that she spent several December 25ths celebrating Jesus' birth working at her A+ Sports office. However, it was clear that she loved helping A+ Sports succeed almost as much as anything else in the world.

One day, as Christmas approached this particular year, Grace noticed large, white, Styrofoam boxes were delivered to all her fellow managers. She did not receive one.

At first, she rejected the conclusions her mind raced to, reasoning that her box was just delayed in shipping. As one day turned into two, then three, her patient positivity changed to, *Oh my gosh, did I not get a box because I'm getting fired?* That fear was followed by a long list of other comparisons such as, *Why did other managers get bigger cubicles when they get promoted and I haven't?*

As much as she wanted to know what was in the boxes in hopes it was something that she could justify *not* getting, she couldn't risk the embarrassment of the other managers realizing she'd been left out.

Fraught with fear, she did some detective work and discovered the boxes were filled with dry ice and several pints of specialty ice cream. It was Wildman's gift to all the managers—well, except for Grace. Her spirit was crushed. Not only was it her favorite brand of ice cream, it was also Poppsie's, and she had none to share.

Now that she had the details, she just couldn't waste any more time on fear; she needed facts. Fortunately, Wildman was working late that night, so after her team left the building, she headed to his office.

Giving help, answers, and service were Grace's strengths. Asking for help or guidance from others... well, that was her Achilles heel. That may shed some light on why she fought Rocketman when he forced things upon her. She could tell him what she didn't want, yet she had to feel like she earned everything she received on her own. (Later, she would teach the *independence motivation* from experience.)

Anyhow, picture Grace somewhat timidly asking Wildman, "Do you have a minute?" while feeling like she's about to throw up.

"Hi, Grace, sure. Come on in and sit down," said Wildman as he walked from his desk to the conference table in his office.

After sitting, Wildman comforted her with a little small talk and then asked, "So Grace, what can I help you with?"

She apologized for seeming so petty, then explained it would take all the courage she could muster to ask him a question. Finally, she asked him to help her understand why she didn't get any ice cream.

He smiled and graciously said: "Oh, Grace, my apologies. Apparently, your name must have been left off my list. It was an oversight and not intentional. I'll make sure you get your ice cream, too." She was so emotionally relieved she fought back tears. That emotion changed to laughter as Wildman affirmed how valuable she was.

With his Wildman kindness, he said, "While you're here, is there anything else you want but have been afraid to ask for?"

"Yes, it would be nice to have a bigger cubicle, so I can have meetings with my team without going to a conference room," she expressed. To which he replied: "We'll reconfigure your office within 30 days, to your specifications. Is that satisfactory?"

"That would be amazing! *Thank you!*" she said with a grateful heart.

Feeling like she was talking with a genie who was granting her every wish, Grace's fear melted into faith that Wildman indeed had her best interests in mind. He never made her feel like she was wasting his time; however, at the conclusion of this meeting, he gave her precious advice: "Grace, in the future, rather than fear the unknown or jump to negative conclusions, simply ask for what you want. With as hard as you work, you'll most likely get it!"

Chapter Fourteen
It's Colorful and Stylish!

"Also he made him a tunic of many colors."
—Genesis 37:3 (NKJV)

To continue its growth, A+ Sports added a predictive behavioral tool in which Grace received extensive training and certification. Because she was so passionate about behavioral sciences, adding this new certification was the whipped cream on the top of her proverbial cake!

Grace's behavioral pattern was called *Scientific Professional*. This meant she was:

- highly authoritative (preferred autonomy)low on the need for social contact or social settings (introspective and individualist)
- impatient for results and able to process information much faster than the average (task-driven, intellectual)
- extremely detailed and reliant upon logic rather than emotions when responding to circumstances (calm, analytical)

- extremely low on expressing feelings or *emoting* (the trainer labeled Grace's emoting score *Spock-like* and used her as a rare example)
- highly motivated (driven)

It didn't require a rocket scientist to observe how Rocketman was similar (head-butting) and different (you seem weird) from Grace. However, understanding the why behind their colorful differences was certainly helpful.

Rocketman received the same training and digested it in his own special way. It was his role and right to keep an eye on Grace, her team, and A+ Sport's customers, even if she didn't like it.

One customer who didn't particularly care for Rocketman's overly focused eye on Grace was Curt, an executive manager for Scheels, a retail sporting goods store.

At a SHOT Show long-long ago, Rocketman interrupted a business conversation Grace and Curt were having. Rocketman attempted to assert his authority over Grace when he tried to take credit for a program that Curt knew Grace had created for Scheels.

"Remember that program we talked about a few months ago?" Rocketman said to Curt.

Before he could finish, Curt held up his hand to visually stop him, then stated, "Oh, I *vividly* remember every word of our conversation." Then, extending his hand toward Rocketman for a goodbye handshake, he added, "Grace has already implemented what we need. Now, if you'll excuse us, we need to get back to our discussion, as I have another meeting to attend."

Wow, it was awesome to have a premier customer help Rocketman find his place and appreciate Grace all at the same time.

Grace loved all her customers, no matter if they were difficult, direct, colorful, or kind. However, Scheels and their associates held a special place in her heart. In her opinion, Scheels was the number one multi-store retailer, back then, largely due to providing an exceptional customer experience, a top-notch manager training program, and the highest standards of business professionalism. For example, in a SHOT Show crowd that was filled with casually dressed retailers, the Scheels management team could be identified by their required shirts and ties.

During 1995–1996, Grace became responsible for selling to all seventeen Scheels stores. Because they were located across several different states, they were initially divided among several different salespeople. However, since Grace understood why Scheels was successful and shared their business philosophy, the individual store managers and executive management team requested she be directly responsible for all their stores. This was also a logical decision, since when the stores operated as one unit, it allowed consistency with pricing and special volume programs. Scheels trusted Grace to effectively communicate the details corporate-wide.

Naively, Grace blamed some of her shortcomings on Rocketman. With her fiery drive, low need for flattering expression, and high need for reliable information based on facts and figures, she often felt friction with Rocketman, who preferred using excitement, exaggerations, and hyperbole to achieve his dreams. In reality, they each had superpowers and blind spots.

Put another way, we all have our own color combinations, and we don't need to be envious or judgmental about anyone else's colors. Biblical hero Joseph was a young dreamer whose favor with his father earned him an ornate and colorful coat. His envious brothers sold him into slavery, but though Joseph endured years of tribulation, he also knew blessing and abundance. His secret: maintaining a kind and generous spirit during the difficult journey. He never condemned anyone but did his best to serve wherever he found himself.

If you grew up in the 1960s or 1970s, you may vividly remember watching crowds of people on television chanting, "Sex, drugs, and rock and roll." Grace was probably wearing a tie-dyed shirt with bell-bottom pants and looking at her mood ring to determine how she felt about these psychedelic times, all while trying to make the colors on her Rubik's cube align. Either "Kodachrome" from the *There Goes Rhymin' Simon* album or "Song for a Dreamer" by Procol Harum was spinning on the record player as brother Pi used Nanny's sewing machine to creatively attach patches to his jacket. Little Gracie referred to it as "his colored coat."

Picturing Uncle George, Rocketman, and Golden Boy's names in the colored boxes she drew from a dream, she envisioned people blending and aligning multiple colors of behavior to create their own individual color palettes. A color palette features different colors; the palate in our mouths helps us discern different tastes. Variety is a good thing for both. Grace's epiphany: Understanding both color association and how to label behavioral style preferences was the key to unlocking a person's potential.

Chapter Fifteen
It's a Chain Reaction!

"Let your speech always be with grace, seasoned with salt, that you may know how you ought to answer each one."

—Colossians 4:6 (NKJV)

January 1996 started with a bang!

The SHOT Show was back in Dallas. Instead of a stadium party, a few Dallas Cowboys football players visited the A+ Sports booth at the show. Grace had a ball interacting with them as she introduced customers to them.

At SHOT Shows, Grace had opportunities for brief talks with Wildman and Cousin Barry. Additional conversations normally took place outside the office during special events or while shooting sporting clays. One day, she was casually asked, "What do we need to do to continue our growth?"

Without hesitation, she answered, "We need to pursue Bass Pro, Cabela's, and the other chain stores. They're a growing market."

Up until this point, A+ Sports had catered to independently owned retailers referred to as Mom-and-Pop stores. Scheels was the exception; however, their store managers still created the orders for their respective stores, so they were unique from other chains.

Grace paid close attention to industry trends. She heard rumblings from customers that Bass Pro and Cabela's, originally known for their catalog business, were gaining traction with brick-and-mortar stores. It was comparable to what had happened with Mom-and-Pop hardware stores when Lowe's and Home Depot arrived.

Before she knew it, that off-the-top-of-her-head comment became a strategic plan.

In August of 1996, Grace and Rocketman had more intel about each other and were getting along much better, which was good. Starting a brand-new chain-store division would be a gamble and a huge challenge. Rocketman presented this to Grace as an excellent opportunity for her. Since she felt it was originally her idea, she had no fear, so there was no fight in asking her to lead the effort.

Grace's new title was national account executive. She had an open operating budget and all the autonomy she needed to get started. Scheels somewhat fit a chain-store profile, so they remained with Grace.

Refreshed was how Grace felt about soaring into something brand new; *rejection* was the meal she was initially served by the purchasing agents from Bass Pro Shops and Cabela's. However, they didn't ignore her, and she wasn't about to go down quietly.

She quickly learned that they were buying firearms and ammunition directly from the manufacturers, and in some cases, at a price that was less than A+ Sports' distributor cost. She had wished for a challenge and a challenge she got!

Grace sharpened her saw—well, more like turned it over to God in prayer—and received just the right words to say to the head buyer at Bass Pro Shops.

Those words were in the form of this simple question: "Steve, where do you get your Rugers from?"

Ruger is the shortened name of Sturm, Ruger, & Company, Inc., an American firearm manufacturing plant that was founded in 1949 by Bill Ruger (as industry insiders called him) and Alexander Sturm. In 1996, Ruger only sold their products through authorized distributors. Rugers were popular and in high demand, but Bass Pro couldn't buy them directly. This was the advantage Grace needed to get her foot in the door.

Bass Pro placed an order for a few Rugers. *Hallelujah*, it was a start!

Then, Grace called the head buyer at Cabela's and said: "Your biggest competitor just gave me a Ruger order. Which guns are you currently out of?" Voila, she got another order!

Getting those first orders wasn't the most difficult part. Doing business their way was. Before the orders could ship, Grace had to review vendor agreements which were *books*, not just a few pages, and if each agreement wasn't followed perfectly, the consequences could be costly. Fortunately, Grace was naturally gifted at thoroughness, and A+ Sports trusted her instinct enough to dedicate whatever resources she needed to make sales.

Grace made regular visits to Bass Pro Shops' corporate headquarters in Springfield, Missouri. She doesn't recall meeting John

Morris, the founder; however, her tour of their state-of-the-art distribution center was unforgettable.

In order to continue doing business together, A+ Sports was required to adapt to Bass Pro's technology, which required electronic data exchange, or E.D.I., capabilities. By adding that capability, both A+ and Bass Pro could make, receive, and track orders electronically rather than by phone or fax. She then convinced A+ Sports to invest in outside resources to make that happen.

A coin has two sides; humans flip coins to help make decisions. In spiritual battles, Grace learned to remind herself that she was the head and not the tail—above, not beneath—to signify that God was on her side, defeating all enemies.

Nanny often said, "It all depends on whose ox is getting goaded." Grace understood that to mean one shouldn't judge another's emotional state before you have enough information. Grace found that understanding all the details often led to a change of opinion or heart, otherwise known as a paradigm shift. To Nanny's words Grace added, "and a story has as many sides as there are people; plus, one—the truth." If you're familiar with how the telephone game works, you may be nodding your head in agreement right now.

It may seem like Rocketman had been doing all the goading thus far, and it's true he did his fair share. But Grace and many others developed as strong leaders largely due to Rocketman's influence and goading; hence his popularity. She became grateful, with a glass-full, abundant, and overflowing mindset toward those lessons.

Gritty Grace caused her own share of havoc for Rocketman.

Before she became manager, Rocketman led the morning sales meeting, which Grace attended. One morning, he was trying to get the team fired up about something, and Grace was in skeptic mode.

After the meeting, she created an email that read, "I see he's got his rose-colored glasses on again." Then she hit send. Oops. In her huff, she had accidentally sent the message to Rocketman rather than her co-workers.

He immediately called her into his office to confront her. "What's this?" he asked.

She lied, he knew it, and she stuck to it.

Many times, while she was a manager, Rocketman would add enhancements to the sales process. Most of those times, she'd stomp into his office and tell him how ridiculous his idea was and then refuse to do it his way. It's surprising that he didn't write her up for insubordination, but then, they both liked to fan fires.

With her sometimes confrontational, sometimes avoidant conflict resolution style, hearing that he had placed negative write-ups in her personnel file wasn't all that surprising—if that was even true.

Rocketman had a reputation in the industry long before he hired Grace, so most of the customers she called on already knew him. Generally, customers either loved him or didn't; there wasn't much gray area. He took her to several of his favorite customers, and she learned a lot from him while having fun. However, when it was her turn to take her team on store visits, some customers abruptly asked them to leave when they learned that Rocketman was her boss.

After documenting a long list of the antics that she had either experienced or heard about, Grace went to Wildman to unload. Spilling the beans felt pretty good while it was happening, but afterward, she felt sick. Saying unpleasant things about the guy who gave her the best job ever really didn't sit well with her. After all, she was also learning what not to do from his example. In fact, in retrospect, she probably would have dismissed all of it.

Wildman took her seriously and investigated the list of concerns that night, calling Rocketman directly. Clearly, she hadn't thought ahead about the consequences of bean-spilling. What did she expect would happen?

The next morning, Grace got paged to a private conference room where Rocketman was waiting. He proceeded to chastise her for going to Wildman and told her that if she ever did that again, he would make her life hell. *Um, hello, that's already happened*, she thought.

It got worse. After her butt-chewing was over, she walked out to the distribution center to get her day flowing in a more positive direction. Only problem: Wildman followed her out the door, boasting about how he had addressed her issues directly with Rocketman. He assured her she would see improvement.

When she stated, "I know," Wildman's expression changed.

"How could you know this already?" he asked. Boy, this was a sticky situation. Wildman (Rocketman's boss) just asked her a direct question. If she answered him honestly, it may appear she was disobeying what Rocketman (her boss) had just told her and there'd be hell to pay. Praying honesty was the best policy, she told Wildman what had just transpired in the private conference room with Rocketman. Wildman left the distribution center in a huff, saying something about not tolerating threats.

Thankfully for her, she didn't hear any more about the second conversation. Little did she know that within a year, Rocketman would be gone from A+ Sports.

Chapter Sixteen

It Was That First Bite!

God has said, "You shall not eat it, nor shall you touch it, lest you die.

—Genesis 3:3 (NKJV)

Have you ever pondered what life would be like if Adam and Eve hadn't taken that first forbidden bite? There is so much to glean from their story.

For one, we're all tempted constantly. Often by food. What foods do you love or crave the most? If it's potato chips, ice cream, or Thin Mint Girl Scout cookies, you and Grace might have been soulmates.

When Grace put on weight, it required either working harder or increased discipline to avoid those carnal cravings. If she had never taken the first bite of chips, ice cream, or cookies, the problem wouldn't have existed, and she wouldn't have been distracted by what she missed.

Adam and Eve were the first soulmates. Since there were no other mates to choose from, hopefully, they stuck together until their end. They set the stage for the consequences of giving in to temptation.

For another, we have the fallout of their decision. After that first sinful bite came first-born Cain, then his brother, Abel. Cain murdered Abel, and I'm not exaggerating (much) when I say that that is sometimes what family members want to do when they work together for very long.

A+ was a privately held family business. Wildman and his cousin, Barry, were the owners. Grace worked closely with Wildman's wife and sat in a cubicle-style office next to his brother's. The vice president's wife worked in sales... and the nepotism went on. Fortunately, there were no murders; however, early on, Grace witnessed soap opera–worthy scandals.

Perhaps not surprising in a male industry, once a buyer got to know Grace a little more, the common question became, "Grace, could you send me a picture?" (Remember, it was the nineties—and social media creeping didn't exist.) The first couple of times it happened was a bit off-putting, so she ignored the question.

To avoid distraction from carnal nature, she developed a canned response: "I'm 5 feet tall, 300 pounds. Still interested?" to which they would uncomfortably fumble for words until she bailed them out with, "My looks have no bearing on my ability to give you the best customer experience. Let's stay focused on business."

To Grace, it was more important to be respected than anything else.

Moppsie did a great job of keeping her humble by frequently reminding her, "In the twinkling of an eye, you could lose your looks. It's what's on the inside that counts." Grace knew Moppsie spoke the truth and didn't take her looks for granted or mock others less fortunate.

The good ole boys on the other end of the phone didn't need to know all that—they just needed to stick to business.

As a manager, Grace had to periodically monitor sales calls for quality assurance purposes. While the veteran females on her team were professional, Grace hired a female or two who enjoyed flirting with the customers a little too much. After several company policy violations, Grace had to fix those problems. Handling those unpleasant situations kept Grace awake at night.

What helped her sleep was thinking about the hysterical first-bite story that involved the head buyers from Cabela's and their initiation challenge. Combining their names sounded like a law firm that served pancakes and ice cream: Robbins, Perkins, and Bramer.

To keep orders rolling in, Grace had invited Rick Robinhood, the vice president of merchandising for A+, to join her on an in-person visit to Cabela's headquarters located in Sidney, Nebraska. Rick was an industry legend and maintained the highest reputation rating in the industry for honesty, integrity, and humility. Buyers adored him, and Grace thought, *What could be better than to have a legendary merchandising executive accompany me?* They flew to Nebraska, then drove about an hour and a half past some lovely windmills to arrive in Sidney late in the afternoon.

Rather than meet at headquarters that late in the day, dinner at Dude's Steakhouse & Brandin' Iron Bar was suggested.

"Dude's? Are you being serious right now?" Grace asked, already feeling like there might be a prank in her near future.

"Yes, Dude's.... They have good food," one of the Cabela's buyers replied. "We'll meet you there."

Rick and Grace found Dude's and were soon joined by the buyers—who, while professional, were also still good ole boys. Before Grace even looked at the menu, the Dude's brandin' began.

"Now Grace, we like doing business with you; however, if you want to keep our business, you're going to have to be initiated into our club," one buyer started, then the others joyfully chimed in.

Grace looked at Rick hoping he would come to her rescue. Instead, he too had a mischievous grin from ear to ear.

We're in a public place; how bad can it be? thought Grace. "Whatever it takes!" came out of her mouth.

"That's the spirit," they said. "All you must do is swallow one big bite of an appetizer we're going to order for you."

The server brought out a plate of Rocky Mountain Oysters (look it up). Not one to be scared away, Grace grabbed an oyster, and down her hatch it went. She was an official member of the Cabela's Club, and the business continued to grow. Rick later told her, "When you took that first bite, they loved it and told me, 'Boy, she's got moxy!'"

Fortunately, the buyers at Galyan's didn't put Grace through any first-bite rituals. However, she did help them open their first two stores in the Twin City area: one in Minnetonka, and the next in Woodbury.

At their grand opening event, her moxy dwindled a bit as she stood at the entrance of the hunting section of another new store. Like excited elephants, she knew there'd be a slew of shoppers charging at her within a few minutes.

Questions from retail customers were tougher than those from retail business owners. Here, Grace didn't have a catalog or computer to obtain definitive answers. She may have looked calm on the outside, but the ducks were a-paddling inside of her. *Today, my folder is "smooth sailor" teal,* she thought.

Her prayers for calm wisdom were interrupted by Johnny F, whose smile and enthusiastic greeting were as bright as a ray of sun! (Prayers answered!) *Johnny's a Golden Glower!* she guessed.

Johnny F worked for RSR, a competitor of A+ Sports. Like Grace, Galyan's was his customer, and he was also there to support them. She recalls their warm handshake, during which Johnny F said, "Oh, you're Grace, I've heard about you! If you need any help, just let me know!" to which she replied, "Would you mind standing next to me for a few minutes? I still get a little nervous during these events, as I'm afraid I won't know all the answers to the customers' questions."

"Of course!" was his cordial answer. He kept his word, and together, the two of them managed the crowd like rock stars.

Johnny F was an angel to her in that moment—and not her competitor. And that is how she consistently found her industry experience to be: People from competing companies loved the industry so they worked together toward a common goal.

Instead of "A Tale of Two Cities," Grace named this Galyan's grand opening story "A Tale of Two Johns"!

As soon as Johnny F left Grace's side, up walked Johnny A, who worked for Galyan's as an assistant manager. His charm was quieter than Johnny F's, but just as soothing to Grace's soul.

Saving her from the questions she was hesitant to answer, Johnny A's tender stroll across the store's artificial turf triggered Grace to mentally place him in her green turf tender folder.

Johnny A continued to put Grace at ease by making her laugh. When he learned that the other guy's name was also Johnny, he asked her, "Did you hear what the one John told the other?"

She thought for a second, then laughed while answering, "You look a little flushed!"

"I know that one because my grandfather's name is John, and he too was supportive and loads of fun!" she added.

Galyan's Trading Company began in Indianapolis as a grocery store that also sold hunting and fishing supplies. Founded in 1946 by Albert and Naomi Galyan, it evolved into a successful sporting goods store that was later purchased by their son, Pat Galyan. Galyan's was special to Grace because it was another family business.

Speaking of family, while in Minnesota, she tracked down her brother, Pi, whom she hadn't "spied with her little eye" since 1985.

While Grace didn't meet Pat Galyan, she heard many positive comments about him. She appreciated Galyan's hands-on displays, theatrical design, and especially their purposeful intent to cater to women in sports. Their stores ranged between 80,000 to 100,000 square feet. The goal was to be The World's Coolest Sports Store. From what Grace could see, they were on their way, and she was delighted to help them.

Figuratively cool, yet literally hot, was the sunny afternoon she spent with Swooperwoman at a company-sponsored outdoor event. There was most likely a politician or three there, along with several of A+'s best firearm retailers.

Cousin Barry had built a fabulous sporting clays range within a few minutes of A+, and it was often the location where company events took place. If you aren't familiar with shooting sporting clays, Grace would highly recommend it. Some described it as golf with a gun but much more fun!

Before working at A+ Grace had no experience with shooting shotguns; however, she was extremely fortunate to work with a man at A+ who was also a shooting coach, and he gave her a few lessons. She could have shot better if she'd paid more attention during her lessons because her teacher became a National Sporting Clays Association (NSCA) Level III professional shotgun shooting coach.

Grace enjoyed teaching Greenhorns how to navigate the course. Her lesson on properly aligning one's shoulder to the gun's rear helped avoid the stock taking a first bite out of their body. One day, at the A+ company event, there was a bit of a lull in the festivities. Swooperwoman and Grace stood quietly as they waited for the last few groups of shooters to finish on the range and gather for dinner. Suddenly, Swooperwoman got excited when she spotted Victor Pierce in the crowd.

Swooperwoman shared that for the last few weeks, she and her team from A+ had been at Pierce's Gun Shop to film some video testimonials. She had gotten to know Victor through the experience and felt Grace would really like him. Grace observed Victor as Swooperwoman spoke. He was laughing, which made his good looks even more appealing; however, she wasn't in the market for a romantic opportunity.

See, a few months prior and for the first time while working in the firearms industry, Grace had allowed a long-time customer to woo her into enjoying weekends with him. During business hours, they remained all business. The weekends were spent traveling the country, going to, of all places, gun shows. *Wow*, she really was a workaholic.

"It's tough to read the label when you're inside the bottle," Grace liked to say, and boy was she inside the bottle, ignoring all the warning signs. Victor was Swooperwoman's subtle attempt to save her best friend from staying in the wrong bottle too long.

Surviving the first bite of retailer romance, Grace considered that trying a bite from a different tree might lead to longer-lasting results.

Chapter Seventeen
It's Worth Trying

Knowing this, that the trying of your faith worketh patience.

—James 1:3 (KJV)

"Try, try again" was a good motto for Victor Pierce, as he was in the process of getting divorced from his wife, with whom he had two beautiful children.

Okay, so Grace was a little captivated by his *pierc*ing blue eyes and his strong sense of self. But when she heard he came with children, she thought, *Next!* She just wasn't ready for that step.

At the end of the event, Grace was stepping across a gravel drive to get to her car, deep in thought, when an SUV nearly ran her over. She heard laughing.

It was Victor Pierce, trying to be funny. Okay, since she didn't get hurt; it might have been a teeny bit funny. They talked, and Victor said goodbye with a promise to call her. "You know where to reach me," she said playfully.

Remember Grace's former hubby, Charming Taz? Well at this point, he had been married to Sweetie for a few years. Grace caught wind that they were going to build a new home and sell the one she had originally lived in with him.

It was a charming house, and Grace decided she wanted it. When she reached Charming Taz by phone, he told her that five people were already in a bidding war for the house. But, before disappointment set in, she could hear Sweetie in the background: "Is that Grace? If she wants this house, we're selling it to her." Grace really liked Sweetie! And that is exactly what happened.

At this point in her young life, Grace was traveling on the weekends for gun show getaways while maintaining straight A's in college. She had purchased a house and was leading a new sales team to the top of the sales charts. She was far too busy to think about a new encounter with Victor Pierce.

A pastor once challenged Grace's logic, when he pointed out that love and hate are *not* opposites. In essence, he explained that love and hate are both emotions that indicate interest. Logically, why would you battle with someone if you weren't interested in them? To her, battling was an attempt to win something or someone over to your side. If you weren't interested, you wouldn't care enough to fight or try to win. So, she agreed the opposite of love or hate is disinterest.

When poor Victor called, he wasn't expecting to be received with disinterest.

Grace was a little surprised when her caller ID at work read "Pierce's Gun Shop" because she had never directly dealt with that store before. Answering professionally, she was almost shocked when Victor Pierce got right to the point: "Grace! I'm calling to see if you'll go out with me this weekend."

"That depends," she retorted, to buy a few seconds to think. "Are you officially divorced?"

He laughed and seemed to enjoy how she got right to the point. "No, not officially; however, we've been separated for..." (She didn't hear the end of his sentence.)

Without hesitation, she replied, "I don't date married men. Call me when you're officially divorced, and we'll see what happens."

Before he could say another word, Grace professionally added, "Thanks so much for calling. I appreciate your interest." And she disconnected.

A few months later, that same number popped up on Grace's caller ID.

She answered in her usual upbeat manner.

This time, Victor's introduction began with, "Hey, Grace, you'll be seeing me Friday night at 7:00 when I pick you up for our first date. Be sure to mark it on your calendar."

You may be thinking, *Wow, that guy was bold.* Or, *Wow, what if she had plans?* Or even, *Wow, I wish a man would say that to me.*

Wow is what Grace thought as she smiled from ear to ear. *He's driven, bold, and courageous; just like me.* What she said was, "Just so we're clear, you are officially divorced, right?"

"I will be on Thursday. See you on Friday night at 7:00. Gotta go!" was Victor's reply. Then, Grace heard the dial tone.

He's going in my red, go-getter folder for sure! Grace thought. *Although his label may change from "Go-Getter" to "Go-Get-Her."*

Touché... Victor had won!

Swooperwoman sat in an office cubicle next to Grace, so she heard their conversation. Grace turned to look at her best friend, who wore a grin. "Yes, that was Victor. Yes, we're going on a date Friday night. Yes, he'll be divorced. And yes, I can see why your instinct told you I'd like him. Thank you for the introduction, but don't get your hopes up," Grace volunteered.

Swooperwoman smiled and quietly said, "You're welcome. I'm excited for you. You'll have fun." And they got back to work.

Chapter Eighteen

It's the Hunt that's Challenging

The lazy do not roast any game, but the diligent feed on the riches of the hunt.

—Proverbs 12:27 (NIV)

Grace was tempted to back out of the date with Victor. She was happy with her life just the way it was. And if Victor had been any other way but his persistent self, she could have easily turned him down.

Grace realized that she and Victor were both driven by challenges. Later she learned that instinctively, humans are naturally drawn to other humans who are like themselves. Or, in Grace's terms, people tend to share the same-colored folder. Yes, opposites may attract; however, in this case, iron sharpened iron—and things were about to get *red* hot. How could Gritty Grace turn down that opportunity?

Well, she couldn't.

So, she dove into her blue, deep-diver folder and analyzed the situation. She decided that if the date started to overheat, she'd throw some cold water on it in the form of truthful details. And that, she did.

Ugh, the first date was a disaster. Grace told Moppsie she'd never go out with Victor Pierce again.

However, a few days later, Victor continued his hunt by spontaneously arriving at her house at 7:00 a.m. to hand-deliver a dozen roses to her before she left for work.

Not one for surprises, Grace responded, "I don't have time for this, I've got to get to work." She drove away and left him standing in her driveway. However, when the surprise wore off, she realized she'd better get busy getting better at being buttered up.

Later that morning, she called to apologize, then sweetly thanked him and agreed to keep him in her dating pool.

"Smile, Smoochie," Victor greeted her as she entered his kitchen the following Friday night. After a long week and an hour's drive, Grace's mind was still deep-diving into the details of why she was there. Victor wrapped her in a huge hug. For the second time that week, her skepticism melted away.

Grace realized she liked sharpening her iron will against his impervious armor. After several months, Victor, along with his two little Piercers, won Grace's attention away from the industry Weekender.

Winning attention by persistence wasn't Victor's only skill. His family maintained a reputation in the firearms industry as incredibly sharp business owners who persevered. Pierce's Gun Shop had been in business since the 1930s. It began as a general store founded by Victor's grandparents. A few guns were ordered to satisfy customers' requests, and eventually, firearms and associated accessories became their core business. Grace loved their family legacy. It was as comfortable as a glove since her hands had always worked for successful family enterprises.

Pierce's Gun Shop also maintained a top position on A+ Sports' independent retailer leader board.

By day, Grace was engaged with top corporate executives from the major chain stores. On occasional nights and many weekends, she voluntarily worked at Pierce's to be close to Victor. You could say that she was fully immersed in the firearms industry. For her, it was heavenly.

Not heavenly was overhearing the disparaging remarks between Victor and his A+ salesperson who regularly referred to himself as "bald, broke, and butt ugly." "Don't say that about yourself," Grace would plead from across the narrow aisle. "Why not, it's true." was his comeback.

Before her promotion, Grace regularly played euchre with Baldy, Swooperwoman, and a few other co-workers including Blondie Bombshell, and a guy named Groovy. They played during work break times; however, when Swooperwoman, Groovy, and Grace were promoted to management, that fun was prohibited during work. So, the group began hosting weekend parties at their homes.

In Grace's opinion, Baldy was lucky that he wasn't forced into management. When she started dating Victor, she regularly overheard the two of them exchanging private details and negative comments about her both personally and professionally. Although difficult to stomach, she realized Baldy and Victor served as each other's therapists and her strength seemed the target of their mutual resentment. Considering how each masked their true opinions when they saw her face, Grace contemplated how her private conversations with Swooperwoman would sound to Victor. To prevent further verbal venting, Grace quietly wrote Victor a letter to clearly articulate what she was hunting for in a mate, including her rules of engagement.

Grace doesn't recollect telling Baldy or Victor that she endured years of hearing their not-so-nice opinions of her; instead, she embraced their critique as enlightenment on how to improve. Years later, reflection on those words helped her explain the gnawing in the pit of her stomach that kept her from marrying Victor. Biblically pondering the consequences of intimacy without marriage prompted this question: *Grace, what would you expect from someone whose true thoughts I've continually revealed to you?*

Whether reverential, real, or imagined, fear and a lack of trust kept her from marrying Victor.

Grace gave Victor a bit of an excuse. In one of the many sentimental cards he wooed her with, he included a line that said, "She tripped his emotional trigger." Another sentence expressed his admiration for her firm spiritual foundation, which was lacking for him.

Grace had no excuse. She had unintentionally made Victor her newest idol, attempting to please him and herself above God. She'd heard this referred to as carnal or fleshly behavior. Looking back, she could kick herself in the rear of her rebellious carcass!

Grace went to Catholic Mass every week to sustain a relationship with Jesus. After a few years, Victor and his children went to mass with Grace several times; however, that commitment didn't stick long-term.

This left Grace with a decision: She could risk marrying a second man who wasn't focused on Jesus, or continue hoping that Victor's heart, in time, would eventually follow hers. If they married, Grace feared the challenge of the hunt would end for Victor, and he might go hunting for someone else.

Her hesitation did not carry over to her business life. Daily she hunted for ways to improve her efficiency in contacting more customers, leading more people, and gaining more business.

In May 1998, Grace was in Key West, Florida, hooking big fish with a rod and reel. Taurus, a popular firearms manufacturer, had invited the key executives from A+ to Florida to tour their factory. Enjoying a few days of vendor-sponsored fishing helped her understand how to develop deeper relationships with her customers.

Two more chain stores based out of Michigan: MC Sports and Dunham's joined Grace's client list. She developed customized special-order catalogs for these chains, giving their customers a broader assortment of products.

Grace frequently visited both corporate headquarters and individual stores, voluntarily training associates on how to utilize their custom catalogs and improve their selling skills.

Wolfman (a.k.a. Jamie W) worked for MC Sports, and he made Grace's life a little sunnier each time they talked. When he moved to Gander Mountain, he introduced her to the team there and the sales began to flow.

Grace will be forever grateful for the connections she made. Hunting for business in this male-dominated field was challenging; however, her customers filled her life with a joy that was easy to pass along.

Chapter Nineteen
It's Time to Party

There is nothing better for a man than that he should eat and drink and make himself enjoy good in his labor. Even this I have seen is from the hand of God.
—Ecclesiastes 2:24 (Amplified)

It was 1999, and with A+'s top-notch support, Grace had grown national account sales to nearly $10 Million. Due to this enormous growth, an administrative assistant was added to Grace's budget for 1999, and a salesperson was added for 2000. She was managing corporate accounts externally and again managing a team internally, making her the only manager with dual roles.

As had been the norm, she had a lot of autonomy and played a unique role within the company.

The Scheels stores were also growing and expanding due to their excellent leadership. Grace proactively sought ways to add more value. For Scheels, that was in-store visits to work alongside their managers and staff. Before grand opening parties, Grace would spend days in the new stores, doing whatever was necessary.

"Whatever" included stocking shelves, pricing merchandise, setting up end cap displays—the list was long.

Remember Curt, the executive from Scheel's who wasn't having any of Rocketman's attempts to steal her thunder? Well, one of Grace's most embarrassing yet favorite stories about Scheels' grand-opening preparation involved Curt and well-intentioned cleaning.

The Scheels team was ahead of schedule for their Lincoln, Nebraska, opening, so there were only minor tasks that needed to be done. Grace couldn't stay idle, so she went to Curt politely demanding: "Give me something helpful to do." He pointed to a Beretta display case, designed to hold several of their Italian-made, beautifully engraved, over-and-under hunting shotguns, and said: "You can clean the glass on the Beretta case."

She was on it immediately. With one side gleaming, she sprayed the other side, and just as the paper towel in her hand touched the roughly six-foot pane of glass, it shattered into pieces. She was devastated. Shocked, she looked at Curt and started profusely apologizing and questioning how that happened, as she had barely touched the glass.

While Curt would have normally teased her unmercifully, he calmly said: "There's nothing I can do or say that can make you feel any worse about this, so let's find a way to make it better." And they did! Good ole Curt. After retiring, he went on to win medals and travel the world as part of the USA FITASC Team.

Y2K universally added stress to many corporations, as their technology divisions prepared for an anticipated computer meltdown. Thankfully, God didn't allow the world to end, and business flourished.

Also flourishing were relationships, as Grace and Victor jetted to St. Maarten for a romantic vacation. They were guests of the heir to an ammunition company who habitually teased Grace by making kissing sounds every time she got close to Victor. He called her Smooch, she called him Smoochie, and that affectionate name stuck. Smoochie succeeded and became the president of his father's company.

During this successful rise, A+ Sports made a few executive management changes, including replacing Rocketman with a manager from one of A+'s satellite offices who was often teased about his accounting background.

Billy Beancounter often jokingly said, "I'm not the boss, Grace is!" Grace appreciated the autonomy Billy gave her. He most likely appreciated that she was so driven that not much was required from him.

On the college front, the spring semester meant taking the required Intro to Speech class. Due to the company speech trauma, she'd suffered eight years prior, this class seemed more punishment than party to Grace.

Dr. Doberman started the first class by making each student write, then immediately present, a sixty-second introduction speech. Gritty Grace decided this time, she was going to rock this class rather than run away.

Week two's assignment was an informational speech. Grace informed her class about her embarrassing first public speech at A+ Sports. Her closing lines: "If I can get up in front of all of you and give this speech after the utter embarrassment I suffered on Friday the 13th, you can do it too! Rather than be afraid—be passionate! Thank you!"

The class seemed inspired. At that moment, she realized how God had used Rocketman's gift of persuasion to trigger a passionate transformation in her speaking abilities. She was grateful.

When it came time for the memorized speech, Grace found a book of poems that contained "Hiawatha's Childhood" and repeated her childhood delivery of the 95 lines, with complete peace. To Grace, the ease of the assignment meant God kept the promise He'd made to her in Jeremiah 29:11.

The last class represented the toughest assignment. Each student had to write about a controversial subject, take a stand regarding their viewpoint on said subject, and then deliver a speech that moved the entire class to be open to agreeing with them on their viewpoint. After thorough research and armed with statistics, Grace educated the class on how concealed-carry laws helped to deter crime and urged them to protect their Second Amendment rights.

Grace got an A+ on every speech. Her mental attitude about speaking to groups completely changed, which was a fantastic reason to celebrate.

In the Fall of 1999, Dr. Alice's psychology class transported Grace to a mentally powerful wonderland. Who knew you could learn so much about human behavior from dogs, cats, bells, and boxes? *Giddy* was the best word to describe how Grace felt about psychology. Her textbook and that class answered all her whys from a scientific perspective. Plus, she could bounce those theories against what she believed about God, and to her, it was all connected and made sense.

Exposure to more methods of assessing and understanding people was helpful when attending the SHOT Show, which consistently ranked near the top of the largest annual events held in the United States. While it was a ton of work, it was also loads of fun, as grand parties were hosted by major manufacturers in the evenings, during SHOT each year.

Even if you're not familiar with the firearms industry, you would likely recognize some of the celebrities Grace was privileged to sight during SHOT Shows.

Glock, an Austrian manufacturer of the popular polymer-framed semi-automatic pistols, selected actor R. Lee Ermey, famous for his role as Gunnery Sergeant Hartman in the film *Full Metal Jacket*, to be at their booth during SHOT. The lines of people waiting to get his autograph were consistently long.

Grace also spotted a well-known advocate for hunting and gun ownership rights, Ted Nugent, a.k.a. The Motor City Madman.

Both R. Lee and Ted made visits to A+ Sports to speak.

One of her favorite photos is of the late R. Lee Ermey standing on the A+ stage with her leaning over his shoulder and laughing. It looked like she was pinching him, but honestly, she wasn't.

Glock threw spectacular parties at SHOT—great food, music, and dancing, which combined many of Grace's favorites. Glock parties were by invitation only. Fortunately, Glock's founder and Wildman were well acquainted. Wildman always made sure Grace got invited and would regularly re-introduce her to Mr. Glock saying, "You remember Grace, don't you? She's sold a lot of your product."

Several other manufacturers such as Smith & Wesson, Taurus, etc. also hosted great parties which Grace was always grateful to attend.

However, one of the best parties Grace attended was Cousin Barry's 60th birthday party, held at his private residence. A well-known musician was the entertainment, and the fireworks show was better than most July Fourth celebrations.

Early in their careers, Swooperwoman and Grace were responsible for the A+ Sport's show booth set-up. That required them to arrive at the convention site a few days early and work with a muscle-bound builder to get the booth physically in place.

One night in Vegas, after a long day of physical labor, Swooperwoman, Grace and Mr. Muscles went looking for a place to relax and unwind. Hearing their desire, the cab driver delivered them to a place called The Beach. It was dark and the building looked sketchy from the outside; but before words could be said, away the cab driver sped. Exchanging silent glances, then looking Mr. Muscles over, the girls smiled in unison, signifying, "We're good."

Once inside, they noticed there was hardly anyone else there. The place looked like a beach! The bartenders encouraged them to stick around, as the party would get rolling after 10:00 p.m.—and that it did! As they were nursing their non-alcoholic sodas, the crowd grew. Then suddenly, the music blared, the dance floor filled, whistles and toilet paper began blowing. That's right, toilet paper. When the girls looked up at the bar behind them, they saw two bartenders wearing only swim trunks, whistles in their mouths, and holding onto a long pole that extended between them. On that pole were several rolls of toilet paper, and behind the rolls, fans blowing.

It was crazy to watch!

The chaos continued, and directly after the blowing was the flowing—of free tequila shots. Neither Swooperwoman nor Grace were big alcohol fans; therefore, neither free booze nor the messiness that accompanied it was appealing. Mr. Muscles was guarding the girls, and he also wasn't interested.

While it was unlike anything they'd ever seen, when the trio learned the explosions were set to erupt every 30 minutes, they promptly prepared to leave.

A guy that looked like a model from the cover of a romance novel had been eyeing Grace. Noticing that she did not take the tequila, he approached her and asked, "May I buy you a drink?"

Politely she answered, "That's sweet, but no. My friends and I are getting ready to leave." Realizing he may not have much time to continue his moves, he persisted.

Before she knew what was happening, Mr. Muscles was in Mr. Model's face, preparing to play the Pal card.

"Listen, Pal, she said she wasn't interested, now walk away," he said. Apparently, like Grace, Mr. Model didn't like to be told what to do, and he pushed into Mr. Muscles with his chiseled chest.

Grace backed up to avoid getting punched or hurt; however, Swooperwoman magically sprouted an invisible cape and gold wristbands.

Instead of a fight, Grace watched her 5'4" bestie make room between the two men by putting a hand on each of their chests and physically pushing them apart with her super strength. Then, in a scolding voice with her fists balled and arms in an X, she repeated the words: "THIS WILL NOT HAPPEN!"

Stunned, the two men continued to back away from each other. Swooperwoman grabbed Grace, then Mr. Muscles by the arms and said, "We're out of here," and to the cab stand they went.

That party was over, and Grace was glad to be leaving. While it was *Wow, interesting*, for Grace, watching all that toilet paper unwinding was wasteful, not relaxing, and it wasn't a place she'd want to be stuck. Her superhero rescue will remain permanently etched in her mind as a powerful exit at the perfect time.

Powerfully impacting A+ Sport's bottom line, the chain stores continued to grow as did their grand opening party schedules.

Being inside the Cabela's Club paid off. Grace was invited to participate in Dundee, Michigan's, store opening in 2000. When she arrived, there weren't many restaurants or other businesses in the immediate area. Grace was impressed by the impact that Cabela's made on that community. Good thing she had the moxy to take that first bite.

In September 2000, Rick Robinhood, who had accompanied her on that first Cabela's trip, took the time to handwrite, "Grace, thanks for the great job you do!" across an email he had been carbon copied on from a Ruger executive to Grace which read:

Thanks for setting up the Iowa Scheels Stores tour. And even though we wish we could have sold more; I think events like this are very positive for A+ Sports and Ruger in the long run. You have a great relationship that I am sure will continue because of all your hard work. Again, thanks. ~Mike

Grace appreciated God, Rick Robinhood, and the firearms industry.

Back on her college's campus, the dean of business invited Grace to his office. He was aware that she was in a leadership position while enrolled. He made her an offer to write a portfolio about her real-life leadership experience that included observations of consumer behavior and operations management, and in exchange, she'd earn enough credits to graduate that May.

To celebrate her seven-year scholastic journey and graduation with honors, A+ Sports hosted a surprise party that Swooperwoman was most likely behind. Words could not describe the appreciation Grace felt.

Chapter Twenty

Obviously, It's Blind

Hear, you deaf; And look, you blind, that you may see.
—Isaiah 42:18 (NKJV)

Are you familiar with the term *inattentional blindness*? How about the sayings, "Love is blind" or "Turn a blind eye?" Obviously, Grace was! She believed female intuition exists and that humans have lie detectors in their gut; hence the phrase "trust your gut." It's whether she had the guts to handle the truth or not that made the difference.

Grace interpreted inattentional blindness as *a psychological phenomenon that occurs when a human doesn't visually see/notice what's right in front of their eyes*. It may be due to lack of attention, or because their attention is so focused on one thing that they unintentionally miss another thing that appears in plain sight. When we say someone "doesn't miss a trick," it may suggest we sense strong cognitive skills in them.

Poppsie, being a wise man who listened often and spoke little, was highly gifted in the cognitive realm and valued thoughtful, observant people. One day, without turning her head, Grace observed Poppsie sitting inside the garage as she pulled in her car. When she opened the door to get out, she calmly said, "Hi, Pops!" to which he replied, "I'm glad to see your peripheral vision works!"

The words *blind* and *peripheral vision* can take you to fascinating places. For instance, did you know that turkeys have incredible peripheral vision? With a flexible neck and eyes on the sides, a slight turn of a turkey's head equals 360 degrees of vision, which makes them incredibly hard to hunt. Therefore, one solution for hunters is a blind. Blinders are sometimes used on racehorses to lessen peripheral distractions and keep them focused. Blinds are used to cover windows so people can't see in. Grace's car was equipped with blind spot monitoring. Sometimes, the blind spot indicator light made Grace think of the song "Blinded by the Light." Grace wanted to live by blind faith in God and avoid blindsiding Moppsie whenever possible. Singing the lyrics to "Amazing Grace" once made her think that her color folders would be hard to find for people who are color-blind.

The point is that what we do and don't see, both literally and metaphorically, can be of great importance. Intentionally, Grace gave God the glory for the visions in her life and the strength to execute them. However, she found herself blindsided by Victor's 12-year-old daughter when she asked, "Can you explain how God works?"

Grace paused kneading the cookie dough they were making and mentally prayed, *Lord help*, and a glimpse of her holy-tricycle rolled by—directing her attention to the rolling pin by her right hand. "Honey, it's like this," Grace began as she rolled cookie dough into what appeared to be a heart topped with flames shooting out of it.

Grace continued, "This flame represents our Holy Spirit, which can burn bright or be dimmed; it is the sacred core of our existence, and like that apple core sitting on the plate next to you, the Earth's core that's staring at us from your science book, and the core abdominal muscles shown in this magazine article I was about to read, it's our innermost layer which protects the seeds of our gut instinct."

Next, Grace added dough to the heart-flame and rolled out a wobbly gingerbread woman. In the middle of Ginger's tummy, she inserted a small circle with two horizontal slits slightly above and on either side of it; making it look like a power outlet. "Honey, this is Ginger's soul layer which conceals her spirit. She uses this outlet in her tummy to connect her heart, brain, and willpower to her Holy Spirit so she can be powerful like a superhero." Grace explained.

Just then, Victor came down the stairs with a grin and pointing to his chin asked, "How do you girls like my new soul patch?" as the radio in the background played "The Devil Went Down to Georgia."

"Daddy, that hair on your chin makes you look mean; we prefer you clean-shaven! And don't come down here trying to steal our cookies or our superpower!" Victor's daughter sternly replied.

Laughing, Grace ended with, "Honey, our outermost layer is our physical body and it's easy to see, love, and—" with that, Victor simultaneously got a kiss, from each girl, on both sides of his lovely soul patch.

Remember Grace's fear of marrying Victor? Afraid that if she let her guard down, or married him, he would hunt for a new challenge? In 2002, that somewhat happened.

The year had started off with a bang—out in a field, where the pheasants fly and the dogs point. It seems important to point out that pheasants also have excellent vision and hearing, hence the need for bird dogs.

This wasn't just any old field, but one owned by a wealthy man. Grace wasn't wealthy, nor had she been pheasant hunting before; but she had Victor, and he had friends in heavenly places, at least when it came to hunting. It helped that his family owned a gun shop filled with all the material things necessary for a hunt—except girl-size clothes and boots. (Don't hate on Victor. Hunting clothes for girls was unheard of back then; Grace kicks herself for not chasing that opportunity.)

"I've got extra clothes and boots that you can wear," Victor told Grace.

"They'll be way too big; I won't know what I'm doing. I'll look like a fool in our industry," she vulnerably replied.

"Relax, Grace. It's a private hunting day. Just you, me, and my buddy who manages the land will be there," shared Victor.

Soon, she was wearing clothes that didn't fit and freezing in a field while looking ridiculous. Tripping over her own feet, in boots several sizes too big, she thought: *If I took a picture of myself right now, I'd see a Clown.*

Buddy was very kind to Grace and helped her hone her pheasant hunting skills, while Victor laughed at their fun. The three of them went hunting a few times before Buddy began dating a girl who became lustfully attracted to Victor. It wasn't long before Victor told Grace, "I'm just not attracted to you anymore."

FEAR can be an acronym for False Events Appearing Real or False Enemies Appearing Relevant. FEAR can also be an action verb used to cause emotional instability, prompting a painful or pleasurable need to escape. "Do not fear," seems a direct order from God, as the words "do not fear" are written in the Bible at least 365 times. By Independence Day, Grace realized her gut instinct, her internal fear, had materialized. Broken-hearted, she blamed herself for not having a holy enough spirit to hold Victor's attention, then punished herself for another failed romance.

During the day, she was a tough and fearless leader. At home, she had stopped eating and slept continuously to avoid dealing with her loss. This went on for several months. Her coworkers and customers visibly noticed a problem as her weight dwindled down to 103 pounds—not enough for her 5'8" frame.

They began asking her, "What's wrong?"

"Nothing, I feel great!" she would chirp, ignoring the hurt inside.

After their split, Grace saw Victor interacting with a manufacturer's representative at a trade show. Then heard Groovy, her old euchre partner and now fellow manager, say, "Grace, how can you stand there and lovingly gaze at that guy after he stomped on your heart like it was mud? He's making you sick. Customers are asking me if you're dying."

"Perhaps I love him unconditionally like God loves me." She replied calmly. "Thank you for your concern. Please tell customers that my unintentional diet plan is still part of God's plan and neither He nor I are ready to turn a blind eye toward Victor."

With a disgusted look, Groovy walked away as he said, "You need help."

Refusing to blindly stand by any longer, Moppsie intervened. As Grace was basking on the couch beside her self-pity pool,

Moppsie said: "You've allowed this situation to kick you for quite some time. How much longer are you planning to kick yourself?" Those wise words worked magic! Grace got up and off the couch—permanently.

In the Bible, John 5 tells a similar story regarding an invalid who had been lying by a pool in Bethesda for thirty eight years, waiting to get healed. When Jesus saw the man, He asked him, "Do you want to get well?" Rather than a direct yes or no, the man gave Jesus a couple of excuses. But Jesus said to him, "Get up! Pick up your mat and walk," and he did.

A few verses later, in John 9, Jesus observed a man who was blind from birth. His disciples asked whether it was the sins of the man or his parents that caused him to be born blind. "'Neither this man nor his parents sinned,' said Jesus, 'but this happened so that the works of God might be displayed in him.' Jesus spit on the ground, made some mud with the saliva, and put it on the man's eyes, then said, 'Go, wash in the Pool of Siloam.' The man went and washed, and came home seeing" (John 9:3, NIV).

Acts 9 tells the story of Saul, a persecutor of the Lord's disciples who was on the road to Damascus when suddenly a light shone around him from heaven. Saul fell to the ground, and then had a conversation with Jesus, whom he was persecuting. Saul went through a conversion process during which he was without sight for three days, and neither ate nor drank. Jesus sent Ananias to lay hands on Saul, filling him with the Holy Spirit and restoring his sight. His name was changed from Saul to Paul, and he began preaching Christ rather than persecuting him.

In Romans 7, Paul admits that even as an apostle, he doesn't understand why he doesn't do what he wants to do but instead does what he hates.

We all have our blind spots

Takeaways: Define

Gracie's story includes many instances when some internal drive thwarted her own best interest. Her fear of losing her brother kept her stuck in a sub-par relationship with him for decades. Her projection of her own failure led to exactly the result she anticipated.

Reflection

Take time to reflect on the following questions. Note that many of them require some thought and elaboration. Consider taking several days to journal about them or discuss them with a friend.

1. What were the formative events of your childhood? What memories bring you joy? Which memories make you sad, angry, or afraid? Who are the people you have yet to forgive for what they did to you?

2. What were your dreams as a child? What did you imagine when you played?

3. What kind of disposition do you have? Would you describe yourself as a passionate fist-pounder, a sunny storyteller, or a never-saw-it-coming gut puncher? Do you color in the lines or do you go all over the page?

4. What "trees" did you run into as a child? What messages did you tell yourself about what you could and could not do?

5. Where has disobeying God (or your own sense of right and wrong) caused burns, hurt, and pain? What can you learn from those events? How can you transform disobedience into obedience that brings healing?

6. Where have you felt separation or disconnection in your life? What got you through it? Can you identify a Bible verse, memory, or proverb that can give you strength and hope in future trials?

7. Think of your friends and the people you have dated. What traits do you resonate with? Which traits turn you off? What qualities may attract you in the moment but have turned out to be problematic?

8. Do you have comfort zones or hidey holes? Do you stay in your comfort zone too often? Where do you need to stretch yourself?

9. Do you have any dear friendships that began with friction? What do you find difficult about interacting with people in your daily life?

10. How do you define success? When have others been able to derail you from succeeding? When have you derailed yourself? How do you react when you fail?

11. Do you find yourself envying others' success or blaming them for your failures? Can you release those negative feelings in order to be open to growth through coaching?

12. Do you celebrate your achievements? How? Which achievements should you celebrate more?

13. How would you respond to the question, "How does God (or the universe) work?"

14. Do you believe you are powerless in your circumstances or that you can make real changes?

What are the underlying forces that are keeping you stuck in your circumstances? Below are some of the forces that presented obstacles in Gracie's life as illustrated in the preceding chapters. Mark any that are also problems for you, and add any additional issues not represented here.

Drilling Down

Achievement	Disobedience	Shortcomings
Adversity	Fear	Transitions
Blame	Insecurity/envy	Unpleasant revelations
Challenges	Projection	Willfulness
Competition	Restraint	
Confusion	Self-reliance	
Discouragement	Separation	

Look at your list of sticking points. If you identified more than one barrier, then your next step is to begin to prioritize them. For instance, if you find you are being willful, projecting negative events, and also fearful of something, then you need to ask, *Which of these is the most pressing problem, and which is least?* Maybe fear is actually behind both your willfulness and projection. Order your barriers and focus on the top three.

Once you define the real source of your problems, you are in a more effective position to plan for real growth. When you address the underlying problems, the presenting problems will often go away, but we'll look at that more in the following pages.

TEACHING to DESIGN

Once we have defined precisely what emotional and spiritual forces are holding you back, we can begin to design a plan to tackle those problems both head on and through indirect strategies.

The goal of the design stage is to answer the question, *What do you want?* Again, this may feel easy at first. You may think:

- I want to have more time with my family.

- I want to grow stronger in my faith.

- I want to get promoted and have more responsibility or leadership.

- I want to start my own company.

- I want to make more money so I can volunteer more often.

As we will see, however, it's best to think of those things not as the goals themselves but the elements that will help you achieve your underlying goals. We're looking for that deeper, emotional and spiritual desire that drives you.

As you follow more of Gracie's story, notice how her choices reflect her core values—or don't!

CHAPTER TWENTY-ONE
It's Off to the Races!

I have fought the good fight, I have finished the race, I have kept the faith.

—2 Timothy 4:7 (NIV)

Like a kangaroo in its mother's pouch, *race* can be found in *embrace* and *Grace*. *Fantastic* re-arranged contains *fans* and *fanatics*. This leads us to the association between Grace and the warm embraces of her *favorites*: Faith, Firearms and Race Fans/Fanatics.

There's an *N*, an *R*, and an *A* in *NASCAR* and you'll find *faithful fans* of both at the track.

Wow, did you know that like *wow*, *racecar* spelled backward is still *racecar*?

At the track is where you would have found Grace in September 2002—standing alone, overlooking the Kansas City Speedway while eating the biggest shrimp cocktail ever. Grace was meditating on the opportunities with which she'd been blessed. Here she was attending another grand opening party hosted by Cabela's.

About that time, a Cabela's purchasing executive walked up and welcomed her. Right behind him came Richard (Dick) Cabela himself. "You must be Grace! I've heard a lot about you. I want to personally thank you for taking care of us," Dick continued with warmth.

"It's an honor to be here, eating these deliciously enormous shrimps, overlooking this beautiful track, and celebrating your success. Thank you for your business! Being here is the best gift I could ask for!" Grace truthfully replied as she held up one of the shrimps.

The rest of the conversation was brief and ended with a friendly handshake. As Dick walked away, Grace remarked, "It's easy to see how that man built an empire—*wow*, he's inspiring!"

The purchaser said: "The way you held up that shrimp tail, I was afraid you were going to tell him about the first bite we made you take at Dude's." They both laughed, and the next day they worked their tails off—in the store, not in the pit.

It was a snowy night in January when Grace observed a different version of *racing* and *pits*.

Raymond, A+ Sport's VP of finance, also enjoyed coaching basketball. Grace had invited him to accompany her on a trip to visit MC Sport's Headquarters in Michigan. He suggested they leave a few hours earlier than planned, as he needed to make a stop along the way.

Raymond's pitstop pleasantly surprised her. Grace found herself seated in the front row of a Notre Dame basketball game. She had a bird's eye view of talented players' pits as they raced up and down the court.

Next, it was off to the Samsung/Radio Shack 500 for the Winston Cup Series at Texas Motor Speedway. As one of the largest distributors of Remington Arms & Ammunition, the A+ Sport's executive team, along with a few high-volume retailers, earned the honor of visiting the Hospitality Village.

There, they had up-close visits with Dale Earnhardt Jr. and Michael Waltrip. Grace didn't ask the questions racing through her mind; luckily, other members of her gang did. One of the coolest perks was receiving headsets that allowed their group to hear conversations between the drivers and their pit crews—a rare positive experience with the pit!

Topping the leaderboard of coolest racing adventures was when Grace qualified for a Richard Petty Driving Experience at Las Vegas Motor Speedway. This time, she would be in the driver's seat—awesome sauce!

She was sooooo excited. Then, her heart crashed into the wall after listening to a voicemail from Victor. He had also qualified. The voicemail was a courtesy call to forewarn her that he was taking a date. To avoid a complete heart attack, she forfeited the opportunity.

Her disappointment was short-lived. Less than 90 days later, Grace was ecstatic to be in North Carolina, standing next to Dale Jr. for group photos. The excursion included a private tour of the facility and Grand Showroom where several race cars were featured.

Dale Jr. was kind and generous with his time—allowing pictures, signing autographs, and answering questions for the A+ Sports group. Grace loved being the only female among her peers and customers. She worked hard to maintain that privilege and didn't take these events for granted.

Just for fun:

Question: Do you know why Speedway got so hot?
Answer: The fans all left.
Question: Do you know why heaven is so cool?
Answer: It's full of Jesus fans.

Chapter Twenty-Two

It's Girl Powered!

A woman from Samaria came to draw water. Jesus said to her, "Give Me a drink."

—John 4:7 (ESV)

Charlie's Angels was another of Grace's favorite, old-school, television shows. Farrah was her favorite Angel, and who can forget the original three's poster featuring girls with guns?

It was time for Grace to surround herself with an angelic team. The A+ Angels became a beautiful mix of blondes and brunettes, each equipped with a different set of talents.

Blondie Bombshell had been on Grace's first sales team; however, after an abrupt conversation with a Scheel's manager named Magruder, she told Grace "I can't do this, he was too intimidating!"

"Blondie, what color is your folder? Grace asked. "Orange!" Blondie shouted with glee. "Correct! You're a passionate persuader, so, to *move Magruder's mountain,* add a few more go-getter red streaks to your blonde ambition and pretend you're a rascally rabbit. Then imagine Magruder is an adorable orange monster and use those persuasive talents to give him a *permanent* reason to do business with you! Remember Scheels Managers appreciate professionalism and speed, and *you* are exactly who they need."

With just that tip, Bombshell blew the roof off sales. Together, the blonde duo expanded the business from Scheels, Bi-Mart, Bass Pro, Cabela's, MC Sports, Jumbo Sports, and several other stores.

To handle all the electronic orders pouring in, the team added Ms. Aimright. She completed the blonde trio. Ms. Aimright's role was to transfer hundreds of items from faxed orders into A+'s computer system. Her speed and accuracy were so impressive that it was like watching a professional shooter win an International Practical Shooting Confederation (IPSC) match.

One day, Ms. Aimright left a quote on Grace's desk. It read, "Remember, God won't give you more than you can handle." Although not Scriptural, it was comforting to Grace.

Aimright's concern stemmed from overhearing Victor's phone calls to Grace, asking her to take him back. Ms. Aimright had watched Grace rebound from heartbreak and didn't want to witness another round.

Victor was driven to win. Grace was saying no, no, no to his attempt at rekindling a romance, but he apparently was hearing yes, yes, yes as he continued to pursue her. Victor's sixth attempt came in the form of an after-hours call to her work desk. Like Grace, Victor was a go-getter, not a quitter—and neither was Ms. Bombshell, who also happened to be working late.

As soon as Grace disconnected, Bombshell exploded. She stood at the door of Grace's office and lovingly commanded, "Do not, I repeat, do not take him back. You nearly died from a broken heart. You won't make it another round!"

Somewhere in that time frame, Aimright married a charming carpenter. She left A+ to help her husband with his business.

A brunette applicant who just happened to share Aimright's skill set was God's gift to Ms. Bombshell and Grace. Ms. Doubtfire dove right in—assisting the team to create wins with the chain stores. Business skyrocketed, creating the need for one more salesperson.

Va-va-va-voom was how it felt when the newest angel entered the room. With her long brown hair came an angelic flare.

Shining as bright as the sun on the tender green turf, all gloom disappeared with Ms. VaVoom. Observing VaVoom's interactions, Grace noticed a pleasant twist. Effervescent, yet humble, Ms. VaVoom made her audience feel like they were standing in the limelight.

Shining bright meant VaVoom might exaggerate compliments or positive emotions to make the customer feel warm and important by expressing what she instinctively felt the customer needed to hear. That gained orders for her.

Quietly deep diving into written order details to ensure accurate shipping, listening to VaVoom light people up frustrated Doubtfire; she interpreted VaVoom's exuberant warmth as lies. That frustration sparked snarky comments like, "You need to quiet down and quit fibbing." VaVoom, detecting the sarcasm or disgust in Doubtfire's snarkiness, punched back with, "Maybe you just need to lighten up and learn how to take a compliment." This example quickly turned into a talent brawl rather than a successful tag team.

To diffuse their conflict, Grace helped them to focus on the talents they had in common. Then, she had them complete an exercise that provided clarity to their differences. The exercise proved enlightening and they realized that adapting and blending their talents made the team more powerful.

This conflict reminded Grace of the Bible story about Jesus taking a direct route through Samaria, to get from Jerusalem to Galilee, which is how he met the woman at the well. While most Jews preferred to keep the Samarians at a distance, Jesus met them with dignity. She reviewed this story for encouragement while leading her team.

Grace shared the following with Ms. Doubtfire and Ms. VaVoom: "Remembering that all of us must play multiple positions in this game called life. It can be very stressful to face our enemies and occasional imperfections. Imperfections or perfections are many times in the eye of the beholder(s) with whom we must interact.

"Considering that we can't take a vacation from ourselves, it's critically important that we maintain our internal peace. If we don't understand our highest value and our occasional shortfalls, we are more susceptible to offense, both from ourselves and others. A person who is easily offended tends to respond with defensiveness.

Did you girls know that I nearly cried when I read the results of the multiple reports about my areas of improvement? Believe me, I understand the conflict you two are having. Rocketman once told me that my biggest flaw was that I couldn't take critique. His advice: 'You have to be able to peel back your layers like an onion.'"

After pausing for a moment, Grace continued. "Rocketman wasn't wrong. I didn't like his words; however, I still listened and learned from him. It took acceptance, time, and vulnerability for me to push past that stress; and the blessing is that I now have that wisdom to share with both of you!"

Immediately after that meeting, the girls blended their colorful talents and produced over 16 million dollars' worth of sales which significantly exceeded their projected sales goal!

Chapter Twenty-Three
It's Trips and Turns

> *"With their hands they will lift you up so you will not trip over a stone."*
>
> —Psalm 91:12 (ISV)

Like Grace, Ms. VaVoom had been raised Catholic. Unlike Bombshell and Doubtfire, who were married, Grace and VaVoom were both single and in committed relationships.

Did you catch that?

Were you hoping that Grace followed Bombshell's advice and turned a cold shoulder toward Victor's advances? Or, were you camped in the Victor Victorious amusement park—hoping Grace gave him one more shot to prove that he could be trusted with her heart?

From a business perspective, Bombshell and Doubtfire flourished in the office, while VaVoom took her turn traveling North, South, East, and eventually West with Grace. Several Scheels stores provided the backdrop for VaVoom to receive her hands-on training. VaVoom's vivacious laughter entertained Grace as they restocked shelves and set up endcaps together.

Tripping with VaVoom gave Grace the escape she needed to avoid deciding how to proceed with Victor. Relationally, Grace's heart was heavy. She had huge doubts that Victor could ever be true and she privately prayed for clarity on what to do.

After Moppsie had courageously helped her escape from the heartbreak pity pool just a few months prior, Grace was afraid to tell her that she was considering a reunion. Moppsie sensed what was secretly transpiring and let Grace in on her own little secret. "A few weeks ago, I called a prayer hotline and requested prayers for you. When they asked for specifics of what to pray for, I told them healing from a broken heart."

Grace was extremely grateful and in awe at the same time. If she realized there was such a thing as a prayer hotline, she certainly hadn't considered it an option for what she was going through. "Thank you, Moppsie. I guess I thought I was on my own in trying to move forward. What did the person on the other end of the phone say when you told them it was a heart matter?" inquired Grace.

"They said they would pray," was Moppsie's answer.

"I'm honored that you called, but I also feel guilty. I consider myself the most blessed girl in the world. Shouldn't the prayer hotline be reserved for serious issues like disease, poverty, or the death of a loved one?" Grace continued.

"Oh Grace, God wants to heal every hurt of every person," said Moppsie. "That's why He lets us know that even the hairs of our heads are numbered. You also know that you have not if you ask not. I called on your behalf because, like God, I love you and want only the very best for you. It is God's will that needs to be done."

And then, Moppsie shared another of her profound proverbs: "Remember, we all have to ride our own horse!"

Immediately, Grace felt a huge sense of relief. Thanks to Moppsie, Grace knew there were armies of angels praying for her. She silently thanked Jesus for His sacrifice and asked Him to remove any guilt she felt about asking for His guidance.

Biblically, she learned from 1 Peter 5:7, that trusting God meant she could cast *all* her worries on Him because of how He cared for her. She decided to take one last leap of faith, trusting that God would turn her past trials with Victor into triumph.

As spring turned to summer, her care-casting resulted in a plentitude of literal fish, as she and Victor went on a Montana fly-fishing trip with Leo Lion and his girlfriend, Penny Peacock.

Working for a manufacturer's rep group, Leo was ferocious at selling Leupold Optics, as well as a plethora of other hunting brands. That group supplied products to both A+ Sports and Pierce's Gun Shop, so Leo had been connected to both Grace and Victor for many years. Penny was such a beauty; she made the fishing waders she wore look like picturesque plumes.

The trip was divine. Facebook wasn't born yet, but if it had been, you would have seen lots of pictures of smiling faces holding fishes from the Little Bighorn, whitewater rafting, bear cub crossings in Yellowstone, and nostalgic memorabilia from the Buffalo Bill Museum.

By the time Grace got back from her vacation adventures, VaVoom was totally in step with the rest of the team.

In July, VaVoom accompanied Grace to participate in an annual hunting seminar that Dunham's Sports hosted for their associates. Mr. Dixon of Dunham's wrote a lovely thank you note that said, "As you know, it's always a challenge to convey a message to your people and still have a little fun."

Grace tried to squeeze in a little fun alongside business when possible. Traveling to California to transition Turner's Outdoorsman over to Ms. VaVoom was a fabulous trip. By day, they strengthened relationships and secured orders. By night, they stood alongside Spiderman at the Chinese Theatre, in front of the lifeguard post on Laguna Beach, and next to some wax figures from The Last Supper that might make you stare.

CHAPTER TWENTY-FOUR
It's Outside Invasions

"Stand therefore, having girded your waist with truth, having put on the breastplate of righteousness."
—Ephesians 6:14 (NKJV)

In the fall of 2003, a new sheriff came to town; that is, A+ Sports named a new president. As far as Grace knew, he was not in Wildman's family. Rumor had it that he bought into the company.

The Hazzard County adventures of Sheriff Rosco P. Coltrane and Boss Hogg, who were brothers-in-law, amused young Grace. Luke Duke was cute, and she liked him a little extra because his name rhymed. Did you know that Rosco's P was short for Purvis?

Purvis starts with the letters P-U—which made Grace giggle. She mentally entertained herself by walking around, holding her nose, as if she were smelling something frightful. Free to cut loose, she acted like she was at a calling contest, PEEEEEEE-EEEEEEEW came out of her mouth. She could be a lot of fun!

Fun rhymes with pun, and both have U in the middle!

The name Purvis reminded her of another word—*impervious*—which then reminded her of the ballistic fiber body armor she once sold. Biblically, impervious reminded her of Ephesians 6, which contains Scriptures designed to keep humans spiritually safe.

Shortly after his arrival, Sheriff P. invited Grace to his office for an introductory meeting. Still managing the chain accounts group at that time, he asked her where she envisioned A+ in the future. She was impressed!

Not one to struggle for immediate thoughts or words, she replied: "Technology is the only way to go. The rapid growth we've experienced with the chain stores has taught me how to develop, manage, and sustain business in this somewhat antiquated industry. So, off the top of my head, I'd start a technology division; and then train independent retailers how to better manage and market their inventory. That edge would help them keep up with their competition. They need to be able to keep their piece of the retail pie, and if we can't help them, we may die."

Sheriff P. made a note. Then asked, "Where do you see yourself in the future?" Not knowing what to expect from the new guy, she hadn't prepared for this meeting. Still direct, she merged into her colorful side and out popped, "As the right-hand to a powerful businessman. I'm single and passionate about business, so implementing successful strategies alongside a strong man—that's my dream!"

SHOOT!... What the heck was that? Grace, you just fancifully shot yourself in the foot! He didn't mean personally, you silly goose! (That was of course her head talk.) Departing la-la land, she was afraid to look at him. Thankfully, Sheriff P. seemed unphased emotionally. *Oh well,* she thought... The truth is the truth. And the Sheriff had helped her reach clarity with just a couple of simple questions.

About a week after that meeting, her boss, Billy Beancounter, appeared in her office. "Hey Grace, Sheriff P. said to tell you that you'll be starting that new division you mentioned to him. He wants the wheels in motion by the first of the year, so I guess you better line up your successor and get rolling!"

"What new division? I don't know what you're talking about," she responded.

"I don't know what he's talking about; I wasn't in the meeting," Billy said with a grin. "What did you tell him?"

Audibly, she replayed the meeting. She uttered, "I'd start a technology division."

Billy B held up his hand, as if to hit pause, and said: "There it is ... now get to it; you don't have much time!"

Although smirking as he walked away, she knew he was serious. Laughing, she yelled out, "Could you at least wish me good luck?"

"You'll be fine!" was Billy's retort.

Billy was correct and very supportive. On November 24, 2003, he sent a letter announcing Grace's promotion to the executives of all the national chain accounts. She appreciated the congratulatory calls and notes she received in response to Billy's letter.

Grace was impressed that the executive VP of merchandising and chief operating officer of Gander Mountain back then (Code Name: Big AL) took the time to write "congratulations!!" to acknowledge her success.

Remember Reba? She was the female Grace promoted as a successful salesperson to Mr. Doughnuts. Well, Grace didn't lie, and Reba didn't disappoint. Grace chose Reba as her successor for the chain accounts.

Within just a few days of the letter going out, Billy called Grace to his office. He showed her an elaborate, yet easy to understand, modeling tool for optimizing inventory. By plugging in a few numbers, a retailer could see instant results. Billy and the company controller had developed this tool so that Grace would be well-equipped to help their retailers soar. This was another A+ Sport's example of teamwork, and how quickly they excelled.

A couple of weeks later, Sheriff P., Billy Beancounter, Grace and the rest of the A+ Sports management team were together to tour the Winchester Olin ammunition factory. Next, they drove to NILO, one of the most prestigious hunting and shooting preserves in the nation. When Grace heard the guide explain that NILO is Olin spelled backward, she thought, *Wow, that's kind of like wow, but different.*

The A+ Sport's management group enjoyed a couple days of team-building fun at that pheasant, chukar, and duck hunting oasis. However, watching the dogs work with superb skills was Grace's favorite part of the trip. When visiting the kennels, she learned the legend of King Buck while observing this regal Labrador's statue.

On the second day of hunting, during the lunch break, Grace was in the lodge relaxing in a leather chair when she noticed there was an interesting taxidermy perched on the table next to her. A split-second later, one of the boys asked, "Hey Grace, do you know what kind of bird that is?"

Sensing it was a set-up, she timidly asked, "Is it a partridge?"

"No," the guide replied. "It's a cross between a pheasant and a chukar. Can you figure out what it's called?"

The peer pressure almost caused her to shout the word they hoped for. Instead, out came, "Oh, I know! It's a *chesant*."

Disappointment appeared on the 12 male faces in that lodge. Nope, those boys didn't trick her into saying a *fowl* word.

NILO was a kingdom full of heritage, hospitality, and phenomenal wildlife making it the best hunting experience Grace had ever enjoyed.

Grass did not have time to grow under Grace's feet. By December 23, 2003, she had presented the A+ Sport's Inventory Management (AIM) system to shooting ranges and retailers in Michigan and Ohio.

Even more incredible; the eleven months spent with her girl-powered Angel Team resulted in over $18.7 million in sales that year.

Chapter Twenty-Five

It's the Big 4-0

> *"And when He had fasted forty days and forty nights, afterward He was hungry."*
>
> —Matthew 4:2 (NKJV)

In 2004, A+ Sports sent Grace to several executive training sessions to aid her career transition from national chain stores to inventory management. By March 10, Grace had completed certification for The Project Success Method: A Proven Approach to Superior Project Management. On March 12, while in the Atlanta Airport waiting to board the plane for home, Grace had a moment to think about the year ahead. That's when it hit her! In her mind, the number 40 in huge, gold, mylar balloons appeared.

"That's it," she shouted as fellow passengers gave her questioning looks. She projected, "This is the year Victor and I will be getting married! I'm turning 40, he's turning 40, it's 2004, which, when reversed, ends in 40... Yes, that makes perfect sense."

In an instant, she got so excited she started pacing around the gate. She even started quietly singing the lyrics to "Chapel of

Love." She saw golden wedding bands along with those gold balloons. "This is a golden idea, during a golden year of opportunity," she said to herself.

Biblically, she knew the number 40 was said to symbolize a period of testing, trials, or probation. In multiple biblical examples, what followed the 40 days, nights, or years was a big change, or as Grace liked to put it, *significant transformation*!

The Bible story of the Israelites taking 40 years to complete an 11-day journey began circling around in Grace's head. She thought of all the trials and tribulations she and Victor had made it through, which switched her mental radio station to: "She'll Be Coming 'Round the Mountain."

Her internal singing made her think of biblical David's 40th Psalm which expressed how he had patiently waited for the Lord who had heard his cry and answered his prayers. If David could go from a lonely shepherd boy to a king in a palace, it shouldn't be too hard going from single to married.

Okay, so there was a split second of fear that popped into her mind, but Grace quickly replaced that with, "Hallelujah, we're getting hitched! Yep, I'm finally hitching my horse to Victor's wagon—woo-hoo!"

Her thoughts continued: "We'll get engaged in 2004, while we're both 40, and since five is the Biblical number for Grace, 05-05-05 will be the perfect wedding date."

During the flight home, she tried to calm down. She closed her eyes, but all she could see was a wedding program with 05-05-05. She opened her eyes and planned her next steps, convinced this had to agree with God's will.

To drive this divine project forward, Grace planned to propose to Victor. She would have preferred it the other way around, but since the numbers had aligned in her mind, she proceeded to the jewelry store. Although her head was convinced proposing was the right thing to do, apparently her heart wasn't completely sold. She negotiated a deal with the jewelry store that if she got rejected, she would get a 100 percent refund.

Thankfully, the ring negotiation was the right thing, as the proposal never made it out of Grace's mouth. After a quiet dinner, as Grace opened her purse to pull out the ring, Victor must have suspected Grace was going to ask for a commitment. "Grace, don't!" Victor ordered in a stone-cold tone. She respected his wish and returned the ring the next day.

The next big transition in Grace's life was purchasing a house not far from Victor's. Her hope was that being five miles away versus fifty five would enhance their relationship, and eventually, they would get married. Instead, the move revealed the truth: Victor had been dating a woman he worked with, he just forgot to inform Grace.

Rather than focusing on relationship rejection, Grace developed a new division for A+ Sports. Deep diving into the due diligence process toward something new kept her from dwelling on the past. By mid-April, she had consulted with many firearms retailers who utilized software in their stores. She had also completed her visits to companies that provided this software. Her new venture required traveling from Minnesota to New Jersey to Florida to meet the technology folks connected with the shooting sports industry.

In the last week of April, Grace completed certification in forecasting/demand planning. Significant because it instantly propelled her knowledge and skill set—a huge benefit to A+ Sports and all their customers. She credits Sherriff P.'s foresight for elevating her education.

When Grace's spreadsheet of distinct advantages was complete, the software company that earned the highest rating won the partnership prize. That company was ARSE Software.

ARSE was based out of Minnesota and owned/operated by the Helland Brothers. Naturally, Grace razzed them about changing their names to the Heavenly Brothers.

She also asked them what ARSE stood for, to which they replied, "Nothing. We needed a name that began with A and just added the other letters to it."

Grace appreciated their unconventional naming method and gave it her own spin: "To me, ARSE means A Really Sweet Endeavor!"

The decision to select ARSE as A+ Sport's partner was based on logic and facts; however, the God winks to Grace were undeniable.

For example, back at that Galyan's opening, Johnny A had rescued Grace from consumer questions. It turned out that Johnny A had left Galyan's and was running the customer support department for ARSE. Coincidence? Grace thinks not and thanks God.

The partnership was a success. Grace made regular trips to Minnesota to meet with the Helland Brothers, Johnny A, and the rest of the ARSE Staff. Then, on one trip, an interesting thing happened. The owner pulled Grace aside and told her that after twenty years in business, he was ready to sell.

WHAT? she thought, totally blindsided.

"You've got to help me find a buyer," were the next words out of the owner's mouth. Followed by, "And Grace, I'm asking you to help me with this, because I want you to run the company for whoever buys it."

She was greatly concerned and honored all at the same time. *Concerned*, because it had been less than a year since the partnership had begun. Now, she had to go back to Sheriff P. and tell him this news. *Honored*, because clearly, she and the owner had built a great relationship, but now it was back to the drawing board. With a sunny smile, she told the owner, "I'll see what I can do."

Thankfully, Grace had so much on her work and life plate, that she had to rely on God to get her through all the events that were happening during her fortieth year on Earth.

"Proactive over reactive," was Grace's motto. It hadn't faired too well with Victor and the marriage proposal, but Grace knew she was much, much better at business. So, as soon as she got back from Minnesota, she walked into Sheriff P.'s office and told him about the owner wanting to sell.

Clearly, God was still guiding Grace's path because it wasn't long after that meeting that A+ Sports bought ARSE through a holding company of sorts. It would have been a total waste of time for Grace to let her concerns rule over God's plan. She was thrilled to be able to move forward stronger than before.

There was only one caveat for Grace to contend with: she had to keep the acquisition completely confidential. While she understood why, it put her in a difficult position, especially with the A+ Sports' customers who relied on her.

Several of the customers lovingly nicknamed her, The ARSE Girl. So, when they heard ARSE had sold, they immediately called her to ask, "What's going to happen to our program?" or "Who did ARSE sell to, and how does that affect us?"

Grace purposely hadn't dug for details about the acquisition, and Sheriff P. provided the script she stuck to. This provided honesty, with the details protected, as if she were a gun vault.

After the acquisition, Grace kept her promise to Mr. Helland by asking Sheriff P. to include managing ARSE under her responsibilities. To which he asked, "Are you going to move to Minnesota?"

She replied, "No, however, I make frequent trips there now. With my existing relationships, we can make it work."

He told her the manager had to live there, then hired a man who lived in Chicago.

Before letting any ill feelings develop over this interesting move, Grace trusted that God had a better plan in store for her. She kept moving forward.

Chapter Twenty-Six
Is It Techy, Touchy, or Both?

> *"And He said to them, 'Cast the net on the right side of the boat, and you will find some.' So they cast, and now they were not able to draw it in because of the multitude of fish."*
>
> —John 21:6 (NKJV)

If you happen to be a fan of skeet, trap, or sporting clays, it's probably a safe bet that you own at least one *side-by-side* or perhaps a sweet *over-under*.

While not technically as far-reaching as her 12-gauge, Grace's favorite shotgun was a Remington 1100, 28 gauge. She named it *Sweet Remi*. The perfect seven men she went dove hunting with one day laughed when she insisted Sweet Remi would be sufficient to deliver results. They became a little touchy when the bird dog laid the first seven birds at her feet.

Truthfully, she admits her success was not due to technical skill; the bird dog just seemed to like that Grace was the only girl in the group.

Although no longer romantically intertwined, Victor and Grace continued to do business together. He helped her get a new gun safe; she trained his staff on A+'s new technology.

With tons of outside-the-industry experience, Sheriff P. launched a long-term strategy. The goal was to become the high-tech, high-touch distributor of choice. Based on extensive research, A+ Sports realized they would have to change the way they did business, or they'd be out of business quickly.

Thankfully, Grace had built solid relationships with the chain stores. Understanding how the chains managed large volumes of inventory placed her in the perfect position to lead a national value-added strategy with independents like Pierce's Gun Shop. The independent retailers had assigned salespeople who provided products. Grace was a bonus resource; delivering high-level, technology-driven, innovative solutions, which most owners weren't aware existed. She quickly realized she was a built-in business consultant to the sales team and retailers alike.

Grace loved traveling to gun shops to share A+'s innovation. While some customers were a little saltier than others, once they saw the value proposition, they jumped on board like ants on a sugar train. And... it just kept getting better. Like fishermen casting their nets on the other side of the boat, A+ Sports was creating new channels of commerce to help retailers grow, and a multitude of requests for additional services came flooding in. The techy part was growing rapidly.

The customer engagement score skyrocketed, creating a positive frenzy throughout A+'s network. Manufacturers, customers, and employees passionately pushed for more programs which meant the marketing touchpoints were thriving.

Grace's bestie, Swooperwoman, had transferred out of sales and into A+'s information technology department years before this explosion hit. By the fall of 2004, Swooperwoman and Grace were back to working side-by-side on several new A+ projects which included launching a retail services division, developing an electronic website for retailers to shop online, and creating an integrated e-commerce solution for larger, more advanced customers.

In brief, this new website gave end users access to A+'s available inventory, which was roughly 80 to 90 percent more product than a physical store could hold. Plus, it saved retailers from having unwanted inventory that collected dust and carrying costs. It seemed like every step along the way prepared Grace for the next one.

Chapter Twenty-Seven
It's Supposed to Stay in Vegas!

"The Lord is good, A stronghold in the day of trouble; And He knows those who trust in Him."
—Nahum 1:7 (NKJV)

The 2005 SHOT Show was held in Las Vegas January 28–31. Grace figured it was, at the least, her twenty-fifth trip to Vegas, also known as Sin City.

Trained that image matters; Grace strived to be a sharp-dressed woman. The red power suit she wore during a SHOT Show training session on ARSE software caught the attention of at least one of the approximately 100 customers in attendance.

Later that day, Grace noticed Freddy Feathers, a premier retailer, and his team of buyers on the SHOT Show floor. They had attended her morning training session. Although her direct contact with Freddy had been minimal, she had visited his store many times. She took this opportunity to shake hands and strike up a conversation.

Oozing with charm, Freddy complimented her training abilities, shared his appreciation for how she helped his business, and then added, "And *wow*, you look hot in that suit."

Grace, appreciative of the compliments, was moved to hug him!

In this good ole boy industry, hugging was the norm—but not for professional, all-business-minded Grace. When they were dating, she even warded off poor Victor, warning, "No PDA during business hours!"

When the embrace was over, Grace stepped back with a bit of shock. Looking at Freddy's face, he seemed a bit shocked too... as was the rest of his team.

With a heartfelt smile, Freddy said, "Wow, thank you—that felt good." A warm tingly feeling came over Grace, it was one of those moments when time stood still. Little did she know that the ice was broken in more ways than just business.

On day two of the show, Grace was in A+'s booth, mentally reminiscing about the many SHOT Shows she had attended with Victor Pierce at her side, and *poof*, her thoughts were interrupted by the literal appearance of Victor and his new female sidekick.

As they entered the booth, Grace's replacement slid her hand into Victor's back pants pocket, while jeering directly at Grace. Bombshell noticed the affectionate display and discreetly whispered, "It appears she's taunting you with her lovey-dovey body language."

Fighting the cartoonish urge to punch Lovey-Dovey right in her kisser, Grace took the high road and tried to redirect her attention toward other customers. Unfortunately, no unattended customers could be found. After several minutes, which felt like hours, the elevation of the high road caused Grace to believe she was having a heart attack.

She went behind a curtained area of the A+ Sports booth and sat down on the floor, trying to catch her breath. Thankfully, her boss saw what was happening and followed her. As soon as she saw him, she exclaimed, "I think I'm having a heart attack—call the paramedics."

"Grace, you're having a panic attack, not a heart attack," he compassionately replied as he sat down next to her.

He conveyed that while Victor was a great customer, the heart problems she had endured from him exceeded the acceptable limit. "You're much better off without him!" he said. "Now let's get back on the Respectable Grace Highway.

Grace's boss stood up and gave her this order, "Stay put, breathe deeply, and remain calm. When Lovey-Dovey is gone, I'll come and get you." Which he did, and Grace calmly moved on with the rest of her day.

With only two exceptions, one accidental, the other an attempt to quiet a chanting room of cheeseheads during a Green Bay Packers game, Grace was not prone to an overindulgence of alcoholic beverages. That night, rather than hosting a pity party in her lonely hotel room, Grace decided to join her fun-seeking coworkers. However, while they were frolicking, Grace wound up playing the role of a brokenhearted human sitting alone at the bar, quietly licking her wounds.

She wasn't there very long when one of Freddy Feather's employees appeared on the bar stool next to her. "Two Scooby Snacks," Grace heard him say to the bartender.

Laughing, Grace teased, "Scooby is a fictional dog. Shaggy, how much have you had to drink?"

"Nothing yet, but one of those snacks is for you. We're in this together," he replied

Normally, Grace would *not* have found herself in this scene, and if she did, she would have replied with a polite, "Oh, no thank you."

This day hadn't been normal. Being at a SHOT Show without the love of her life wasn't normal. Hugging a customer, who was also the boss of Shaggy—the friendly, drink-buying guy sitting next to her at a bar—wasn't normal. Like Elvis, "normal" had left the building.

Suddenly the song lyrics to "Bad Day" began playing in her head, and she decided to try a Scooby Snack to help her turn it around. Determination replaced sadness, and out of nowhere, Grace asked Shaggy: "Where's your boss?"

"Well, I don't know. Let's call him and find out," Shaggy replied as he dialed Freddy's cell. After connecting, Shaggy added: "He says he's brushing his teeth and getting ready to go to bed."

"Give me that phone!" Grace ordered as she held out her hand. Faking liquid courage (the Scooby Snack was awful), she told Freddy, "Get your clothes on and get over here ... the Lady in Red needs to talk with you."

"Okay, I'll be right there," Freddy replied.

Grace handed the phone back to Shaggy again in shock at her abnormal behavior—mentally reminding herself that Freddy was one of A+ Sports' very top customers. What had gotten into her?

Whatever it was, it was exciting. Another warm feeling came over her. She was still 100 percent sober, so it wasn't the alcohol.

She mentally worked to calm herself down, skeptically thinking: "Freddy hasn't made it to any of the business meetings I've scheduled with him; why would tonight be any different?"

"If he does show up, what am I going to say?" she thought.

Now, feeling the need for some real liquid courage, she exclaimed: "Shaggy if you're going to buy me shots, make it straight tequila." In her mind she bounced back and forth between *Game on* and *What the heck are you doing?*

Shaggy bought: she drank. Soon, she felt happy and was ready to dance!

As she approached the dance floor, something red caught her eye. It was Freddy in a red plaid shirt. She stopped in her tracks as her heart was about to jump out of her chest with excitement. Wow, he didn't disappoint her this time, and another wave of warmth flowed through her. For Grace, the emotion was overwhelming to a biblical proportion—a *Gone with the Wind*-category movie moment.

Freddy came directly to her and asked, "Do you want to dance?"

Grace had been taking ballroom dancing lessons to help her get over the loss of Victor, so her "*yes*" had never been more confident. Freddy was a fantastic dancer. They moved together better than any man she'd ever danced with before, including her dance instructors.

Grace's mental mood changed from "It's been a rough day" to "I might be in heaven." And as she was dancing cheek to cheek with Freddy, she was giving God credit for the turnaround that evening, not Scooby or his snacks.

Intermittently, Grace was interacting with her coworkers, who appeared to be having fun. Grace observed two of her fellow male managers doing a "dirty sandwich" dance with one of their wives. *That's interesting*, she thought, but didn't make much of their actions for several reasons, not least of which was that she understood how close-knit the managers were and she wasn't about to cast stones when she was acting out-of-character herself.

Seeing the dancing sandwich trio triggered Grace to return to age seven when she philosophized that "99.9 percent of the time, people aren't joking, kidding, or teasing; they're revealing a version of their true thoughts." Around age 17, she added, "Alcohol is like truth serum... The more serum that goes in, the more hidden truth, either beautiful or ugly, comes out."

Whether wise philosophy or interesting observation, Grace's words were about to ignite in her own life.

She seized the cheek-to-cheek dancing opportunity to prod Freddy about why he blew off so many business meetings with her over the years. He claimed he didn't realize that he had, then Grace remembered several relevant past conversations she'd had with some of Freddy's employees.

The employees had pleaded with Grace to tell Freddy that a person close to him was blocking vendor meetings along with other suspicious activities. Grace encouraged the employees to obtain proof and take it to Freddy themselves as she didn't want to get involved. Besides, she couldn't get to him herself... and *poof*, the lightbulb lit up. Maybe there was truth in their claims.

Applying her truth serum, but without exposing the employees who pled, she began questioning him about other happenings that quickly heightened his curiosity. Freddy excused himself saying, "Now I need a drink."

Grace has full recollection of that night and the next night when she and Freddy continued their business conversation 100 percent sober. While she may have appeared out of control to onlookers, and her behavior was not normal compared to the professional self-conduct she preferred, she believed God accepted her repentance.

Clearly, however, what happened in Vegas did not stay in Vegas!

Instead, one of the dirty dancers decided that Grace should be reprimanded for her cheek-to-cheek dancing with Freddy and reported her to the Sheriff. Grace's indiscretions were addressed according to A+'s corporate policy during a brief in-person meeting. She accepted full responsibility for her actions, stayed calm, and did not deny the accusations.

This confrontation caught her off-guard, and during the meeting, she didn't know who had snitched. While the question crossed her mind, it really didn't matter, and she didn't ask. She also didn't try to take down any of her coworkers. Instead, she thought about how Jesus compassionately, yet unemotionally, dealt with the adulterous women when his opponents were attempting to trap Him.

Grace's acceptance and non-emotional honesty seemed to trigger Sheriff P.'s anger. She doesn't recall her boss, who was there as a witness, uttering a word. However, when threatened that if she spoke of her punishment to anyone she would be terminated and possibly sued, Gritty Grace appeared. Still as calm as a cucumber soaking in an ice-filled tub placed at the entrance of an igloo in

Iceland, she placed strategically folded arms on the conference room table and leaned in toward Sheriff P.

Looking him directly in the eyes, she nearly whispered something to the effect of: "Please be aware that *if* you feel the need to sue me over this one minor incident, there are a mountain of truths to be revealed with detailed documentation to back up every indiscretion that I've witnessed over the last 15 years." And, she wasn't joking, kidding, or teasing!

Chapter Twenty-Eight
Which RUT Is It?

"What profit is there in my blood, when I go down to the pit? Shall the dust praise thee? Shall it declare thy truth?"

—Psalm 30:9 (KJV)

In the hunting world, the word "rut" often describes the season when deer and elk display the urge to breed. In the human world, a rut can be used literally or figuratively to describe something a person has fallen into or is stuck in; somewhat like the pit as mentioned earlier in this story.

Did you realize that the word *rut* is, perhaps purposely, smack dab in the middle of *truth*?

Grace couldn't take back what she had done. Although it may or may not have tarnished her reputation, she was grateful that an uncontrolled urge, displayed on the dance floor, led Freddy to an investigation for the truth. What ended inappropriately began with Grace whispering words of wisdom in Freddy's ear. Ultimately her questions saved him and his business from getting stuck in a much deeper rut.

Because Freddy owned his business, he wasn't at risk of getting terminated or sued for sharing his story, which he apparently did, with many of the people Grace was connected to. On a regular basis, and for several months, Grace would be asked: "Did you hear about Freddy Feathers and how he almost lost his business?"

"It is what it is," Grace often heard people say.

One day, she heard a pastor comment that he was not fond of the saying, "It is what it is." It seemed he considered that saying as passive. Often surrounded by pastors, Grace believed she understood his point. Her takeaway: God gives us dominion and authority over the enemy. Believers are to stand in victory, not passively accept defeat. It's a daily battle; however, if you're truly seeking God's will ... you'll find *it* ... and that too "is what it is."

Grace found Moppsie's saying, "The past is the past and it doesn't change," enlightening and akin to "It is what it is." Grace added: "What can change is your perception of the past, your behavior in the present, and your outlook for the future." And: "A human has to want to change in order to—and that first requires a change of heart."

Freddy's life drastically changed after dancing with Grace. He showed his appreciation to her in many amazing, sometimes hysterical, ways. They became close friends, something that could not have happened without the perfect chain of heart-pounding events and a dash of inappropriate behavior.

While Grace couldn't reverse her less-than-perfect behavior in Vegas, her experience triggered the positive consequence of staying on the Respectable Highway. You escape an internal beat-down from guilt and shame and external beat-ups from demons of jealousy, false impressions, and condemnation.

So, simply questioning Freddy regarding her suspicions about his business ended up:

Revealing
Ugly
Truths

This bold, yet risky choice appeared to have temporarily landed Grace in a:
Really
Unpleasant
Trench

But God, for Freddy and Grace, used that risky revelation for good, returning a higher level of:

Respect
Understanding
Trust

When Grace stood firm during the Sheriff's threat to derail her, his demeanor changed. In fact, he smiled and said something like: "You know, Grace, I once made a similar mistake in my career. The consequence that I had to face because of it changed my life." They shook hands and moved on with their day.

Chapter Twenty-Nine
It's Elevated

"Instead of your shame you shall have double honor, And instead of confusion they shall rejoice in their portion. Therefore in their land they shall possess double; Everlasting joy shall be theirs."

—Isaiah 6:7 (NKJV)

Grace rededicated her attention to keeping her professional career professional and her private affairs private, and her responsibilities were expanded.

Either directly and/or indirectly, she interacted with over 5,500 firearms retailers and 300 vendors across the United States. Now that ARSE was owned by A+ Sports, Grace worked with that team to create a turnkey system. It was designed to promote an enhanced customer experience. A success, this partner-style selling approach created the need for an additional associate. Grace reeled in her beautiful fishing buddy, Penny Peacock, to help.

Under the Sherriff's guidance, they hosted professional dealer shows and formed a dealer advisory board. Grace was responsible for creating programs, training, and facilitating several leadership sessions during those events.

The business consulting method was well received, and Grace's next assignment was to find and hire a third-party provider to continue elevating A+'s retailer success.

Like the ARSE software project, Grace enjoyed meeting and interviewing companies to partner with. This time, her due diligence led to a consulting firm: Strategy Business Partners (SBP), based in Chicago. Grace loved creating these strategic business partnerships for several reasons. Providing unique value for A+'s customers was exceptionally fulfilling. Interacting and learning from business consultants and psychologists outside the industry... that was an intellectual thrill ride on her favorites elevator.

There were three men that Grace interacted with at SBP: Larry, Charlie, and Dr. French. To introduce their new offering, Grace invited them to attend A+'s dealer show. Dr. French, the group's psychologist, was selected to give a presentation.

Sitting in the audience next to Freddy Feathers, she was elated with Dr. French's teaching style and the message he conveyed. Much of what he shared, she'd learned in her psychology courses; however, the way he applied it to how employees think and behave in the workplace was stellar, in her opinion.

For example, and not verbatim, he shared that if an employee heard that their employer made five million dollars, they would likely think that meant five million dollars' worth of profit. He suggested education and communication as ways to overcome these incorrect conclusions.

Grace's biggest takeaway was when Dr. French pointed out that a human's number one mental need is to be right! She elbowed

Freddy to make sure he was catching this life-changing spark with her.

Someone in the audience asked, "What about the need to be wanted?"

Dr. French answered that the need to be loved or wanted was high on the list, but "to be right" was number one.

This wisdom was a pivotal point for Grace and she hoped A+ Sport's retailers found it as valuable as she did. However, not all retailers put as much emphasis on training and growing as Freddy did. He was a brilliant and engaging leader who led by being in the trenches with his troops. His employees couldn't outwork him.

Although competitors, Freddy and Victor seemed to greatly respect one another. Often, they shared wisdom and worked together toward common goals. This warmed Grace's heart, as she loved win-focused relationships.

Detached from Victor, Grace switched from voluntarily helping Pierce's Gun Shop in her spare time, to helping Freddy. She was not only a workaholic, but it was becoming clear she was also a people pleaser.

A few A+ Sports customers signed up for the new consulting program. Receiving positive feedback, Grace also discovered a seed in her heart to become an independent consultant, and each good review was water on the soil.

Already a volunteer consultant to Freddy, she told him her dream. He said, "You can't be a consultant until you've owned your own business; no business owner will listen to you until you do."

While his candor figuratively hit her upside the head, she laughed as she pointed out, "You're a business owner and you listen to me—as do hundreds of others."

Freddy continually fanned Grace's competitive fire, for which she was grateful to God.

Since she'd contracted SBP on A+'s behalf, she thought, I've got the best resource on consulting at my fingertips; I'll ask Charlie how to become a great consultant. Coincidentally, they went to Charlie's Steak House for dinner. During appetizers, Charlie mentioned he had written a book. "Is the book about how to become a consultant?" Grace excitedly asked.

It wasn't.

When Grace shared her consultant dream with Charlie, he told her, "You hired us, so you're certainly talented enough; however, you're not old enough. Wait until you're at least 50."

Grace was amassing a mountain of *you can't* and *you aren't enough* advice, but she trusted God's grace to elevate her if that was where she was meant to be.

Unfortunately, SBP went out of business within a year of their strategic partnership with A+ Sports. It appeared consulting was a tough business to sustain. What Grace learned from that experience was enormous. Most of all, she learned that she possessed enough to become a professional consultant and speaker someday. She just had to muster up the courage to do so.

In the meantime, Grace had more than enough to focus on, as she was selected to be part of the New Product Launch for KRISS rifles. Her role was to coordinate and support launch events with ranges across the U.S.

Connecting A+'s customers with innovative ideas and new brands propelled her to reach new heights!

Many retailers knew who "Grace from A+" was; however, with all the new roles she was taking on, they also knew her as the KRISS Girl, the ARSE Girl, the Retail Services Girl, and the Gun Girl. Her highest joy came from being God's Girl first!

Several staffing changes occurred around this timeframe. A new man, from a toilet manufacturer, took Billy Beancounter's place. Ms. Bombshell left, and a few new team members were added to support the growth the retail services division was experiencing. Technological enhancements at A+ Sports exploded in 2007. Terms such as *value-added reseller* and *omni-channel marketing* were added to Grace's sphere of responsibility.

A forward-thinking company that sold a planet's worth of optics partnered with A+ for innovative growth. Swooperwoman and Grace drove the project that helped that customer capture additional market share by integrating A+'s inventory with their e-commerce site, and then shipping inventory directly to their end consumer.

Swooperwoman and Grace continued working in unison, helping A+ to elevate their in-house e-commerce platform. A+'s online business grew exponentially from upgrades that were impactful, informative, and extremely user-friendly.

Grace was honored to be part of several other technological advancements.

Takeaways: Design

Gracie's path wasn't a straight line, and yours may not be either. That's okay. The point isn't to have it all figured out and to march straight through everything like the Terminator. The point is to know where you're going so that when you get off course, you'll recognize it.

What do you want? If you had the money, if you had the time, what would you do with it? What is the thing that is so worthwhile to you that you would lose sleep, skip meals, or spend your last dime on it? Don't sell yourself short! One thing Gracie always had was a strong sense of self-respect and personal dignity. For her, this came from her personal faith. She wasn't about to let others tell her her worth; she knew who she was and felt confident that God loved her. It may be harder for you, but if you're going to overcome your obstacles and grow, you need to believe that you're worth it.

And guess what? You *are*! If you're a human being (and I feel safe assuming you are), then you are an amazing creation roaming this earth with great depths of love to give and a capacity to make the world a little better than you found it.

So, what do you want?

If your first answer was, "It would be easier to tell you what I don't want," You are in good company as other humans have answered the same way.

To test that you really want it, ask yourself a yes or no question: Do I want *this*?

Keep revising until you can answer simply, "Yes!" No caveats, no ifs, ands, or buts. Just *yes*. Whenever you cannot say yes, ask, *Why not? What is missing, or what isn't right?* And hone in on the most precise statement of your desire.

Once you can say yes, it's time to design your plan. This part can be frustrating for people because there isn't one plan for everyone. You need to design a plan that can move you toward your defined desire within your current circumstances.

For some people, that means putting aside or spending some amount of money. For others, it's about time or how they schedule their day or week. It may be an activity you add in or something you take out. Something you do every day or something that happens weekly or monthly.

It doesn't matter if you use SMART goals, HARD goals, CLEAR goals, or DUMB goals. Use the model that makes sense to you, so long as the specifics point you toward your deep underlying desire—and help you to confront your primary barriers.

Reflection

1. Pick the top obstacle from the Define stage. Imagine a situation when that obstacle thwarted you. Now reimagine it with a positive outcome. Do the same with an event you are anticipating: Imagine you perform your best and things turn out well.

2. Which description fits you best: a gutsy go-getter, a monstrous mountain mover, a likeable lime-lighter, or a detailed deep-diver? How does choosing one of those help you understand the best way to design your plan?

3. What does it feel like to *not* get what you really want? How did you get over that, and how could you help someone else get over it?

4. Has stress ever led you to overindulge or lower your inhibitions too far? What was the consequence? What can you do to avoid the negative consequences next time you're stressed?

5. Do you feel any shame or guilt about past choices? Take a moment to repent of those things and then let them go. Rededicate yourself to your core goals and values.

A big part of designing well comes from learning from your mistakes. Think about what hasn't worked and then come up with a better plan. Grace experienced sadness, rejection, temptation, and failure but kept going. As a result, she also found new insight into herself through working with new leaders and learned to innovate to solve problems and to set bold goals.

With your obstacles and your desires clearly defined, set yourself a big goal for the next year and then five years. Then set three smaller goals for the next day, week, and month. The smaller goals might be habits or routines that will help you reach the larger ones.

PRACTICING to ALIGN

In the previous two sections, we defined the emotional and spiritual barriers to growth as well as your core desires for your life. Then we began to develop a plan to achieve what you desire and face down your obstacles. Now we need to look at matters of alignment both within yourself and within your family or organization.

I want you to think about alignment as both internal and external. Internal alignment means the goals you set and the plans you make correspond to your intrinsic drive, character and values. You're pursuing change or growth because it makes sense for you, not because someone else wants you to.

External alignment means getting your team or family on board with you. It's how you help others understand the plan and its goals and then get them not only to accept but hopefully to get excited about them so you can all pull together.

Chapter Thirty
It Remains a Choice

> *"Today, I have given you the choice between life and death, between blessings and curses. Now, I call on heaven and earth to witness the choice you make. Oh, that you would choose life, so that you and your descendants might live."*
>
> —Deuteronomy 30:19 (NLT)

Do you realize you have a choice in what you think and how you respond to circumstances? What we fill our mind and bodies with is our choice, and it's our choices that make a difference in our results.

Moppsie taught Grace to avoid watching scary movies, or as she put it, "anything that boggles your mind." Pi had done his fair share of giving her scares when she was little, so focusing on pictures of the Sacred Heart instead of Pi's scary eye took her mind to happier places.

Being raised Catholic was healthy for Grace, as repetition of the Lord's Prayer provided daily comfort. In troubled times, her mind automatically defaulted to "Our Father who art in Heaven, hallowed be thy name. Thy Kingdom come; thy will be done!"

Hallowed ground for hunters is often their sacred hunting spot. Over the years, many men have told Grace that when they're in the field, or in a tree stand, they feel the most spiritual or closest to God. Having quiet, peaceful time surrounded by nature soothes their spirit and soul. They are in a watching-and-listening mode. When Grace was first invited to go hunting, she was conflicted and couldn't sleep. She knew the experience would be beneficial to her career, but taking any life... She felt that was up to God, not her.

Victor was a phenomenal help in educating her on how and why hunting was important to sustaining human and animal life. When she understood the whole picture, she was able to reframe her experience.

Spring turkey season became something she looked forward to, and yet, she never shot a turkey. After the first time out, she didn't complain about getting up early or going out in the cold. She had a cushy seat, the best guide, and a great spot. Warmed by the sun with her head in the clouds, she napped with a smile as turkeys danced right past her.

Grace never cared for Halloween, but during Halloween season 2008, she learned she was being let go from A+ Sports, which felt like a cruel trick. She was walked out the door and handed documents, the top one of which informed her that she was being released as part of a re-organization and insisted, "This is in no-way a reflection of Grace's performance." Still, she couldn't help but remember Vegas in 2005. Did that blemish on her record lead to this result? Ultimately, there was no sense in trying to discern whether it was the past haunting her, an unknown evil, or simply an impersonal business decision that had devoured her position; it was gone. She was now free to move on.

After shocking Moppsie and Poppsie with the news, she cried for a few moments to mourn the loss of a long, successful career. Then, green pastures appeared in her mind, and she told Moppsie, "Let's go to Walmart."

They went shopping and ran into several people whom Grace had worked with. Practicing emotional control, she laughingly talked with her now former coworkers—not revealing the secret they would soon learn.

She bought some Twizzlers for the kids—trick-or-treaters who were hopefully still innocent to the twists that happen during the Halloween seasons of real life.

Chapter Thirty-One
It's Birdy Dancing!

"Look at the birds of the air; they do not sow or reap or store away in barns, and yet your heavenly Father feeds them. Are you not much more valuable than they?"
—Matthew 6:26 (NIV)

Having been kicked out of A+ Sport's proverbial nest, Grace needed a bit of time to spread her wings and her talents. She wanted to re-create her success outside the firearms industry. She turned down several lucrative offers to work for other distributors and took a flight of faith to grow outside the firearms comfort zone.

A couple of weeks after she was released, Poppsie encouraged Grace to use her severance package and start the independent consulting practice she'd dreamed of creating. When quick stepping back into November 2008, Grace could literally be found waltzing her way across ballroom dance floors. Instead of being sour about her A+ separation, she enjoyed lemonade, laughter, and an occasional Jive.

A proper Tango was the closest she came to repeating that night of too-close dancing with Freddy Feathers. She wasn't looking for any trouble or dates, just good dancers to improve her fancy footwork. Perhaps you remember the drinking bird from your science class that bobbed up and down dipping its beak in water. Well, that bird reminded Grace of Steve, who was also a "tall drink of water" and taught dance. Steve invited Grace to different dance venues, several nights a week. He also invited her to church one Sunday morning.

Consuelo, another dancer, had been attending this church for some time and had invited Steve to join her. When Grace heard Steve say, "We'll save you a seat in the seventh row," she knew it would be perfectly divine. And that it was.

Not divine for some, including Grace, was the stock market crash that occurred on September 29, 2008. One of the articles Grace read stated the Dow Jones Industrial Average fell 777.68 points in intraday trading. The crash caused her 401K to plummet, which was not helpful when combined with the re-organization that hit a month later. Seeing that 777 now provides insight into what happened next.

The auditorium of the church sat roughly 3,000 people, which overwhelmed some, but excited Grace. She made her way to the enormous stage, then counted back seven rows. There she found signs that read *saved* rather than *reserved*. She laughed as she rewound to the blind date where she learned what saved meant.

Seated with the Seventh Row Savers, Grace's heart pounded with excitement. As soon as the worship music began, the entire church stood and celebrated. Grace felt inexplicable joy in her spirit. Immediately, she knew this was the church home she'd been seeking.

When the pastor announced there'd be a special offering taken for the church's recession response, Grace got chills and was compelled to contribute $300, even though she didn't know where her next check was going to come from. In her heart, she felt God would bless this faith-filled response in ways she couldn't imagine. And He did!

It was a couple of weeks before Christmas when Grace exited the dance floor after a heel-kicking, country two-step. What she stumbled upon was a divine introduction to a sweet woman named Tammy, who was married to wonderful man named Don. While sipping punch, Tammy asked Grace: "What are your holiday plans?"

"I'm not sure. I lost my job a few weeks back, so I'm free as a bird," Grace cheerfully chirped.

Tammy turned and summoned Don to join her. Arriving with his hand extended, Grace could have sworn she heard his angelic wife say, "This is Grace. She's a dove who's lost a wing. You've got to help her."

Don immediately took Grace under his wing and placed her in a new nest with one of his lofty connections.

After landing in the restaurant industry as vice president of strategic sales for a SAAS (Software as A Service) model software company, Grace soared.

On May 7, 2009, during a planning meeting with outside executives, Grace feared she was caught in a time warp, as she repeatedly heard the words "NRA show."

Noticing she was dazed and confused, the president, Jim, laughingly stopped the meeting and said, "Grace, we're talking about the National Restaurant Association." He then explained, to the rest of the room, Grace's affiliation to the National Rifle Association.

Both NRAs were associations heavily weighted with males. Being the only female golfer at several outings, Grace concluded that the restaurant industry may be even more male-dominated than her previous home. Although the franchisees seemed to prefer golf over sporting clays courses, she quickly nestled in.

Grace was racking up more frequent flier miles than ever before, as she raced around to various restaurant conventions. She had another déjà vu experience when she saw a plethora of black-and-white checkered flags. Only this time, she wasn't in Kansas. She was making a pleasant pit stop at the Checker's/Rally's convention. The theme was how to create a "WOW in a bag" customer experience. *Wow, indeed*, she thought, when she learned about the Women's Foodservice Forum (WFF) from a group of highly impressive females attending this same convention.

Grace was admiring the Rally's/Checker's floor when Conrad danced into her life. Conrad was a franchisee for this brand and owned a Popeye's. Both a lovable burger and bird man, Grace was ecstatic to gain his business. Chickens are tasty birds, and in 2010, God's claim to fame for Grace in the restaurant roost was a sale of software to 700 Popeye's restaurants. Clearly divine, because she was told, "The request for proposal window is closed, and there's no room for you on the presentation agenda." Miraculously, Grace closed the sale during a one-hour presentation and spontaneous lunch at Popeye's headquarters in Atlanta, with six of their top executives. God had moved mountains for that meeting to take place. The deal was sealed, and Grace didn't see the Popeye's group after that.

More mountains moved, as Grace was mesmerized by the crowds of people who participated in the altar calls at the new church. It wasn't long before she found herself accepting the pastor's invitation to come forward if you want prayer for healing.

Grace needed to pray for healing for Poppsie, who had been diagnosed with cancer. When she had heard, she could hardly process this news right in the middle of her career rebirth. Now, she went to the altar to ask for prayer for her beloved father. In the presence of God, her self-will vanished, and Grace allowed God's will to penetrate her tough exterior. Peace flowed through her during the prayers she received for Poppsie. Her prayer was that his cancer would be removed and he would remain healthy and with her. In her spirit, she felt God's healing plan would be Poppsie developing new, invisible, wings.

God gave her family strength, while planting new seeds for the future in Grace's brain. She thought or received the words, *Prepare to fly solo,* as well as, *Endings trigger transformation.*

Before Poppsie began his transformation, Grace wanted him to know she had taken his advice to heart. She prayed and prepared to launch a sole proprietorship.

Simultaneously, week after week, Grace heard the pastor repeatedly ask, "What is Jesus calling you to do?"

She kept thinking, *I wish that I knew!*

In the bookstore, located in the lobby of the church, a daily devotional book grabbed her attention. With an outstretched hand on the front cover, it felt as if Jesus were personally inviting Grace to dance with Him. She accepted the offer by escorting the book over to the cashier and then out the door. It remained her daily seed for dancing through life.

Poppsie's wings sprouted, and he flew to his Heavenly coop. It wasn't the outcome she had prayed for; however, she had peace that Poppsie was still with her in spirit and empowered to help more than ever before. With her heavenly and earthly fathers together, she believed she'd succeed.

Grace walked away from a huge commission to answer a higher calling from above; even though she didn't quite know what that calling was. Now, for the second time, Grace had no job and no concrete plan. This time, leaving the work nest was by choice. And by no means was that decision easy. She spent emotional hours on her knees asking God, "Are you sure this is what I should do?"

Grace didn't claim that God spoke to her out loud however, she felt He validated or answered with uncoincidental happenings. For example: On that first day, when she was on her knees, second guessing and seeking God's wisdom, she heard no reply at all. Nothing, zero, nada... big fat goose egg on the sound scale. However, a peace came over her, and she decided to turn on the television.

She came across a Bible teacher named Joyce, whose tell-it-like-it-is style spoke to her. The Bible verse John 10:10 was on the screen: "The thief does not come except to steal, and to kill, and to destroy. I have come that they may have life, and that they may have it more abundantly" (NKJV). Joyce was explaining that it was one of her favorites.

The next morning, Grace purposely watched Joyce's program. On that day, Joyce was interviewing a man named John who was a renowned authority on business leadership.

"*Now* we're talking!" Grace yelled as she jumped off the couch and did a way-to-go-God happy dance–followed by a not-so-good moon walk. When the program ended, she turned off the television and said, "Thanks God. I've got it. I want my business to be full of Jesus, with a teaching platform that resembles Joyce's strength and John's success."

That boost of vision kept her going for the next several days. She positively prayed, and at times temporarily agonized, over what her business would be called. How would she brand and market it? What value would she provide? Who would her clients be? Which niche would she focus on and how would it be funded? The list was long.

If you've ever started a business venture, you can likely relate.

Grace had no answers. The temptation to quit before she devoted any more energy to this seemingly insurmountable idea put her back on her knees with this plea: "God, I left a perfectly good job to fulfill what I believe is your will. I need Your help! Help me help You, right now, please!"

Within seconds, the Bible verse that she had seen on her television screen quick-stepped into view.

Wow! "Okay, my business will be based on verse John 10:10. John's my grandfather's name, so it's like a legacy business; that makes sense. The apostle John was memorable for telling everyone he was the one that Jesus loved, so that fits. Many of the men who helped me in the gun business were named John... seems perfect!" Grace said out loud.

Swooperwoman was super good at marketing, so the next call for help was to her. "I need a name and logo for my company, so I can put a brand and marketing plan together. You're the best I know at that, so what comes to mind?" Grace asked her bestie.

Without hesitation, Swooperwoman said: "Your gift is providing solutions, so the name has to include solutions or strategies."

Later that evening, Grace was at home, fixing dinner for another female friend, Jazzy.

Although not known for her jazz dancing skills, the two girls were connected via Dancing Steve. By night, Jazzy was known as a songbird. By day, Jazzy was a director of strategy for a large corporation. These two had a lot in common, and together, they had a lot of fun.

In the kitchen, which was open to the living room, Grace prepared Jazzy's salad as she told her about Swooperwoman's suggestions. Suddenly, Jazzy's work position occurred to Grace: "Hey, you're a strategist. What do you think I should name my business?"

"You're direct, so it needs to fit you. How about Clear-Cut Strategies?"

"That's it!" Grace exclaimed.

Chapter Thirty-Two
It's All in the Name

> *"For where two or three gather in my name, there am I with them."*
>
> —Matthew 18:20 (NIV)

One Saturday night, Grace was seated next to Jack at a Safari Club International banquet. Years later, Jack and Grace reconnected and went duck hunting. Learning of her consulting dream triggered Jack to ask Grace for help with his municipal supply and software start-up businesses.

At a hockey game, through a man connected to Jack, Grace met a man named George whose persona reminded her of her favorite uncle. During this intro, she learned Jack and George had been as close as brothers at one time. By the middle of June 2011, George and his son-in-law, Bo, became clients who immediately felt more like family.

The core value/mantra that George claimed for his business was also referred to as The Golden Rule. The version he preferred was

"Do unto others as you'd have them do unto you," which is an adaptation of the Biblical verse found in Matthew 7:12.

Like A+ Sports, George's primary business was distribution, and he had survived by being the best of the best. His niche was residential, commercial, and automotive window film, so Grace's knowledge of optics and sunshades came in handy when understanding the glass business.

Just for fun: Do you know why George's scarecrow won first prize?

He was outstanding in his field!

George and Grace had something in common. He was the last independent distributor standing in his LLumar-branded field, where he had invented several tools helpful to film installers. By this time, Grace, too, had invented some things of her own. She had put together several systems and models to help humans understand themselves and others.

Like A+, George had connections to the car racing world. There were pictures of racecars prominently displayed in the halls of his office space. The annual convention for his company was SEMA, which stood for Specialty Equipment Market Association. Like A+ at SHOT, George hosted a booth at SEMA.

Grace had been hired for succession planning, organization, and training. Like Grace and her family, George had a litany of favorite sayings, one of which was, "I'm getting ready to hand over the keys to the castle." So, Grace called him King George.

From Grace's perspective, King George had a heart of gold, which sometimes led to hostage situations, because he struggled with carrying out consequences for poor performance. George ranted to Bo and Grace about how some subjects should be fired, never intending to pull that dismissive trigger.

One day, during a George rant, Grace grabbed his attention by using both names, you know like your mom does when you're in trouble. "George Louie!" she sternly cried, and that's when it hit her: "Hey, did you know that my two favorite uncles are George and Louie?"

In typical George fashion, he replied to her question with a question: "Did you know my favorite uncle's nickname was Doc? While we're on the subject of interesting coincidences, guess who inquired about buying one of our warehouses?" asked George.

Grace took several incorrect guesses, then gave up.

"Victor Pierce. Seems they want to open another location with a gun range," George told her.

All she could say was, "Wow!" They decided to jump in George's car and go visit Victor at his store. Victor wasn't there, but Grace had a delightful chat with Victor's dad, who confirmed that he had handed his kingdom keys over to Victor. When Pappa Pierce said, "Victor's the boss now, you'll have to talk with him!" she was praying that George was paying attention.

Instead, George was eyeing the Glocks and asking about a shotgun that they had on a super sale.

Even though Bo and George didn't benefit from hearing about Victor's successful succession story, George did contribute to the Pierce legacy of success with his gun purchases.

Several months later, Grace was shopping in one of the anchor stores of a local mall. Whence on her way to the potty, Rocketman she did spotty. No time to chat or to stall, first came nature's call.

Can you believe this? she was asking herself, hopefully not aloud. *Rocketman, of all people, and after all these years? Oh well, he'll probably be gone by the time I go back by.*

Nope, there he stood, at the cashier's desk in the teen girl's department, and this time, he noticed her. "Hey, Grace, what are you up to?" Rocketman asked.

"I started my own company, and I have a contract with a nearby client," was her reply.

"Who's your client?" he asked.

Feeling invaded a bit too quickly, she answered, "I'd prefer to keep that confidential."

Seeming to sense she was uncomfortable, Rocketman added, "The reason why I ask is I also started a company when I left A+ Sports. We installed specialty lighting for a client close by. The owner's name is George Louie."

Grace nearly fainted. She mentally held smelling salts to her beak to stay upright.

The population of the metropolitan area referred to here was over two million people, and Rocketman immediately named the one client they had in common? Grace was convinced this one-in-two-million collision had to be God's handywork; she just couldn't explain the why.

Rocketman seemed genuinely happy to see her. He invited her to grab a glass of wine and catch up; however, she already had plans and therefore declined.

She was excited to tell George about another coincidence. He reacted somewhat calmly: "Yes, I know him, and we were a customer. Have I told you about my customer who says he's god with a little G?"

"No" grace replied, wondering which branch he was flying off to this time.

"It stands for George's Oldest Dealer," he cheerfully chirped.

King George wore many crowns, including the jester's. He always had a story or a quip when a situation needed comic relief. The King was no fool, though, when it came to quoting the Bible, and he would regularly pepper his speech with appropriate passages, Psalms, and Proverbs.

Depending on which foul word escaped his mouth, he would either justify it with, "That word is in the Bible, you know," or act like it didn't happen.

"George!" is all Grace could say, as it was his kingdom after all.

One commandment Grace couldn't allow to be broken was using her Lord's name in vain. Boldly, she wrote an addendum to her consulting contract that stated breaking that commandment would result in *poof*, she'd be gone, and she'd be taking her Godly wisdom with her.

Thankfully, George and his employees complied, although, it did prompt a story of how he had gotten kicked out of Catholic school. Seems he fibbed to a nun about putting his peas in a milk carton and throwing them away.

Chapter Thirty-Three
It's an "I" Conundrum

"And why do you look at the speck in your brother's eye, but do not consider the plank in your own eye?"
—Matthew 7:3 (NKJV)

After more than 18 years of answering the phone, "A+ Sports—This is Grace, how may I help you?" or, introducing herself as, "I'm Grace with A+ Sports," her identity became synonymous with her employer. She was proud to be part of that team—it was her family.

She thought back to her early years at A+, recalling how the locked security door between the warehouse and the office area caused more than just a safety divide. As expectations, sales, and the number of employees rapidly grew, so did the we/they mentality between the associates of the same company. For example, when a customer claimed an order was wrong, the blame game began. The correction process started with "Whose fault was it?" "Was it ordered wrong (office) or picked wrong (warehouse)?" When the truth was uncovered, someone, somewhere was held accountable, and there were consequences.

Unintentionally, Grace had played the blame game too, when new to management. While at an after-hours cocktail party, Wildman inquired: "Grace, how are things going with your new sales team?"

She answered, "Well, if the merchandising department did better at getting the products we need, we'd be exceeding our goals."

She hoped that Wildman would go to work the next day and give merchandising an encouraging pep talk! Instead, he asked her another question, "Grace, is your ship in 100 percent tip-top shape?"

Humbled, she answered, "No sir."

With a warm and gentle manner, he suggested, "Perhaps you need to focus on what you're responsible for first."

She couldn't help but admire his instant yet polite way of illuminating the telephone pole in her eye. She replied, "Yes, sir, I understand your point."

Well, this familiar division and blame game was happening with George's company. Fortunately for him, Grace's precision rifle was already loaded with an accurate solution. It had to do with how people communicate with one another and especially with how they interpret one another.

"I, I, I... me, me, me!" was another of King George's expressions. Depending on whom he was referring to, it could have been interpreted as a positive or negative statement. The timing and meaning depended on George's emotions. The good news was that, since Grace didn't seem affected by George's emotions, he generously shared them with her. As his trusted advisor, Grace became the proverbial cat to kick, hopefully saving his wife from hearing about those work problems. She also saw that she needed to break people out of "I, I, I" thinking.

"I" at the beginning of a sentence points the attention to the person making a proclamation, appropriately labeled first-person speech. The person behind the *I* could be crowning themself with glory, taking responsibility, offering a challenge, or simply sharing a fun/helpful experience. The true intent can be difficult to discern. In general, it is a good idea to phrase a comment or criticism as an "I statement," but in Grace's experience, problems could still arise with how the receiver perceived the I statement. It was a common communication problem that Grace wanted to help the people who were willing to improve.

Grace had studied leadership, business, and psychology, and was certified in disciplines of human behavior. Through applying her learning to her work with George's team, she developed what she called her *clear cut change resistance principle*, which says that people resist change for two reasons:

1. They don't want to change, or

2. They want to change, but don't know how.

For example, Mr. Art Aerophobia lived in Atlanta, Georgia. Due to his fear of flying, he had never flown and refused to change his ways. That was until Art's favorite uncle Anthony offered to pay Art $7,000,000 to fly to Gnarabup, Western Australia, for a visit. There were two conditions attached: one, Art had to travel by plane, and two, he had to arrive within the next ten days.

Art getting to see his favorite uncle, along with the monetary consequence, prompted change. Instantly, he switched his mindset from refusal to asking, "How can I get over my fear of flying?" Fear made him unwilling to change, but when the consequences for changing became impactful enough, Art found motivation to find a way to change. Seven perfect days later, Art and Uncle Anthony were walking together on Gnarabup Beach. Their lively discussion centered around Art's plan to travel the globe since discovering he loved to fly.

Here's the question: Was Art's fear real, or an artificial hurdle that he had used to avoid change?

Another of Grace's clients, The Fictitious Fig Farm, was owned by two men, Phil Fitasafiddle and Stanley Stretchypants. During the executive interview, Phil claimed the company's most important need was for Mr. Stretchypants to change his drinking, vaping, eating, and exercise habits. Phil's highly spirited "I, I, I, me, me, me" insisted that his lifestyle habits were perfect; therefore, it was his business partner who needed to make *all* the changes. (It's common for "I, I, I, me, me, me" attitudes to include a "you, you, you" judgment or two.)

After Phil voiced his concerns, some of the emotion behind them dissipated. Calmer, he asked, "Grace, why can't Stanley see that he needs to change?"

Grace compassionately asked, "Phil, is your performance at The Fictitious Fig in 100 percent tip-top shape?"

He blurted out, "No, but," then stopped himself. After pausing for a moment, he said: "I see what you're getting at. My focus on Stanley's personal habits is blocking me from improving the way we operate. Grace, thank you for opening my eyes!"

Silently, Grace passed the glory for that victory on to God and Wildman!

Through the succession/change process, both Phil and Stanley realized the organization's primary need was a step-by-step strategic plan to keep their business alive and healthy just in case one of them suddenly wasn't.

Sin, *lie*, and *die* are three words with typically unpleasant connotations. To Grace, it seemed appropriate that an *I* was smack-dab in their middle, since when she had sinned and lied, she needed that fleshy behavior to die.

The words *pride* and *alive* have an *I* in their middle, too. During interviews and trainings, Grace observed that the word *pride* sometimes bred micro-expressions of contempt. Digging deeper into why the word *pride* was viewed positively by some and negatively by others, she found a correlation to the core beliefs a person held about themselves, their family, and who they believe God is.

One example, Subject A believed God was his Creator and viewed Him as a punisher. His perception of Subject B, who consistently conveyed, "Look at me, I'm as happy as can be," was "He's full of himself and should be ashamed of his pridefulness."

From talking with Subject B, Grace learned his "look at me" projection was a result of viewing God as an all-loving creator. He revealed, "by allowing my Holy Spirit to shine, it helps others to see God's goodness and light." His perception of Subject A: "He's a great guy. It's just sad that he's become so critical and skeptical that no one wants to be around him. He says he's a believer, but it's like he forgot that Jesus died so he could live an abundant life."

In this example, both subjects claimed they believed in God, yet the differences in how they identified with God internally caused a different external projection. Grace learned her secret to shining required surrendering her will to God's (also referred to as dying to self) and understanding that an identity in Christ alleviates the negative "I, I', I, ... Me, Me, Me's" in life.

For situations in which she was unable to discuss her spiritual beliefs, having top-notch behavioral tools was extremely beneficial in helping humans understand their identity and value.

George and Grace continued to work on a succession plan for his business. She shared, "Agreement is a key to healthy relationships, resolving conflict, and getting teams to engage." Then, she asked George this question: "How does one get what they want if they don't know what they want?"

"Good question!" George replied. "If you didn't know what you wanted, you'd have to be happy with whatever you got."

"Do you think most people are satisfied with what they get, or do they tend to want more or something different?" Grace asked.

"What do you think?" he replied.

"In my experience, a person's response is based on several thinking factors. For example: Level of complacency, conditioned behavior from childhood, and outlook regarding the future are just some of the factors that determine whether a person accepts the circumstances they're dealt or are driven to reach their full potential," Grace shared.

She added, "George, did you know thinking styles and change can be measured?"

She paused. "And have you ever thanked God for what you thought you wanted, but didn't get? I have! If I were still at A+,

I wouldn't be sitting here with you, George. God's plan seems better."

George just looked at her. He was processing all the knowledge coming at him.

"George, before we identify our team's value, potential, and the ideal roles for them, I'd like to understand what you truly want," Grace injected.

"I want you to make sure Bo is prepared to succeed. He doesn't seem to want to listen to me anymore, so I need you to help him," was George's reply.

Bo seemed clear that he wanted to accept the keys to George's proverbial castle.

At age 60, George was mentally sharp and physically going strong. His passion and hobbies revolved around his family, and his identity was good father, then good businessman, in that order. He loved sharing his family identity with Bo.

Claiming heirs weren't ready was a hurdle that owners often used to postpone a change or transition. Real or imagined, the hurdle could be identified, measured, and conquered—*if* the figurative king or queen was willing. When he realized that change was possible and Bo was proving himself worthy, George's readiness to change waivered daily. His *yes, no, maybe* bullets spun around as if they were in the chamber of a revolver.

When George's *yes* flipped to Bo's *not ready*, Bo's flopped to, "George is never going to give me what I want. I'm going to quit!"

George constantly remarked how brilliant his son-in-law was, and Grace agreed.

However, when those two didn't agree, Grace heard, "Bo thinks he's smarter than me!"

Bo would simply confirm, "I am."

Bo was brilliant because he used few words and made concepts or things simple to understand while keeping his emotions detached. George was equally smart; however, his need to explain details and express his emotions sometimes made whatever he was trying to convey more complex. Grace advised that both styles were necessary for success as the people in their kingdom came with a variety of needs.

From this exchange, Grace conceived the philosophical question, "Would you rather be smart or brilliant?" How one answers that question gives Grace insight to their style. One answer is not better than the other, it simply indicates people are both similar and different from other people.

Grace combined George's industry knowledge and Bo's brilliance with her plethora of experience. Together, they created a variety of customized training programs for their dealers and internal team. Incorporating her years of helping A+ Sports host the best dealer shows, Grace also helped implement improvements for George's customer events.

Then she presented an interactive communication/leadership seminar entitled "Getting Engaged" to many of George's dealers. She had a whole slide deck prepared using elephants, lions, and monkeys to illustrate behavioral and leadership concepts and from prior use, anticipated it would go over well.

As she peered into the audience of roughly 80 business owners, Grace realized the window film industry was exceptionally male dominated. The highlight for Grace was when the only female business owner, a very short and spunky gal from Michigan, was selected to be the spokesperson for her table.

When Grace asked her, "What's the number one problem with communication?" Ms. Spunky stepped up onto her 8' round table and exclaimed, "The problem with communication is: People lie!" To which the crowd roared, and Grace heard a few people shout, "Now that's the truth!" The presentation was a big hit.

Truthfully, it wasn't until a few days after that speaking engagement that Grace realized her dream to become a professional business consultant and speaker outside the firearms industry had come true. She thanked God!

Next dream: return to her beloved industry and speak at SHOT Show!

As she pictured her name on the SHOT Show banner, her eye caught the mouse pad on her desk that read, "Don't lie for the other guy." It's a warning not to make what's referred to as a straw purchase, which means buying a gun for someone who can't. Grace contemplated this:

- The word *criminal* has two *I*s, and all eyes should be focused on criminals when it comes to gun control. A gun doesn't have any eyes.

- *Firearms* contains an *I* and *arms*, but no legs, so they can't walk away by themselves.

- *Handguns* contain the word *hand*, but no physical hand; therefore, they can't shoot themselves in the foot.

Then, Grace contemplated this:

- *Me* has an *e*, and no *i*.

- An *eye* has two *e's* and no *i*.

- *Self* has an *e*, and no *i* until you turn it into *selfie* or *selfish*.

- *He, she, we,* and *they* all have *e's* and no *I's,* and a *finger* has both and literally, it can point toward anyone. *Anyone* has a *y* which rhymes with *I*.

- There's an *I* and a *me* in *time*. Some clocks have hands, not fingers, to point to their time.

- At one time, a popular saying was, *There's no I in team...* and then a wise artist rendered a drawing that made an *I* appear. Perhaps that creative individual was challenging the status quo, which is also a talent.

- In Exodus 3, God said to Moses: "I am who I am." In John's gospel, Jesus makes seven "I AM" statements referring to who he is, was, and always will be.

She couldn't be sure where all this was going, yet, but she was starting to see her way to making more dreams come true.

Chapter Thirty-Four
It's Forgiveness with a Twist

> *And whenever you stand praying, if you have anything against anyone, forgive him, that your Father in heaven may also forgive you your trespasses.*
> —Mark 11:25 (NKJV)

In 2011, Grace started her first spiritual journal where she wrote reflections on how events in her life impacted her faith. After a year of this, she reviewed some of what she had written. Her spiritual notes boiled down to these seven themes:

- Daily, renew your mind with positive affirmations and keep it set.

- Remove competition, comparisons, and excuses by positively renewing your mind and keeping it set.

- Replace condemnation, shame, and lies from the enemy by receiving only grace and mercy from God... which requires positively renewing your mind and keeping it set.

- Remember J.O.Y. = Jesus, others, you. Joy and peace are found in receiving and believing... not self-beating.

- Do not allow weariness, age, or perceived past failures to steal your dream. Fix your mind on the gift Jesus gave you and keep it set.

- Remember freedom is the ability to say yes to God and no to people-pleasing behavior and negative feelings. This requires a habit of moment-by-moment mind renewal.

- Forgiveness: realizing freely you have received, so freely you may give.

Forgiveness was *not* something Grace struggled with, except when it came to forgiving herself for an occasional rebellious nature, some paralysis from over-analysis, and non-compliance with God's manual for living the brightest and healthiest life possible. Living free, day in and day out, was an area she desperately wanted to improve. She often beat herself up instead of receiving what had been done for her over 2,000 years prior.

Groundhogs commonly invade gardens to innocently eat in order to survive. If you're the owner of said garden, this survival act may feel more like destruction or robbery. The hunters and owners who couldn't forgive their destructive nature called them varmints, and Grace had a solution to their problem in a variety of calibers. The twist was in the rifling of the barrel. Without getting into the weeds, here's the bottom line: How the barrel is twisted or grooved defines where the projectile goes.

Like Groundhog Day, when the SHOT Show rolled around every year, Grace regretted that one night in 2005 when she had let her guard down due to seeing the shadow of her former happy life with Victor. Daydreaming, she saw Groundhog Phil emerge from his burrow. Slowly, he completed a 360-degree circle looking for his shadow. Then looking directly at her, he said "Grace, spring and Easter will arrive early this year. My friend Jesus says stop living in your shadow of punishment and step into His abundant light."

That daydream positively twisted her mental projection from internal self-loathing to the external love of Jesus. She realized that one night had triggered new twists of happiness for Freddy, his new wife, his employees, and his new life.

The person who revealed Grace's 2005 indiscretion was eventually made known to her; it was none other than her trusted ally Groovy. In industry parlance, he ratted her out, but she had never confronted him, nor did she hold the slightest bit of contempt. *Why not?* You may ask. Because he wasn't the problem. And although he was one-third of the dirty dancing trio, Grace didn't wish to cause any grief for anyone else. Her disappointment was in herself.

Overall, rat or not, she still thought her former euchre playing pal was mostly groovy.

In December 2011, Grace ran into Groovy Ratatouille. They exchanged pleasantries, and he said, "We should do lunch soon."

"Absolutely," Grace replied, and she walked away.

The ah-ha moment hit. "We're approaching February 2012, seven perfect years after punishment day. *Forgiveness*—you've freely given it to Groovy, but he doesn't know that!" Grace thought.

She could hardly contain her excitement as she imagined Groovy breaking bread with her—and getting the chance to finally ask for forgiveness for telling on her!

Her mental film reel started to roll, along with her enthusiasm. *I'm going to get the forgiveness party started by inviting and paying for lunch*, she thought. *Yay, I won't have to carry this secret around with me anymore!* She was literally celebrating out loud.

Over the next couple of days, she praised God for the opportunity to plan and execute a forgiveness lunch and confirmed a date for early 2012.

Ignited is the best word to describe how Grace felt when she woke up that morning. She pictured herself and Groovy sitting at a table, an awkward pause, and then before he even took a bite, the words, "Grace, I've got something to tell you," Exiting his mouth. Followed by: "Years ago, I couldn't stand watching you make a fool of yourself, so while I'm not sorry, just to clear the air, I wanted you to know that I'm the one who squealed."

Grace envisioned him looking at her with a poignant pause. Out of her soft, smiling lips, she would compassionately exclaim, "Groovy, thank you—I forgive you." Then, she'd casually take a bite out of her turkey sandwich and change the subject to ease any pent-up discomfort he had dealt with over all those secretive years.

Poof, like magic, he'd be somewhat surprised, yet relieved. Then, they'd be free to tell their story of forgiveness to help anyone struggling with regret or embarrassment from the past.

They sat down. Grace thought she'd go the extra mile by breaking the ice with a little small talk. She asked about his wife and kids. He said they were good. Things got quiet, then she noticed his posture change.

"Grace, there's something I need to ask you," Groovy started.

Hmmm. Ask was one word off. He was supposed to say *tell*.

Grace refers to the next line as *the hostage phrase*: "But, you have to promise not to tell anyone, okay?" Groovy added.

Uh oh, only two sentences in, and the forgiveness plan was already off course. Surprised that Groovy's words weren't verbatim to those in her head, she replied, "I can't promise you anything until I hear what you have to say."

"You have to promise to keep this a secret!" urged Groovy.

For a split-second, her curiosity was piqued; however, it was quickly replaced with discouragement. Besides believing a secret isn't a secret if more than one person knows about it, she was annoyed at the possibility of more hidden motives.

"Just spit it out and let's not play games here," she said.

Groovy paused, as if taking time to process whether he should trust her with his secret, then came the twist—a line so shocking to Grace, she mentally fell off her chair.

Chapter Thirty-Five
It's the Secrets We Don't Keep

> *"The secret things belong to the Lord our God, but those things which are revealed belong to us and to our children forever, that we may follow all the words of this law."*
>
> —Deuteronomy 29:29 (NKJV)

"I'd like to date you."

Those were the words Grace thought she heard. Stunned, it felt like she was in slow motion. Looking at Groovy, she leaned in, praying she would hear something different come out of his cherry-pitted pie-hole.

"What did you just say?" Grace asked.

"I'd like to date you."

Yep, that's what she thought he said. But certainly not what she came for, nor what she wanted to hear. To remain calm, she dialed up Jesus on her mental hotline. She focused on remaining a cool blue, rather than fanning the red-hot fire she was feeling.

"You'd like to *date* me?" she asked, looking at him like he had lost his mind. *It's a joke, he's just trying to divert you while he gains the courage to tell you the truth*, she wanted to believe.

"Yes, I'd like to date you, and I've wanted to ask you this question for a long time," Groovy very calmly replied. Now he'd admitted that it was pre-meditated.

Embarrassed for him, yet attempting kindness, she said, "I'm flattered. And I assure you, there's *no way* that's going to happen."

Flattered? Now she was lying and wanted to eat those words, rather than her lunch, as she wasn't flattered, she was unimaginably disgusted.

"One more time, let me ask you. You *are* joking, right?"

"No, I'm serious," Groovy said. "In fact, I figured since you don't work at A+ anymore, I can just drive the safe distance to your house and, you know... date."

Grace, (in her head): *Run... this is a trap, not a secret!*

The man who had reported her "scandal" was sitting in front of her saying more scandalous things. *Scandal* comes from the word *skandalon*, which means things like "the trigger or part of a trap to which the bait is attached;" "stumbling block, snare, an offense, cause for error;" "the enticement or occasion leading to conduct which brings with it the ruin of the person in question." She certainly felt like a trap had been sprung on her.

As reality set in, she felt nauseous. She went on to explain that while she hadn't been a saint, she had repented, and founded a business devoted to following the ways of Jesus. She asked Groovy "Why would you throw your vows away after watching what Victor's unfaithful behavior did to me?"

While he was quietly justifying his position, she began to connect the dots. Was it possible that he ratted her out hoping that she would get fired so he could date her?

You may be asking why Grace didn't simply walk over to Groovy's desk in 2005 and say, "I heard you ratted me out. Thank you, I needed that to set me straight."

Good question! The answer is two-fold. For one, she'd been threatened with termination, or worse, if she spoke a word. Second, she chose to avoid any more drama, conflict, or shame that day.

Or you may be wondering why, if she was so excited about telling Groovy that she'd forgiven him, she didn't start lunch with, "Groovy, I forgive you."

Answer: Looking back, she wished she had.

Anyway, think about it: Would you rather read a book about an always saintly, goody two-shoes or one about how God helped Grace overcome defeat and gain joy?

Lastly, Grace asked herself, "What if those who told her Groovy was the squealer had fibbed?" It seemed easier to avoid any awkwardness altogether.

On March 28, 2012, Grace volunteered her time to answer the phones at a Christian radio station fundraiser. During the two hours she was on call, she noticed the phones were eerily quiet. She also observed that business donations inviting the audience to match funds made the best impact.

This observation spurred her to make a monetary donation. To remain as anonymous as possible, she asked that only her business name be used.

Around 5:07 p.m., Grace was told, "Your match will be next."

She watched twelve other volunteers quietly wait for the phone to ring when suddenly the hairs on the back of her neck and arms stood up as a feeling came over her that was indescribable.

At roughly 5:14, Mary, the on-air personality, went wild promoting the "female business owner who's ready to take your calls." Instantly, *all* the phones lit up like a Christmas tree. Bewildered, Grace focused on the call she'd answered. It was a female donor who felt led to give *all* her $350 tax refund to help Grace make a difference. The generous donor didn't realize she was talking to Grace, who was far too humbled to mention it as she fought back tears. Grace gave a little, and this woman was called to give it *all*.

Grace was grateful and reminded that God is in *all* ways, in charge of what stays hidden and what is revealed. In a five-minute segment, her donation broke the record for funds raised. Overwhelmed by the experience, she melted into the arms of Mary and David, her two new angelic friends.

It was a hair-raising, hallelujah, can-I-get-an-Amen moment that solidified for her that you can't be held hostage when you're trusting and beholding the One who's already won the war.

Chapter Thirty-Six
It's No Longer a Crime Scene

"But his wife looked back behind him, and she became a pillar of salt."
—Genesis 19:26 (NKJV)

In November of 2012, Grace was still working for King George when her cell phone rang. The number that popped up looked familiar, but no name appeared. When she answered, she heard: "Grace, this is a voice from your past." She recognized the voice; it was Johnny B, a firearms industry connection that dated back to 1996 when he worked for Gander Mountain.

"Wow, it's so good to hear from you. How did you get my number?" Grace asked.

"It wasn't easy. It felt like you went black ops on us!" he answered, then added, "I went to the A+ Sports booth back in 2009. They told me you left. Not one person seemed to know where you went or what you were doing."

"I'm so glad you hunted me down. You know you've always been one of my favorite people, right?" Grace stated with glee.

"Yes, and Grace you're one of mine, which is why I'm calling. When are you coming back to the industry? We need you!" Johnny B replied.

"I'm not sure. Right now, I'm in contract with a King! Any thoughts on how I could help the most?" Grace inquired.

"Yes, you need to assist retailers and software companies with reporting and integration," was his excellent suggestion. Then he added, "Come to the SHOT Show and meet with me."

On New Year's Day, 2013, Moppsie told Grace she sensed that either A+ or another firearms company was going to make her an offer. "Perhaps," Grace replied. "I've received six unsolicited calls in the last 40 days. I'm waiting on the seventh for perfection. With SHOT just weeks away, I need a badge, a direct flight, and an available hotel room. When God makes that happen, I'll be on my way to Vegas."

As those words left her mouth, Grace got a text from Johnny A. It read, "Grace, I've got a SHOT Show badge for you. Can't wait to see you in Vegas!" (Johnny A had helped Grace at Galyan's grand opening, then at ARSE.)

Grace's mouth dropped open. Closing it to a smile, she said, "Thanks, God!"

Ecstatic, she called Johnny A for details and thanked him for being a perfect angel.

The next day, King George extended her consulting contract for another year. With God, that's how a girl rings in the New Year!

Rich, Grace's beloved pastor, taught her that "you live the Christian life left foot, right foot." She agreed as the left foot, right foot trust-walk was working for her!

A smile was plastered on her face as she walked the SHOT aisles, which were so crowded that she could barely get through. On her last full day in Vegas, there was an eerie silence as she entered the convention show floor. Grace saw giant crowds gathered around the television monitors. As she got closer, she realized the public announcement being broadcast could negatively impact the audience.

She disliked seeing the concern that was washing over neighboring faces. She momentarily closed her eyes and prayed.

When she opened her eyes, she saw an angel toward the front of the crowd.

Well, more like the back of 6'5" Commander Bad Axe's head. She hadn't seen or talked with him for years, even though she'd considered him a favorite friend.

She tapped him on the shoulder. When he turned and saw her, his facial expression was priceless!

"Grace! What are you doing here? Where have you been? How's your mom?" Yep, he hadn't changed a bit.

"Great! How are your wife and sons?" she asked.

After a brief catch-up, they exchanged contact information and went on their way.

Takeaways: Align

Sometimes people ask me if I'm a business coach or a life coach or a relationship coach or a spiritual coach—or what? The fact of the matter is that I am all those things. True growth happens at every level of your experience. Think about a chocolate milkshake. You can't separate the chocolate from the milk; they're totally mixed up together. You can change the type of chocolate or milk you use, or the quantities, but any change affects the whole package.

Grace discovered that God had a design for her life: to drop her into the middle of people's problems so she could use her unique brand of empathy and no-nonsense to help them. Once she realized that, she had clarity about what she wanted to do and was able to align her desires and plans to find the right path for herself.

Whether you stumble into your own insight or get help from a friend or coach, it may feel like a revelation for you, too. Hey, enjoy the ride! Not everyone gets to have the experience of discovering what they are here to do.

Reflection

1. If a person you secretly admired asked, "Who are you?" or "What makes you unique?" how would you answer?

2. Do the people you work with feel more like family, strangers, or a pack of wild animals?

3. Have you ever had to hand down knowledge or authority to someone else? How did it feel? Was it easy or difficult? What made it so?

Another piece of alignment is checking yourself as you go. When you find yourself straying, get back on track. When you successfully achieve a goal or take steps toward your goal, allow yourself to track and celebrate those little wins.

As your wins compound, consider creating a wall of wins (WOW) where you post all your victories. Take a picture of your initial wall to establish and document your baseline. At the beginning of each quarter, update your wall with your cumulative wins, then take a picture so that you can see your progression.

Before you know it, you'll realize you are achieving your dreams and desires, one right after another.

REPEATING to REFINE

We're all human; no one is going to get it all right the first time. If you still haven't solidified your plan, it's time to do so. And I have good news for you perfectionists: The perfect plan is the one you have written down. That's because trial and error is not a sign of imperfection at all—it's built into the system. The last phase involves taking action to follow your aligned plan, then periodically taking stock and deciding if the plan is working or you need to make a change.

Learn, teach, practice, repeat, and you have yourself a growth plan!

Chapter Thirty-Seven
It's Marching Madness

God has given me one new commandment that I should love others just as He has loved me.
—John 13:34 (AMP)

It was just days away from SHOT Show 2014. Unlike the previous year, Grace hadn't received any God nudges to indicate a need to attend. Quite frankly, she was so happy with King George, it wasn't on her mental radar. That was, until she pulled into her local Kroger parking lot.

Grace's cell phone rang while parking her vehicle. She was excited to see Commander Bad Axe appear on caller ID. She hadn't spoken to him since their encounter in Vegas.

They exchanged a few pleasantries, then the Commander shared the reason for his call. He needed to schedule a meeting time with her. "That won't be possible," Grace shared while smiling.

"What do you mean that's not possible?" asked the Commander in a serious tone. "You must go to SHOT. I need to meet with you!" he commanded. Déjà vu of 20 years prior set in.

Oh, these wonderfully strong men, they inspire me! she thought to herself.

"There's no need for me to go. My client just signed on for another year, and they'll have my full attention," she cheerfully shared.

"You are going. I need to meet with you!" he adamantly expressed. "I'm going to hang up and call my travel agent to book your arrangements."

"That won't be necessary; I'm not going," Grace confirmed.

"You are going. I need your help! I'll call you back." And her phone disconnected.

She glided through the grocery, glad to have heard from her friend. Then she checked out, packed her car, and was about to back out when the Commander called back. Grace stayed parked and prepared to let the Commander down as easily as she could.

Sounding extremely frustrated, he told her that his agent couldn't find any reasonable flight times, and the rates were astronomical. By the time he had reached the end of his bad news, he'd already arrived at plan B. Like flipping a switch, he began negotiating a meeting for the last week of January at a distributor's dealer show, only two hours away from where Grace lived.

Known for his unusual yet contagious laugh, Grace nicknamed the owner of the regional distributor Shotgun Jack. Businesswise, she considered him to be a friendly competitor of A+ Sports.

The show was smaller than those she'd hosted with A+—enjoyable, as it made for a more intimate customer experience. And speaking of intimate, while seated in a dining area and talking privately with the Commander, who happened to appear but—you guessed it—Victor.

Victor hadn't moved six feet from the table, when in walked Freddy Feathers. Seeming shocked, he asked, "Grace, what are *you* doing here?"

"I'm here as a guest of Commander Bad Axe," she replied.

Just then, the loudspeaker announced that all guests should proceed to the hotel tavern for happy hour. A few hours later, Grace watched as happy pals Victor, Smoochie, and Leo Lion entertained the crowd by attempting to play the washboard, kazoo, and tambourine on stage.

Grace drank *only* hot water from a coffee cup.

Victor, on the other hand, seemed snookered. He stumbled upon Grace and asked her, "would you like to see a picture of my grandchildren?" "Yes!" She answered. They moved away from the music and crowd. Victor shared the photo—and said, "Grace, I apologize for all that I put you through. I never meant to hurt you." Laughing, she said, "I think you're loopy; however, I forgave you a long, long time ago."

Seeming suddenly sober, he added "Recently, it hit me that when we were together, I resented you for articulating what you wanted and standing firm in your faith." He was referring to the letter she'd written outlining her rules of engagement.

John 10:10 appeared on her mental teleprompter, which was no surprise at all. Approaching ten years of separation, Grace was overjoyed that Victor was able to validate the enemy behind their divide. She was also pleased that it seemed he'd found the right wife for a happy life.

When Grace returned to the tavern, the Commander asked, "Grace, is everything all right, I saw you talking to Victor, then you disappeared. I was worried."

"Things couldn't be more perfect. Now, let's get back to why you needed me," she said.

Briefly, it seemed there was some family love lost due to resentment and the stress of operating a family business, and he wanted her input. Clearly, God had just used Victor's validation to set Grace up for success.

The next morning, the Commander seemed more like his normal self. "Grace, I know you have your planner with you; go get it so we can schedule the start date of our project." And he was right. Her planner always traveled with her.

Not moving, Grace reminded him that she had a year-long contract with King George. With 300 miles between them, she didn't find it feasible to accept him as a client. "You probably just need to get a few things off your chest, then you'll be fine. We can do that right now while I'm here," Grace tried to reason.

As he pulled out his checkbook, he repeated his request: "Open your planner, please."

She didn't want to argue with her friend, so she pulled her planner out of her Winchester Olin attaché. Scooting beside him, he saw how full her February was; almost every day had plans of at least three bullet points. "See, I'm not kidding, my calendar is full. There aren't enough consecutive days open for a new project," she shared.

"Let's look at March," was his solution.

She flipped a few pages to reveal that March 12, 13, and 14 had no bullet points—they appeared to be wide open. The Commander put his finger on the March 12 date and said, "Write my name in here. This will be the day we get started." Then, with pen in hand, he opened his checkbook and asked, "How much will it take for you to not argue with me?"

Remembering how he had given in to her request to accept a new salesperson 20 years prior, she laughed. With no idea of how she was going to manage helping King George, a few other small clients, and make a regular 300-mile trip, Grace wrote his name in her planner and prayed.

They separated for the rest of the day, so the Commander could complete his show orders. Grace merrily skipped from booth to booth, catching up with tons of manufacturers' reps and previous customers. She was so happy that she sang, "Here Comes the Sun," in her head. Jesus, Son of God, filled her heart.

When they reconvened the next morning, Grace thanked the Commander for inviting her to Shotgun Jack's show. Then she shared, "You know, my business is very different from my executive role with A+. It's centered around relationship coaching, team-building, and love legacies. So, before I make the trip, what is it that you want me to do for you?"

That question triggered tears in this incredibly strong man's eyes. "My family doesn't use the word *love*."

To avoid crying with him, Grace smiled and confidently said, "Well then, I know exactly what to do and where to start." Next question: "How will we define success?"

He replied: "Success would be having everyone in the same room, calmly communicating instead of cussing and flipping each other off. But that will never happen."

Grace silently transmitted, *Dear God, it seems we're returning to the land of "it will never happen"... Apparently the Commander just doesn't know You yet.*

Standing, she said, "Well, I have my marching orders. I'll see you on March 12."

After a hug and a "Don't worry, it's all going to work out" pat, Grace raced out the door and headed for home. Before she reached the end of the resort's snow-covered parking lot, her phone rang. She pulled into a parking spot thinking it was the Commander. She was shocked when she looked at the caller ID crossing the screen. *Wow, could this really be...?*

Chapter Thirty-Eight
It Overflows

"I have come that they may have life, and that they may have it more abundantly."

—John 10:10 (NKJV)

The call Grace received was from Freddy Feathers. Seeing her at the show triggered him to realize that she was the best solution for a technology transition project he had coming up. All business, he got right to the point: "Grace, I need your help. How soon can you start?"

Stunned at the possibility of working with Freddy again, she told him, "I'll need time to think about that one!"

Grace's two-hour drive home overflowed with praise to God!

As she jumped back and forth between celebratory yipees and, *Yikes, how am I ever going to serve all these clients?* it was as if she heard God say, "Relax, we've got this!" So, she turned up the radio volume and sang along with Mandisa's "You're an Overcomer."

The next day, King George summoned her to Bo's office. She could tell from his facial expression that something was weighing heavily on his mind. Not wanting to waste any time, she asked him: "George, what's wrong?" He motioned for her to sit down. *Uh oh, this is serious*, she thought.

Again, she asked, "What's wrong? Did someone quit? Did we lose a customer? Oh my gosh, did someone die?" He hardly reacted, which was unusual.

"No, it's nothing like that," he said solemnly. "Grace, as you know, we're getting ready to do a major expansion on the warehouse." He stopped as if to maintain his emotional composure. "Well, that's going to require a sizable loan." He stopped again, giving her time to jump ahead to what he was preparing to say, which she did.

BINGO! WOO-HOO! HALLELUJAH! floated through Grace's mind like massive floats at a parade.

"George, are you trying to tell me that you need to cancel my contract?" she asked. In her mind, this was God's answer to *Yikes, how am I ever going to...?* God was revealing His answer right then and there. She was ecstatic.

George was doing his best to not disappoint her. Giving her a confused look, it was almost as if he wanted to change his planned words.

"Well Grace, the bank..."

Trying to let him off the hook without further pain, she interrupted him: "Cancelling our contract is not a problem at all."

Then, George interrupted her: "Whoa Grace, slow down! I didn't say we want to cancel your contract. I'm just making you aware of the financial process we must go through."

"Oh!" she said, as she realized how overzealous she may have been. "So, you anticipate our contract will run the full year as planned?" she slowly asked.

"I'm not sure yet. We haven't had much time to think through all the details. Since you're our advisor, I wanted to hear your input. If you had let me finish, you would have heard me say that the bank saw 'consulting fees' and inquired, 'How long do you anticipate needing this outflow?'" a happier sounding George trumpeted.

"Awww, that's a good thing!" a gracious Grace commented, before thinking: *Wait a minute. If that was a good thing, then why did George look and sound so downtrodden?* As it came out of her mouth, the look on George's face indicated what his heart might have felt. He wasn't prepared to let her go *just yet*.

When George heard that she had another opportunity and realized he wasn't hurting her, they settled on a wrap-up date in April. It was a win-win-win for everybody.

Another of Grace's connections, Gabriel Greystone, co-owned a technology consulting firm. Gabriel's father worked for the National Rifle Association. Grace and Gabriel had met while they were both helping Freddy Feathers.

While meeting with Gabriel one morning, a colorful wheel on the wall attracted Grace's glance. "Wow, what's that?" She asked. Grace knew the letters DISC meant Dominance, Influence, Steady, and Compliance from already being DISC Certified; however, Gabriel's wheel resembled a dartboard with a bullseye in the middle.

The eight colors of the circular wheel were arranged in the same order as the color-filled square boxes from Grace's childhood creation. Unlike Grace's original diagram, no gray or boxes existed. However, the colors coming together in the bullseye reminded her of the kaleidoscope she loved and of the dual-labeled, rainbow file folder system she had customized years before.

Picking up on her enthusiasm, Gabriel encouraged Grace to use the same DISC assessment provider as they did so she could train his team, which she immediately did. That suggestion shot Grace's behavioral arsenal up to an expert level.

In early 2009, Grace attended a skeet shooting event that Gabriel's company hosted for their clients. It was a huge success. As a participant, Grace was thrilled as she watched novices having a blast while safely shooting skeet for the first time.

Inspired by this experience, Grace created corporate shooting event packages, hosting them at several of the ranges around her area. She absolutely loved transitioning people with a fear of firearms into fearless folks having safe fun with guns.

George's wife and daughters heard about Grace's "safe fun with guns" program and asked her to schedule a private event for them. It was intended to be just the girls, but they couldn't leave the King out. Grace's heart overflowed with joy!

Without trying, Grace was fully loaded and overflowing with business. She was convinced it was her focus on Jesus and His message from John 10:10. To recap, as the year progressed:

- She transitioned from George's castle to the Commander's Hunting Center.

- She helped Freddy Feathers transition his operation from one software platform to another, while transitioning a long-time manager to retirement.

- She was transitioning firearms virgins to victorious enthusiasts.

And then, it got better!

The Commander witnessed immediate success. He told a couple of the manufacturers' reps how helpful she'd been. One of them suggested she visit the Fabricated Firearms Factory on her drive back home, which she did.

Upon arrival, she noticed the Fictitious Firing Range just a couple of doors away. Grace realized that she had visited this location over a decade earlier. She sat silently, trying to recall the name of the owner of the Fabricated Factory. The indoor range didn't look familiar.

Ferdinand Fibalittle—that's it, that's the owner's name, Grace recalled. Excited, she bounced out of her car and through the door like a red rubber ball.

"I'm here to see Ferdinand," she told the receptionist. "Then you're several months too late," was the curt response.

"Oh, my, what happened to him?" Grace asked with concern.

"I'm not at liberty to divulge those details," said the reluctant receptionist.

"Well, clearly you're still in business. If Ferdinand is gone, who's the owner now?" Grace pleasantly persisted.

"If you don't know, then clearly, you're soliciting and missed the sign on the door," Ms. Reluctant retorted.

Grace wasn't a pastor or preacher, but in this moment, she needed to imagine that she was. She pictured the Apostle Paul talking to her like he did Timothy: "As for you, be calm, cool, and steady" (2 Timothy 4:5). *Here's an opportunity for kindness training,* thought Grace. The forced thought replaced her temptation to unleash an un-pastor-like tongue lashing on Ms. Reluctant and her rude 'tude.

She heard an apt paraphrase of John 10:10 in her mind: "Don't let this enemy rob your joy. Grace, it's not about you... Remember who I am and why I came!"

Grace couldn't precisely say she wasn't soliciting, so she tried the *melt her with kindness* angle.

"Well, I respect how you protect your company's privacy. Have you considered becoming a security guard—you'd be wonderful at it! I bet the new owner appreciates what a great job you do!" Grace went on, encouraging.

Ms. Reluctant melted like snow on a 112-degree day. "Do you really think so? I do pride myself on keeping solicitors at bay."

"Yes, I can see that! Where did you get your training?"

"I worked a couple of doors down at the Fictitious Firing Range," Ms. Reluctant-Getting Warmer beamed.

"How interesting..." Grace shared her A+ Sports background with Ms. Warmed Up, and within minutes, it felt like they were long-lost sisters.

Grace learned that Ferdinand Fibalittle had his firearms license revoked due to some discrepancies with governmental rules. The license was transferred to Ferdinand's nephew, Frank Fantabulous.

Once Ms. Warmed Up realized that Grace was there to 100 percent help and 0 percent harm, she said to Grace, "I think Frank might be available. Would you like to meet him?"

"Why, of course!" Grace replied, and off to Frank's office they went.

For several hours, Frank and Grace talked about the firearms industry, things that had changed, and some that had stayed the same. Frank repeatedly thanked Grace for going out of her way to stop by. "I feel like I've known you all my life, like you're one of my favorite relatives!" he expressed.

"That reminds me, one of my favorite clients owns a business named The Fictitious Fig Farm. I did a double-take when I saw the Fictitious Firing Range sign. Do you own that too?" Grace asked.

Frank looked flabbergasted.

"Is there something I should know?" Grace inquired. "It is a firearms range, right?"

"You've got to be kidding me," Frank said.

"So, it's not a range?" she asked.

"This is unbelievable, what a small world," Frank said while shaking his head with disbelief.

Grace watched Frank pick up his cell phone, and silently hit the speaker icon.

"Phil Fitasafiddle here," Grace heard from Frank's phone. "Uncle Phil, you're never going to believe who's sitting in my office."

Chapter Thirty-Nine
It's Tongue Twisting Victory

> *"I have victory wherever I go."*
>
> —2 Samuel 8:6 (AMP)

Turns out Grace's client Phil had an older sister, Franny, who was Frank's mother. Here's a diagram of Phil and Frank's family tree:

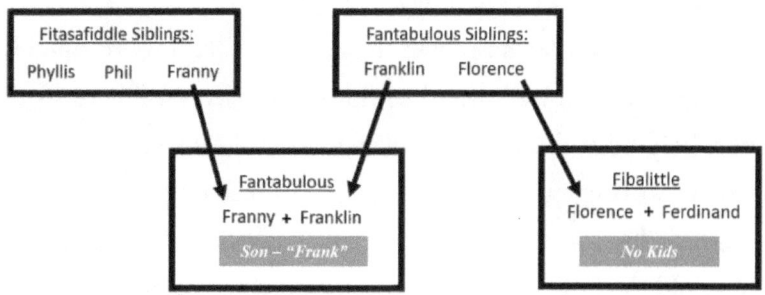

Once Frank divulged that it was Grace in his office, Phil was elated! Phil gave Grace a quick update on his staff and confirmed that they were still using the processes she'd put into place. Suddenly, he stopped mid-sentence and asked, "Grace, how in the world did you end up in Frank's office today?"

She replied, "A manufacturer's rep referred me."

"Are you sure it wasn't God?" Phil asked.

Laughing, Grace said, "Yes, indirectly, I'm sure it was."

Phil continued, "Frank, I can't explain what it is that Grace does... However, trust me when I tell you, she saved my business and changed my life. There will be times when it is tough to hear what she shares. She'll pull out hidden emotions, and it's likely that you'll cry... and you won't be the only one who does. However, I promise that, if you can be vulnerable enough to listen and follow her advice, you'll be grateful that she appeared out of nowhere."

Frank simply replied, "Okay," and shortly after, they disconnected. Frank invited Grace to join him for dinner. At the restaurant, they were seated at a quiet table secluded in the corner. After they had ordered, Frank confirmed that he accidentally owned both the Fabricated Factory and the Fictitious Range. Since his Aunt Florence, who had married Ferdinand Fibalittle, had no children, Frank was the closest relative she had to a son.

Uncle Fibalittle had grown the Fabricated Factory to roughly 50 employees. Just 18 months prior to his license being revoked, he wisely built the Fictitious Range. It had 10 lanes and could have easily been rated a 5-star facility. Fourteen employees worked there. Sadly, Uncle Fibalittle's lifestyle had led him into a pit that he couldn't climb out of. Frank intervened to save the businesses more out of family obligation than willingness.

Grace asked, "What were you doing before you agreed to help your uncle?"

"I was living out my dream as a guide in Alaska, and Grace, you have no idea how hard it was to choose to help my aunt and uncle over staying in paradise. I had no intentions of leaving my dream to take on what's now become a nightmare," he painfully shared.

Their salads were delivered.

Frank asked Grace if she had met his Uncle Phil's twin sister, Phyllis. She hadn't.

He explained that his Aunt Phyllis married an exceptionally tall pipe-smoking man named Pete Padiddle. Grace heard herself mentally snort as she thought, *Perhaps Pete should change his last name to Piper.*

Speaking of pipes, Pete's one eye squinted when he lit his; so, Phyllis nicknamed her hubby Popeye. Hearing that prompted Grace to tell Frank her Popeye's Chicken story and to explain that she walked away from a successful career and a sizeable commission to follow a call that wasn't clear.

"Can you see how my story relates to yours?" she asked.

"Yes, you also made a tough decision, so you do understand what I went through," he answered.

"Exactly!" Grace agreed.

Following family tradition, Phyllis named her four children Phee-phee, Phifer, Pho, and Phylum. At home, Phyllis made her life a little simpler by shortening her children's names to Phee, Fi, Pho, and Fum.

The family lineage was necessary for Grace to understand because Fi, Pho, and Fum all worked at the Fictitious Firing Range.

Here's a diagram to help you stay connected:

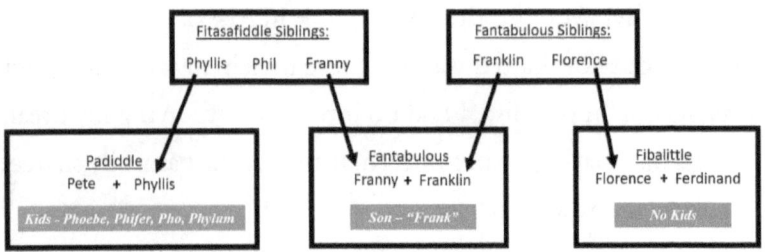

Practicing full transparency, Grace asked Frank if he was familiar with her background.

She was excited about the chance to help him and was tempted to go into the many stories from her past. Instead, she kept it to her three favorites.

"Frank, I love your name!" she started. "I don't want you to feel like I'm making fun of your name, light of your circumstance, or unfair comparisons. So frankly, Frank," she paused to see if he could take her humor without offense, "to help you decide whether we should move forward together or say goodbye, I'll share my testimony. I'll start with the ugliest things I've done, and end with how trusting Jesus replaced ashes with blessings."

Frank's response was, "Thank you, Grace. I made my decision to move forward with you the second you said Fictitious Fig Farm. However, your willingness to be vulnerable makes me want to get started right away. How do we do that?"

"First, we'll need to pray," said Grace.

"I may have already done that. I think it's the reason you're here. You saved me!" Frank excitedly informed her.

"How so?" she asked.

"Last night on my drive home, my thoughts were filled with such darkness and despair that I began uncontrollably sobbing.

The snow-covered trees that lined my route grabbed my attention, and I could no longer see the road. Then, I remember an urgent push to wrap my truck around a tree and end it all." As Frank told Grace this, his complexion faded to a pale-gray color and tears began streaming down his face.

"I hit the gas and headed off the berm, but the gravel caused me to just miss the tree. Confused, I thought I was slamming on the brake, but apparently, my foot was still on the gas pedal. My truck accelerated through the grass and onto the pavement, and all I could see was a brick wall. It all happened so fast.

Somehow, my foot got to the brake and I slammed to a stop. I've never been so disoriented in all my life. It occurred to me that I should put the truck in park, and as soon as I did, trembling and convulsing took over. I thought I was going to throw up but was too terrified to open my eyes." Frank's micro-expressions were so vivid that Grace felt his fear as if she were with him.

"Then, a peace I can't explain came over me. Slowly, I opened my eyes, and in front of me was a flashing sign that read, 'JESUS is the expectant HOPE of what's to come. Hold on for one more day.'

At first, my eyes were blurry from crying, so I just stared at the words until my vision became clear. As I looked to my right, all I could see was the red brick wall I almost hit. I looked back at the sign and then realized I was next to a small church. One that I drive by every day but hadn't noticed." As Frank told this portion of the story, his demeanor displayed peace and his face hope.

Perfectly timed, their spaghetti and lasagna arrived.

While hearing these stories of despair wasn't pleasant, God had empowered Grace to teach people how to overcome certain adverse circumstances.

"Frank, are you able to share the thoughts you had leading up to your near-fatal experience?" Grace empathetically asked. Following is a summary of what Frank shared.

His wife of many years was threatening divorce because she wasn't happy raising his four children by herself. She blamed him for making a stupid decision to help Uncle Fibalittle over considering how it would affect her.

Although he made sure that his family had a large house in a safe neighborhood with a pool, tennis and basketball courts, dirt bikes, and land to ride on, every night his children moaned about how he wasn't around to play with them. This guilt pushed him to carve out a couple of hours each night for them, even though most nights, he was so physically and mentally exhausted that he could barely stand.

When he finally made it to bed, his wife, who had once been the most fun-loving, positive person he knew, started in on him: "Did you make sure the door was locked? Did you let the dog out and make sure he had water, or do I have to do everything? You know, I haven't played tennis with my friends for weeks, because I'm stuck in this house all day being everyone's slave..." her list sounded long and consistent.

Then, there was the business drama. Every decision he made seemed to be wrong.

Uncle Fibalittle couldn't accept responsibility for the loss of his license. A man who had originally praised Frank for helping him was now telling him he didn't know anything about business.

Uncle Fibalittle's rage got the best of him. Shortly after Frank changed the locks, Fibalittle stood in the parking lot to yell at his former employees. He screamed: "I blame Frank and all of you idiots for ruining my fabricated fortress!"

After the first time this happened, Frank purposely arrived 30 minutes before the employees. He tried every tactic he could think of to calm Ferdinand and get him to leave. Eventually, it was necessary for the police to intervene.

Frank's Aunt Florence was the reason he agreed to help in the first place. She had placed the S.O.S. call to Frank, as her husband had too much pride, but no other options. Since she had no children, Florence gave Frank loads of love and attention his entire life. As the best aunt a person could wish for, he couldn't let her down.

With the rules Ferdinand had broken, there wasn't much time for Frank to acquire his license and save the business. It had moved so quickly that Frank didn't realize the audaciousness of this commitment. The pit that Ferdinand Fibalittle had dug was so deep and wide, that the stress from uncovering his details put Aunt Florence underground.

On the day of Aunt Florence's funeral, Frank's best friend from high school accidentally overdosed on painkillers. While he was still in shock from the news, his wife told him, "If you would have spent more time with him instead of at work, this probably wouldn't have happened. You're always so focused on yourself."

When Frank acquired the Fictitious Range, the employees working there seemed to be doing a fairly good job. However, as soon as the team felt safe that Ferdinand's license would never be renewed, the truth about what had transpired came to light.

One example: An employee had footage of inappropriate behavior between Ms. Reluctant and Uncle Fibalittle. She claimed she had been a victim and was contemplating a lawsuit. To salvage the situation as compassionately, quickly, and quietly as possible, and without dismissing her accusations, Frank moved her to the Fabricated Factory. He felt horrible about his uncle's bad behavior and implemented an employee assistance program to help her and any other employees who may have felt victimized.

About a week after Ms. Reluctant had been transferred, she passed out in the middle of the factory floor. Unfortunately, the doctors claimed her symptoms matched several chronic conditions; therefore, they had no clear diagnosis or solutions for her.

To keep her employed and everyone as safe as possible, Frank promoted her to the receptionist position. He installed an additional camera and panic button and made the office into more of a booth. That way, if she lost consciousness, the walls would keep her from falling and someone could see her if she passed out.

Quadrupling the business chaos were Frank's cousins. Hearing he'd lost a few employees; well-intentioned Aunt Phyllis texted him every couple of days to say: "I've got three boys who can help you." Aunt Phyllis wasn't accepting his soft "no thank you," and finally he couldn't endure the pressure. He caved on his personal commitment to never hire family or friends. Overwhelmed, and with spots to fill, he took the path of least resistance over his preference of putting interviewing, hiring, and onboarding processes in place. Fi, Pho, and Fum each came with a unique set of issues, and their family entitlement was becoming more than the senior experienced managers, or Frank, could bear.

Frank felt like he was being held hostage in every direction he turned. Because family was involved, there wasn't a single person he could trust to help him, not even his wife. Convinced his marriage, family, and financial ships were all sinking, hitting the tree appeared to be his best way out.

"If you hadn't arrived when you did, Grace, I'm not sure what would have happened. But, last night, before I put my truck in drive, I said to that church sign, 'If you want me to have hope, it's going to take a miracle.'"

Chapter Forty
It's More Than Miraculous

> *"But their minds were blinded. For until this day the same veil remains unlifted in the reading of the Old Testament, because the veil is taken away in Christ."*
> —2 Corinthians 3:14 (NKJV)

By the time Frank had finished his story, it was 11:35 p.m. The restaurant closed at midnight. Having been Grace's client, Uncle Phil predicted she would want to extend her stay to help Frank. He also understood how she worked. To assist her, Phil booked a room for Grace at a local hotel, then called Frank's wife, Fiona, and offered her a deluxe, all-day spa package with only one condition: She had to enjoy the day with his business advisor. Fiona accepted.

During dinner, Grace received this text from Phil: "Should you be inclined to accept Frank as a client, your spa-day with Frank's wife is booked for tomorrow morning. Coincidentally, Frank uses my accountant who is scheduled to meet you in the hotel lounge at 4:30 p.m., and my attorney who plans to have dinner with you at

7:00 p.m. By the way, when they heard it was you, they both told me they'd take it easy on my checkbook, because you are so much fun to talk to!

"Oh, and one last thing, by the time you arrive at the hotel tonight, the desk clerk should have your usual drink ready to hand you. Thanks Grace, you're the best!"

That was sign enough for Grace.

On the 20-minute ride back to the Fabricated Factory to get her car, Grace said to Frank, "I'm curious, how would you describe your spirituality?"

"Do you mean like religion?" he asked.

"Just try describing whatever comes to mind," she answered.

After a very long silence, Frank shared: "When I hear the word *spirit*, it takes me back to Alaska. As a guide, my closest friends introduced me to customs and rituals indigenous to their culture. I miss that connection, as it was very loving and peaceful."

He continued, "My mom and dad weren't churchgoers, and they didn't talk about religion. When I met my wife, her family was Catholic. I went to church with her one time and didn't care for it. To be honest, it wasn't really the church, but more how her dad acted on the car ride back to her house. He was in a foul mood and cursed like he just came from a bar. Upon arriving home, he cracked open beers and drank until he was drunk. When he became belligerent, I thought, *if that's what being religious means, I want no part of it.* My parents *never* acted like that, so I decided to follow their path and not attend church."

"So, when you think about God, what description appears on your mental teleprompter?" asked Grace softly.

"Have you ever seen the game show, *Let's Make a Deal?*" he asked.

"Yes, I have," Grace answered.

"That's what trying to figure out who God is for me. Only I don't like to waste my time with guessing games; it's hard to explain."

"Keep going. You're doing great, and I'm intrigued," encouraged Grace.

"Okay. To me, picking a religion to follow is like picking the right curtain. Behind curtain number one is Baptist, curtain number two is Methodist, and then once you've finally settled on a curtain, you're tempted with more boxes and envelopes to determine your fate. Rather than wasting time, playing games, or guessing wrong and getting zonked, I'd rather not play at all."

Waiting to make sure she didn't interrupt him, Grace said, "Thank you for sharing that great analogy. You're painting realistic pictures for me. Boxes and curtains are terms I frequently use. If we move forward, we'll put measurements for responsibilities, performance, productivity, etc. in grids. Grids are made up of numerous boxes. Humans are spirits made up of unique values. Like your game show reference, humans play guessing games. We make judgements based on a person's costume and try to guess what's hidden behind their curtain or veil.

Jesus, who's name you stared at last night, tore a veil when He died on a tree. That is a deep and serious subject and probably best saved for another time. Have you ever seen the game show *Hollywood Squares?*"

"Yes, I have," Frank answered.

"If we move forward, your employees will feel like celebrities when we match their most valuable talents with their best starring role. The past zonks that have been dealt to the Fabricated Factory and Fictitious Range will be replaced with predictable X's and O's," continued Grace.

"Grace, I noticed you said, *if* we move forward. In my mind, we've already started, and we need to keep going. What am I missing?" Frank asked.

By this time, they'd reached the Fabricated parking lot. Grace asked Frank to hold his question for a moment as she opened the truck door, jumped out, and grabbed a small book from her vehicle. Then, she jumped back in his truck.

"What you were missing is an understanding of who really saved you last night. It wasn't me," Grace answered.

Then, she handed him a hardback book that was roughly 4 ¼ x 6 ¼ in size. Frank noticed there was an inviting hand on the cover with the name "Jesus" below it. Before he could ask any questions, Grace suggested he open the book to any page and read what it said.

While he did what Grace asked, she noticed the clock on the truck's dash showed midnight. She took this moment of silence to pray for the Holy Spirit to lead both Frank and her in the direction they needed to go.

She looked over at Frank. The book was in one hand, his other hand was wiping tears from his face. She waited.

At 12:07, Frank handed her the book opened to February 27. "Grace, read this," he said. The two short paragraphs spoke directly to him, as if it were Jesus doing the talking. It reiterated, in more detail, what the flashing sign said. Frank was getting a full-on dose of why Jesus is the answer.

When he noticed she had finished, he asked her to also read April 5, May 3, and June 2—which she did. When she finished, she closed the book and without saying a word, looked at him.

Fighting back more tears, Frank asked, "Grace, each page you read spoke directly to my life. What's happening here? Those dates are my children's birthdays. If I had succeeded in that milli-second urge last night, they would have been fatherless. I'm so ashamed of what I've become. How could I have possibly been tempted to do something so horrific?"

Calmly and softly, Grace said, "Frank, I can't work with anyone whose self-pride keeps them from accepting help or attempting transformation. It seems you've been emptied, which presents a great opportunity to refuel with a new fire! Let's view this moment as the start of a brand-new race. Here's your first lap; when I say go, name all the words you can think of that start with *de* or *dis* until I say stop. Go!"

Frank was off... "Destroy, despair, disaster, demolish, dismiss, deceive, deception, destruction, disappointed, discouraged, dismal, decompose, decay, disengage, destroy... wait, I think I said destroy already—did I?"

He heard Grace say, "Stop! Frank, for lap two, I'd like you to name words that start with *re,* and the rules are the same. Go!"

"Remodel, replay, response, resurrect, refresh, *refuel*, reposition, revitalize, redo, reorganize, repair, repossess, rebuild, reconnect, rekindle, renew, resurgence, resurrect... wait, did I say that before?"

Grace said, "Stop! Frank, that was excellent! It's after midnight, and those words were firing out of your brain! Now, to answer both of your earlier questions, yes, you did say *destroy* and *resurrect* more than once. In fact, you were going so fast, I could barely capture them." To add levity, she asked, "Hey Frank, did you hear what happened to the man who forgot to pay his exorcist?"

Laughing, Frank thought for a few seconds and answered, "No, I did not. What happened to him?"

"He got repossessed!"

Laughing harder, Frank told Grace she was giving him exactly what he needed.

She added, "If we continue racing together, expect a lot more fun accompanied by exercises, laps, and homework. Lap three is also your homework. When you get up tomorrow morning, I'd like you to take a fresh look at the words I've captured for you and tell me what you see. As for me, I'm exhausted and I'm going to my hotel. Thank you for sharing your story."

Grace got out of Frank's truck, and off she went.

Chapter Forty-One

It's One More Day

"You will be secure, because there is hope; you will look about you and take your rest in safety."

—Job 11:18 (NIV)

"You must be Grace! Welcome!" said the hotel's front desk clerk. She handed Grace a white porcelain coffee cup of hot water and with a warm smile asked: "I take it you'll be with us until Sunday?"

"Absolutely!" Grace replied, as she took the warm cup and headed for her upgraded queen suite.

The next day, Saturday, went exactly as planned. Grace spent six straight hours listening to Fiona, who didn't hold any details back regarding her personal perspectives. The next six hours were spent between the accountant and attorney, who already knew Grace from working with Phil. They too revealed all the information they felt she should know.

At 10:45 p.m., she was just walking in the hotel when she received this text from Frank: "I heard you've had quite a day. I'm pretty sure my thank you needs to come with an apology. You must be exhausted, and I hate myself for being this selfish; however, I won't get any sleep tonight until I know what our next step is."

Her reply: "See you at 9:00 a.m. tomorrow morning in the lobby. No apologies necessary, I'm grateful to be of help. Your homework is to rest assured that God's got this, even if you don't know exactly who He is."

His return text was a thumbs up emoji.

Having gone through these types of client scenarios before, Grace anticipated that Frank would be anxious to talk with her and would arrive early. She went to the lobby at 8:00 a.m. hoping to eat a continental breakfast and get her one cup of coffee in before Frank arrived. She had just settled at the table and taken her first bite when Frank walked up and said, "Good morning, Grace. I'm sorry I'm so early, but..."

Grace held her hand up to stop him, then asked: "Are you really sorry, or is there a better word to describe how you feel?"

Silently, Frank took a few seconds to process her question then said, "I'm here so early because I just couldn't wait to see and talk to you. But, if someone cut into my time like that, I would think it rude."

Grace asked, "So is the one word that truthfully describes your intention *rude*?"

"No, I didn't intend to be rude, but then I realized that it might appear rude to you, and I felt badly," Frank shared.

Patiently, Grace asked, "What one word describes why you're here early? And please do not be concerned about my thoughts regarding your answer; simply share your truth."

"*Excited* and *hopeful*... but that's three words... I'm sorry Grace," Frank said.

"Frank, it's my intention to be helpful, not rude, with what I am about to share. It appears we're working together, so here's an improvement tip: please stop saying the words *sorry* or *I'm sorry, but* for things you're intentionally, excitedly, or purposefully doing.

"Saying *sorry* and *but* as part of everyday communication is a habit many of my clients had. We'll work on the *but* portion another time. For now, here's how to improve. If you are truly apologizing say, 'I apologize.' If you are expressing true sorrow or sympathy for a loss, then 'I'm sorry, I was wrong' or 'I'm sorry for your loss' is certainly appropriate. Sorry can come across dismissive when it's not sincere. Habitually saying, I'm sorry,' may project a victim mentality or imply you've been abused or feel attacked, are avoiding conflict—or something else. Replacing sorry with sincerity leads to better outcomes and healthier relationships. As leaders, paying attention to our words and their semantics help us paint proper pictures in the minds of others. Years ago, I developed this mantra: Words have meaning, so say what you mean, mean what you say, and don't be mean about it."

Grace paused before continuing. "Frank, have you ever been to Times Square?" Grace asked.

"Yes" he replied.

"Great! Picturing your thoughts and words going across one of those huge billboards will help your effectiveness immensely." Grace continued: "My mother taught me that 'what the mouth says, the ears hear, and then the brain does.' Example: if a person continually says, 'I'm stupid,' it won't be long before they'll have themselves and everyone they communicate to convinced. Conversely, if they changed 'stupid' to 'loved'... their audience would eventually feel that love. That love would spread, and the impact of one person's thoughts and words could change the world. Now that you understand the why behind my coaching, are you willing to incorporate that tip into your daily life?" Grace inquired.

"Yes ma'am, I'm sor... Wow, I see what you're saying," Frank said, catching his own words.

Grace used body language to communicate "take a deep breath and try again," which he did. "Grace, I was so excited to see you that I arrived early. If that's unpleasant or rude, I'll be happy to return at 9:00 as planned."

With a huge smile and a thumbs up, Grace invited him to sit down. "Oh, I forgot something in my truck. You're never going to believe this... I'll be right back," he told her.

He returned with a basket of home-baked brownies. "These are for you. Fiona got up at 4:30 this morning to bake them for you. She said she was so energized by your visit that she couldn't sleep. She wanted you to have these for your ride home. Grace, Fiona hasn't done anything like that in over a decade. It was like she was the woman I fell in love with."

Quite Frankly, Grace was a little surprised too. Her female clients and wives of male clients often made her treats or gave her gifts; however, Fiona had shared a lot of pent-up frustration. Her change of heart must have been God. To Frank, Grace simply said, "How lovely. Please hug and kiss her when you get home, and tell her she's appreciated."

"Oh, and you should have seen the texts I got from my attorney and accountant. They were almost identical. They basically said they loved seeing you again and they'd do anything they could to help us," Frank excitedly added. "Your surprise visit and spontaneous help has given *all* of us hope!"

Grace had placed her cell phone on the table. At 9:07 a.m., her notification bar flashed an angel emoji from Phil. At that exact moment, Frank placed a blank check in front of her. He waited a split-second for her attention, then said: "I don't know how your fees work, but I imagine it'll take a hefty retainer to return. After all you've been through to save us, what amount is required to get you back?"

"I'll make you a deal," Grace started, then stopped as she was cracking up at her words. "Oh my gosh Frank, I didn't mean to sound like Monty Hall." Then he started laughing, and they both couldn't stop. When one gained composure, the other one snorted. Literally, they both had to use napkins to wipe the tears from their faces.

Finally, she got out what she needed to say, "I'm going to leave this daily devotional book with you. If you agree to faithfully read it before you begin each day, I'll return."

"Done!" he shouted as he stood up. Before she could get to her feet, he hugged her. "You saved my life!"

"The glory, for one more day, doesn't belong to me." she replied.

The brownies were *out of this world*, as were the doors of opportunity God was opening for her.

Chapter Forty-Two
It's Switching

"The thief comes only in order to steal and kill and destroy. But Jesus came that I may have and enjoy life, and have it in abundance (to the full, till it overflows)."
—John 10:10 (AMP)

The Commander referred Grace to another family business close to his heart: Deed's Dairy Equipment. This business was well-established in the dairy/agricultural field. The owners expressed a need for team building and organizational structure.

Mimicking her other clients, Grace discovered their needs revolved around these CORE areas: improvement in Communication, Organization, Relationships, and Engagement.

Unlike her customers whose livelihood revolved around guns, Deed's focus was on helping herds of livestock go round as their milk flowed down. Deed's specialty was installing sophisticated rotary milking parlors which Grace found very cool.

Specific to Deed's clientele, Grace learned this: "To avoid brown poo-poo from a black and white moo-moo ruining your shoe-shoe, wearing rubber boots was a wise thing to do-do. And, to avoid getting shocked, she need *not* touch the colorful wires located in an electrical box.

Grace helped Deed's DEFINE measurable gaps within their organization; DESIGN project teams to divide and conquer the issues that were revealed; and ALIGN their people with their purpose, projects, and processes to sustain success; then taught them how to REFINE these areas for continuous improvement.

One of Deed's owners made a 300-mile trip to visit with King George. The purpose was to understand how following Grace's process had been beneficial. This was an experience Grace had dreamed of: One client helping another to build stronger businesses and relationships.

With a repeatable/sustainable structure secured and project plans/teams in place, the final transformation was triggered during a customized behavioral training session which Grace retitled: "How Now Brown Cow?" Simply stated: In roughly 18 months, the Deed's team building was a success. The owners expressed that they were pleased with the results which led them to a family succession plan years later.

Frank and Fiona's project lasted a little longer. It was as far as one could get from simple due to the multitudes of spiritual battles and emotional chaos that had been erupting for months.

One of Grace's most memorable employee interviews took place with Frank's cousin, Pho. She was on her third question when she noticed Pho's clenched hands and jaw. Chin slightly lowered; his glaring stare appeared to be mentally burning holes through her.

Reading his expression, Grace shifted from a question to an observation: "Pho, you look like you're ready to hurt somebody."

"I am," he fired back, in a tone that was not his own.

While unpleasant, she had received similar reactions to the interview process a time or two before. And, like Pho, the people making the "I am" statements had visible weapons handy to make good on their words.

Before Pho, her reaction was to lightheartedly say, "Well, I know it's not me that you want to hurt because I'm a lot of fun!" which usually broke the ice. The reactors clarified that they were merely unhappy about being questioned. By jumping in their behavioral box, Grace immediately shifted the atmosphere to a comfortable place to share.

This time it wasn't Grace or the process that was triggering friction for Pho. Instinctively, Grace reacted differently. When Pho's burning stare didn't break, she pushed her notebook to the side, put down her pen, and removed her reading glasses from her face. It was time to get spiritually serious.

Logical Grace left the scene, and spirit-filled Grace appeared. She didn't think; she moved—following the picture that was being painted in her head. She saw a basketball coach, sitting in a rolling chair like she was. He turned to a disgruntled player, then scooted his chair toward the young man. She did the same in real life. She saw coach lean down, placing his forearms on his thighs and interlacing his hands. Grace did the same. She looked Pho directly in the eyes and firmly said, "Talk to me... let it all go."

Pho mimicked her body language, and started talking so fast, she could barely grasp what he was saying. He talked non-stop, for almost 90 minutes, describing a car accident that he'd been in during his teen years. It had claimed the life of his best friend.

As he talked, she watched his emotions undulate in waves of hysteria, rage, guilt, shame, panic, and eventually, peace. Like a steam engine grinding to a halt, Pho stopped talking. He sat back in his chair and let out a huge sigh of relief.

Grace had been intensely listening to Pho and silently praying for Jesus to come to his rescue. Pho's 90-minute transformation was mesmerizing.

When Pho leaned back, Grace mimicked his posture. After his sigh, she asked him to describe how he felt in one word. It was *released*.

She watched as Pho seemed to be grasping for his thoughts by repeatedly running his fingers through his hair. Seeming bewildered, Pho asked, "Grace, what just happened?"

It had been ten years since the traumatizing accident. In that span, his family didn't know how to help him. They didn't attend church, nor had they experienced anything like he had. Pho had lost hope that there was anywhere or anyone he could turn to for help. He felt alone, dismissed, and when he had tried to express his pain, misunderstood.

Having a third party to express all those pent-up emotions to seemed to help him break-free from years of anxiety.

Grace explained her goal with the Fictitious Range was to help people understand themselves and replace business chaos with results. Now that she'd heard his story, she had one that he could probably relate to. She shared her teenage loss of handsome Remi, and how God had carried her through the grief.

Each of Grace's interview sessions has a "vision" segment of questions. That segment opened Pho's eyes to something he'd never considered before. He discovered his passion was to share his testimony to help other youths.

The bottom-line result: Pho left that room a powerfully changed man.

Unchurched Pho left Frank's company to pursue a career in youth ministry. Pho thanked Grace for helping him find his passion. "You're welcome, and thank Jesus!" she would say, realizing *soon*, he'd understand exactly what she meant.

Fum's interview session followed Pho's. Other employees had described Fum's work performance as ho-hum. Apparently, he moped around the range complaining about what they didn't have instead of realizing how many benefits his workplace had. Giant-like in stature, Fum was viewed as an asset when moving and delivering gun safes. According to coworkers, Fum had the biggest entitlement mentality, and he was often found in the back room fumbling with his phone.

The science that Grace used was successful in pinpointing the whys behind Fum's described behavior. However, the scientific results were only one component of a multi-faceted approach to transformation. Within the first few questions, Fum was providing external blame for why he wasn't successful. Extremely common in Grace's world, she knew exactly how to turn Fum's excuse frown upside down.

The interview process revealed that Fum felt his stature made him naturally gifted at football. An injury had killed that dream during his sophomore year. Associating his identity with success on the football field, the separation left Fum feeling "like a useless ox." He developed an emotional eating habit and gained more weight than was healthy, driving his self-image deeper into a sea of hopelessness.

From Pho, Grace knew that Fum's foundation didn't include a church, so she drew a football field diagram on a piece of paper.

Grace explained that the goal posts represented behavioral extremes, and the 50-yard line was the mid-point. There are no right or wrong behavioral patterns, simply players standing in different positions on one field. Then, using X's and O's, she visually pointed out which yard lines Fum's pattern fell on, and where his strengths were in respect to his fellow teammates.

Visually seeing a future strategy for the Fictitious Range that included goals and written plans of how to achieve those goals, Fum's demeanor changed from ho-hum to "what's next, coach?"

"We're going on an exploration to find your dreams," Grace shared. They discovered that Fum's high-school football coach was now involved with a group known as FCA, Fellowship of Christian Athletes. They contacted the coach, arranged for Fum to get involved, and soon his identity transformed from useless ox to faithful follower. At work, his performance shifted from ho-hum to humbled service, and in less than 30 days, he was a top producer at the Fictitious Facility.

Fi was scheduled to meet with Grace the next morning.

When Fum told Fi that he'd seen a bright future for the Range, Fi asked, "Does it include random drug testing?" Fum answered, "Maybe," to which Fi responded, "I quit," and he walked out the door.

Grace suggested Frank utilize Fi's block of time for a brief update. Frank bounced around his office like a kid at Christmas.

With only a third of the employee interviews completed, Frank informed her that numerous positive shifts had already occurred. He concluded with, "It's a miracle—just keep going, Grace!" And he headed off to a meeting.

It took several weeks to complete the first round of assessments and interviews. Purposefully, owners are the last to complete their portion of Grace's process so they understand what their team has gone through. Frank's interview date fell on the first Friday in May. Thinking back to the Friday they first met, Grace suggested they celebrate with lunch at the place they'd had their first meal.

After ordering, Grace asked, "How have the daily devotions been going?"

He replied, "Fantastic! It's how I start each day. Today, I asked my phone to look up the two verses that were at the bottom of the page, so I could get a deeper understanding."

Wow, Grace did not see that coming. From reading the same devotional, she knew that John 10:10 was the verse at the bottom of that day's page. There was no mistaking who'd opened this door.

Grace asked, "By chance, do you remember either verse?"

"The first one was... dagnabit, I forget. Oooooooh, but the second one was John 10:10! You'd be proud of me, Grace; I think I memorized it."

Their lunch arrived at their table. While they ate, Grace asked Frank to share his observations of the "de, di, and re" exercise. He pulled out the list of words and said, "It's interesting that all the de words I gave you seem dark and negative; the re words seem positive and light."

Not much further into his observation, an epiphany hit him. "Grace, I ended the first list by repeating *destroy* and the second list by repeating *resurrect*. Frank grabbed the paper with both hands and pulled it close to his face while shaking his head. "The de of evil was the thief trying to destroy me. It was a resurrected Jesus who saved my life that night."

"Absolutely!" Grace said smiling. "Check please!"

Chapter Forty-Three
It's Something Else

"The end of a thing is better than its beginning, and the patient in spirit is better than the proud in spirit. I do not hasten in my spirit to be angry, for anger rests in the bosom of fools."

—Ecclesiastes 7: 8-9 (NKJV)

Fiona Fantabulous wasn't forgotten. Grace met with her privately several more times and learned of a list of fears that drove the change in her behavior from loving wife to not-so-nice.

Living in Alaska, Fiona was familiar with icebergs. She also liked that variety of lettuce in her wedge salads. Grace handed Fiona a blank piece of paper and asked her to draw a large iceberg. Seems Fiona had artistic ability. After being complimented, Fiona giggled and said, "Hey Grace, let's go out for a salad after this exercise!"

Fiona's next step was to picture all the interactions she'd had with Frank, her family, and friends since their move from Alaska. From Fiona's eyes and posture, Grace could tell she was thinking of those people and taking this exercise seriously.

Next step, in the part of the iceberg that was above the waterline, Fiona was to write all the adjectives that her spouse, family, and friends would use to describe her behavior during that time.

To confirm, Fiona asked, "What Frank and my family and friends would say?" Grace's answer was: "Yes, that is correct."

She wrote these words: *cold, rigid, distant, whiny, complainer.* Then, she stopped and looked at Grace. Her eyes were filled with tears and a fearful expression.

Grace had the tissues ready, and quietly put the box in front of Fiona as she had an enormous emotional release. About 98 percent of the time, whether male or female, this exercise netted the same type of result. Fiona captured a special spot in Grace's heart when, through her tears and red stuffy nose, she sweetly asked, "Grace, can you hug me? I feel so sad, broken, and alone."

The time it takes for people to regain their emotional composure after this step in the exercise differs. The critical words here are *time, regain, emotional composure.*

Grace explained to Fiona that "while an emotional release may happen in an instant, overcoming the junk we've been storing in our elephant-sized trunks, usually does not. It's easy to slip and fall on the icy wedge that sometimes becomes our life."

Then Grace asked, "Ever been deep-sea diving?"

"Yes."

After a few substantial dives below the waterline, Fiona captured the root cause of the behavior she was projecting. Fear and wedges of resentment, stemming from childhood experiences, surfaced. Fiona felt her family was losing Frank's attention due to his work. Because she had six siblings, her father had to work multiple jobs to provide, so he wasn't home much. When he was home, his time was consumed with gambling, alcohol, abuse, and anger. She sometimes felt it was her fault for being a burden. Her father's behavior took a toll on her mother because she didn't know how to help and eventually gave up trying. In Fiona's words, "I grew up in an environment of avoidance and fending for myself."

Like Frank's Uncle Phil, Fiona appeared to be fit as a fiddle from the outside. She credited her love of tennis as the catalyst for maintaining her physically fit shape. Fiona went on to explain that her parents were too poor to pay for her high-school team uniforms, etc., so she spent her teen years working to support her passion.

"I was really good and might have gone pro if I hadn't messed up," Fiona shared. Seems on a dare, she'd shared her bare derriere out the window of a school bus. Her teammates convinced her that the tinting of the windows on the boy's bus would prevent them from seeing her fleshly flash. After her suspension, shame stopped her from pursuing a higher level of play.

Naturally, Grace told Fiona: "One night of too-close dancing almost derailed my dreams. But God stepped in, and here we are, unlocking your hidden potential."

Unlike Frank, Fi, Pho, and Fum, Fiona had been raised Catholic, and her family seldom missed church. De-churched, she understood who Jesus was; however, she described her relationship with Him as a distant memory. As Fiona shared her pain, it became clear her view of God reflected her relational experience to her dad.

After more exercises and much discussion, Fiona came to this realization: Frank didn't drink, had no bad vices, and went above and beyond to make others feel loved. When they lived in Alaska, he had devoted a great deal of quality time to his family.

She determined that what had changed was their environment, revenue source, and her response to it. Fiona told Grace: "I've been acting like a spoiled brat. Frank's not the problem. I am." Then, she tucked in her bottom lip as if to chew on her words, and went into silent mode for several minutes. Grace watched as Fiona's facial expression shifted from disappointment to hopeful determination. Then Fiona asked: "Grace, can you help me positively adjust to my new circumstances?"

Grace answered: "Absolutely, I'm honored you asked. While the process will, at times, be difficult, we'll make it fun by pretending we're well-equipped warriors. In essence, we're going to *war* against negativity with *positive power!*"

Grace continued: "My W.A.R. means Willing, Able, and Ready to implement change, keeping our Ephesians 6 armor on until we succeed! Here's an example:

WILLING—From your heart, you must be willing to reframe past negatives into positive projections, which requires focus, time, intention and effort every day.

ABLE—From your mind, to cognitively understand that your degree of difficulty is based on the choices you make in each step of the process.

READY—In your spirit, be ready. Like tennis, my job is to observe, encourage, and coach you on how to gain wins. Your job is to determine what winning means and to keep working until you reach your goals.

Fiona chose to rekindle her relationship with Jesus. She and Frank began their day by reading his devotional book together.

They ended each day by reviewing the Bible verses shown on that day's devotional page, for a deeper understanding.

Frank and Fiona's relationship was transformed. Family members, friends, and employees noticed a huge improvement and started asking them, "What are you doing differently?"

Considering that they were at the beginning step of their restoration and didn't want to spiritually offend anyone; they gave this truthful, yet secular answer: "We're executing the process our coach, Grace, taught us which includes:

- Practicing unconditional love and obeying boundaries within our family;

- Setting expectations, rules of engagement, and sharing results and feedback within our business;

- Protecting our spiritual and emotional peace by *not* allowing anyone or anything to offend us!"

If the person, or group, they were answering to looked confused, they'd paint the mental picture Grace had drawn for them by adding, "We're pretending we're joy-filled clowns that simply can't be knocked down!"

Grace believed the biggest compliment she could receive was a client referral and/or when a client referred to something valuable learned from her. Frank, Fiona, and their associates paid Grace many compliments by repeating her rhymes, questions, quotes and emulating her teachings.

Fiona's favorite Grace question to repeat was, "Yes, and what color is your folder?"

Her favorite Grace rhyme, "Whether red, yellow, green or blue; God loves you and Grace does too!"

Fiona's favorite Grace quote was: "Success is not hindered by age, gender, or the color of your folder. It's hindered by refusing to grow in God's wisdom and grace as you get older."

During one visit, Frank directed Grace's attention to a huge sign he had hung next to the range. It had a picture of bullets in the middle and read: FREE AMMO TOMORROW!

Grace had jokingly created that sign and labeled it "A genius marketing strategy for the holders of yellow folders." In truth, it was Frank's tribute to Grace and her constant reminders to not procrastinate like Pharaoh did in Exodus 8 when plagued by frogs.

When teaching this Bible-based lesson, Grace handed students fake frog "pets" and encouraged them to make up stories about them. In her mind, she went back to sitting in front of the TV and watching the Looney Tunes frog dancing on a stage. Grace believed all the students and their stories were created, orchestrated, and connected by God.

Like Grace, Fiona was happiest when efficiently redeeming her time and effectively organizing things by placing them in proper boxes, bins, barrels, baskets, and bags. When Fiona learned Grace could accurately place people's behavioral talents in different colored folders with fun-filled labels, or on a chart that resembled a football field, without making people feel less than, limited or boxed in, she wanted to emulate Grace's style.

In addition to her business coaching, Grace had rolled out a Relationship Remodel program to a few other clients. Frank and

Fiona became participants. Every Sunday, they faithfully kept their focus. No business concerning the Fabricated Factory or Fictitious Range was discussed on Sundays.

"Finding a church home that fulfills your spiritual needs can be difficult and time consuming." Grace explained. Fiona and Frank agreed that they wanted to find a Bible-based church that was grace focused. The first church that popped into Grace's mind was the one Frank landed upon, unintendedly. So, she scheduled a visit with the pastor.

After hearing Frank's story, the pastor was emotionally moved. He welcomed the Fantabulous Family with warmth, kindness, and love.

Uncle Ferdinand Fibalittle also wasn't forgotten. During Grace's third visit, she was reviewing the range's standard operating procedures when Uncle Fibalittle's vehicle appeared on the parking lot's video surveillance. "Oh boy, here we go again," said the range officer. "That's Uncle Ferdinand," he told Grace. "We need to call Frank immediately, and then call the police."

Grace had bonded with this range officer. She said to him: "Please do me a favor, call Frank and ask him to meet me outside. Don't call the police, or draw any other attention to this situation unless directed, okay?" He agreed and called Frank.

She rushed outside to Uncle Fibalittle's vehicle with a huge smile on her face. She wanted him to feel like a ray of sunshine was heading his way. As she got closer, she could see that his window was down and he was smoking a cigar. She wildly waved at him to project happiness.

Once she reached the empty parking spots next to him, he extinguished his cigar and rubbed his eyes as if he were trying to clear his vision. "My dear friend, so good to see you. It's been a long time!" Grace sincerely said.

"Grace, from A+ Sports, is that you?" he asked, as if she might be a ghost. He swung his door open and got out, just as Frank was crossing the parking lot that separated the factory from the range.

When Frank saw the door open, he began frantically running. Grace caught him doing so in her peripheral vision. Her head snapped toward him and up went her hand as if she were a traffic officer saying "STOP!" She then gestured a friendly wave to indicate she was safe. He approached gently.

She extended that waving hand to Uncle Fibalittle. He shook it like it was a pump handle from a dry well. Unexpectedly, she got hugged!

"Grace, I haven't seen you since the '90s; what are you doing here?" he asked.

Before she could answer, he reminded her of their first meeting. Apparently, he'd gruffly asked her to leave the premises when he learned that Rocketman was her boss. She vaguely recalled it. He added: "I'll never forget that visit. You looked me right in the eyes and said, 'Why should we punish ourselves for what someone else did or failed to do? I'm different, and you won't know what you're missing if you don't give me a shot.' Grace, your logic hit me right between the eyes, and I gave you a big order. Don't you remember?"

"Well, yes, now that you've filled in the details, I do recall that. Thank you for a nice walk down memory lane," she replied. Frank was standing at the back of his uncle's vehicle, silently observing.

"To answer your question, I'm here helping Frank. A better question might be, what are you doing here?"

Uncle Fibalittle emotionally broke down. Grace suggested that he drive to a nearby coffee shop. She and Frank would meet him there so she could hear his side of what had transpired over the years. And that is what they did.

A transformation took place that day that's only possible with divine intervention. Uncle Fibalittle began Bible studies with Frank's family shortly after that meeting. Roughly seven months later, Uncle Fibalittle bought the small building that sat between the factory and the range and turned it into a bakery/coffee shop. He called it: Fibnomore's Fixations. The pastor from Frank's church helped Uncle Fibalittle start an early morning men's Bible study that met in a cozy back room. Business thrived.

Frank fully implemented the processes Grace created and purchased a new computer system. Previous chaos was replaced with measurable results both at work and at home. Thanks to better efficiency, Frank was able to devote quality time to his passions again.

With her youngest child in school, Fiona decided to work part-time at the range for a stronger connection to their family business.

After learning how to shoot, Fiona became an enthusiast. Grace helped her with event planning, and one of the first groups was Fiona's tennis pals. Fiona's love for event planning spilled over to the coffee shop next door. She and Uncle Fibalittle remodeled the second story of the coffee shop to host coffee and art classes which were a huge hit.

Fi, Pho, and Fum's sister, Phee-Phee, graduated with top honors from Imagination College. As a medal winner for the shooting sports team, Phee-Phee was a fantastic fit for ownership. Frank helped Phee-Phee grant company stocks to the employees and form an ESOP, a.k.a. an Employee Stock Ownership Plan.

Chapter Forty-Four
It Never Crossed My Mind

> *"She is a tree of life to those who take hold of her, and happy are all who retain her."*
> —Proverbs 3:18, NKJV

What do you think happens when you die? It's a question Grace asked clients who retained her for succession planning. Many business owners reply, "It's never crossed my mind."

She would then ask another difficult, even painful question: "How about your business? Will it expire with you or be extended through your family tree?"

And then: "If we tested your people on their understanding of your rules of operation, how pleased would you be with their grades?"

Politicians are a people group; and they may make or influence the rules other people are supposed to live by. Their mindset may be visible or masked by the words they say and the written rules they make. Grace experienced, firsthand, how people in the firearms industry were affected by the decisions of politicians.

Like political parties, some parents exercise their control through rules. And since all of us must be children before we become adults, how we respond to our parent's rules can be displayed multiple ways. Grace divided those multiple ways into four rough sections: rule makers, breakers, followers, and fakers. And like behavioral factors, she found people tend to bend and blend those rules, however they need to, in order to survive.

The Bible also has rules. The wisdom contained is said to come from God, but He, too, used people to put His thoughts and words into written rules for success.

Divided into two-parts, the Bible is chronological in nature. The Old Testament contains information which flowed directly from God. In the New Testament, Jesus enters as the Son of God. The Old Testament is full of rules and direct control by God. The New Testament is filled with miracles and sacrifices of Jesus, out of His Father's love, which extends an invitation to follow Him into a world full of mercy and grace.

Whether Old or New, Father or Son, the constant remains that we, the people of the earth, have free will regarding rules. The choice to make or break, follow or fake, is our individual responsibility. The consequences of our choices remain our destiny. We can make life complex and burdensome or easy and simple depending on whether we follow the biblical plan or our own individual creations. Both obedience and disobedience determine the size of the divide between a Father who art in Heaven and life on earth, from what Grace has witnessed.

In Grace's A+ Sports days, running a gun shop without a plan was called *flying by the seat of your pants.* Lack of planning, reporting, and clarity was the pain point Grace recognized when she compared how chain stores were operating versus how Mom and Pop Shops did business.

A rule breaker, Ferdinand Fibalittle was a prime example of the consequences for a man without a succession plan. He had The Golden Rule posted on the wall of his business, but his truth was: "Do as I say, not as I do." That disconnect caught up with him and resulted in severe consequences. Without Frank Fantabulous, both the Fabricated Firearms Factory and the Fictitious Firing Range would have withered and died like the fig tree Jesus cursed.

Death hadn't crossed Frank's mind until he felt he was failing at keeping his family and business thriving. The permanent consequence of the milli-second fix Frank attempted hadn't crossed his mind until his life nearly expired. It was Frank's near-death experience that helped him see the sign that pointed to Jesus.

For Fiona, "What happens when you die?" brought instant tears. Intending to redirect, Grace expressed her personal picture: "Jesus will be there to welcome me with a smile unimaginably bright. Joyfully laughing, we'll exchange stories like, 'Remember that day when you and Fiona were giving Me glory, honor, and praise? Well done, My good and faithful servant!"

Fiona later shared, "Forcing me to think of what happens at my end and then reframe my picture was one of the most valuable lessons I learned from you, Grace!"

Whether an independent business owner or chain store operation, Grace observed that in business, planning and preparing with the end in mind are wise strategies to lessen or eliminate the business burdens any death leaves behind. Emotionally planning, projecting, and preparing for what lies ahead in life and business caused chaos and stress for many of the business owners that crossed Grace's path. Replacing that chaos with results became her tagline and God-given talent.

Under calm circumstances, Frank believed in perfecting plans and processes; however, when chaos felt like it was closing in on him from all sides, his emotional plan of escape was to hit a tree.

Young Grace survived hitting a tree with her motorcycle.

At age 16, a loved one hit a tree and died.

She was honored and understood why she was called to help Frank.

Jesus, dying on a cross for our sake, is unfathomable, and HE crossed her mind all day long!

Frank Fantabulous implemented a full strategic plan for his business, which included the company's purpose, standard operating procedures, and promotional plans for both his people and products. His operation created clear written standards by which productivity, performance, profits, and power were measured and driven. Like Frank after his awakening, his business came alive.

Frank gave the credit to Jesus for saving him, then pointing him in the Kingdom direction with both his family life and his business.

Ferdinand Fibalittle fibbed no more and attributed his transformation to a new understanding of what Jesus did for him when He died on a cross. That cross was made from a tree.

Grace encouraged clients to research the significance of trees in the Bible with the hope that their life would be as positively impacted as was the case for Grace, Frank, Ferdinand, and everyone they've touched with their tree stories.

Chapter Forty-Five
Time, It's Running Out

But of that day and hour no one knows, not even the angels of heaven, but My Father only.
—Matthew 24:36 (NKJV)

Completing her fifth year in business with a whirlwind of client success, Grace was compelled to make another trip to Vegas for the 2016 SHOT Show. With her *why* unclear, she didn't plan, she just went.

The SHOT Show was hosted by the National Shooting Sports Foundation. NSSF also hosted Shot Show University, which focused on education and support for firearms retailers. NSSF was one of the industry's largest organizations, and Grace had dreamed of being a speaker for them.

Upon arrival in 2016, she received a special invite to attend one of the SHOT University Seminars, which was presented by a female. So, she went.

Grace found the presenter inspiring and thought, *I want to be a presenter here next year.*

When the seminar ended, Grace introduced herself to a man with an Irish name who appeared to be in charge. Rather than inquiring how to get on the speakers list, she rapidly explained her A+ Sport's history. She then suggested he ask several gun shop owners if they knew "Grace from A+ Sports," and if they did, what would they say about her.

Mr. Irish pleasantly replied: "Okay, I will."

They shook hands, and Grace walked away.

Grace often gets her best ideas and answers to prayer while showering. The next morning, while singing in the shower, it occurred to her that she was in Vegas with nothing planned for the rest of her time. Suddenly, she remembered that it was Jenifer Lopez's opening night in Vegas, and that it was advertised as already sold out.

"That would be an interesting show to see," she said out loud.

Before drying her hair and on a whim, she texted Commander Bad Axe with these words: "Do you know what I think would be fun and interesting? Going to J. Lo's sold-out show."

When she met him in the lobby of the hotel less than an hour later, the Commander handed her an envelope. "Here you go," he said.

Later that night, Jennifer Lopez held Grace's hand as she sang to the crowd, and a few days later, Grace and the Commander were on *The Today Show's* footage of those next to the stage for opening night.

Even more interesting was that the Commander had no idea of who J. Lo was before Grace's text. Apparently, God heard Grace and helped the Commander deliver an unbelievable performance.

Grace believes the Commander works for God as her promoter and sometimes, guardian angel.

Several months went by, and Grace's situation had changed, prompting her to have a serious shower conversation with God.

Extremely frustrated at the difficulty she was having closing contracts, Grace asked God to help her decide whether to invest more money into promoting the business He'd given her or go to work for someone else. "Please God, make it clear *today* which direction I'm to go," she pleaded.

Less than an hour later, as she sat down at her desk, her phone rang. A fellow business consultant called offering her an opportunity.

"You're an angel with my answer to prayer," Grace exclaimed. She proceeded to tell him what she'd prayed for and why. Instantly, the consultant suggested Grace visit a man named Bob.

Wow! she thought. *Like wow, Bob spelled backwards is still Bob!* When she learned that Bob's office was conveniently located 1.5 miles from her home, in a building that she had visited and dreamed about having an office in, she was compelled to visit him that same day.

Entering Bob's office, his first words were, "God must have sent you!"

"Apparently so," Grace confirmed.

Bob and Grace talked for over five hours. He provided biblical teachings about things she comprehended, but didn't recall learning before—for example, the Year of Jubilee. Near the end of their meeting, Bob asked her if she was afraid of success. Followed by, "What do you need to keep your business going?"

Without hesitation, the answer crossed her mind and flowed out of her mouth in three, crystal-clear bullet points. To each point, Bob replied, "I can help with that." Grace was awestruck by Bob's generosity and accepted his offer, returning to his office the next day.

Less than 30 days later, Mr. Irish from NSSF called. He shared that, per her request, he had asked several retailers about her and was impressed by what he had heard. Her professionalism, breadth, and depth of knowledge and experience both inside and outside the industry, brought rave reviews from the retailers he spoke with.

Then, she was invited to speak at the 2017 SHOT Show University.

Her dream came true—validation that God never runs out. He sent legions of angels to help Grace run toward a bigger dream.

During this time, Grace found herself working alongside a plethora of pastors. She observed that prayer requests for restoration boiled down to three main categories: health, family, and finances. Grace also found that those blessed with healthy bodies, families, and businesses sometimes struggled to answer: "What are you most grateful for?"

Grace made this connection: Being mindful of continual blessings is a critical step to transformation.

The idiom "you don't miss your water till your well runs dry" was one she used to prompt a thankful mindset. After surviving the 2020 toilet paper shortage, that could shift into: "You never miss your toilet paper till the store runs out."

Speaking of running out, in 2020, that happened in the gun business. For example, in January 2021, a 50-round box of ammunition that her client was selling for $7.99 a box (pre-pandemic), sold for up to 10 times that amount *if* you could find one.

While the political effect from changing red to blue was nothing new, the level of demand in the gun business was unprecedented. Politically driven fear and the stress caused from supply/demand issues were two things that Grace disliked about the industry she appreciated.

Grace's personal experience inspired this transformational question for her clients, "What are you about to run out of?"

Hope and *time* were the two most common answers Grace received.

While working with Bob's team to prepare for her speaking engagement, a man named David introduced her to a device designed to homeopathically improve foundational necessities in the human body. As she witnessed miraculous happenings with pastors and people who worked for God, it occurred to her that it was possible to trigger powerful transformations in the physical health and mental hope for people who believed and were willing to work toward improvement.

Remember Ms. Reluctant, Frank's receptionist? Well, she was one of the first people Grace thought of. Ms. Reluctant's undiagnosed health condition produced unpleasant complications to her physical and mental well-being. Her unpleasant state often created stress and anxiety for those around her.

Witnessing the empathy and compassion Frank had shown Ms. Reluctant convinced Grace that God was revealing one more tool for her restoration arsenal. So much so, that she purchased a device, then drove to the Fabricated Factory to show it to Frank.

You may also recall that Ms. Reluctant was considering suing Ferdinand Fibalittle.

After hearing Grace's God story, Frank convinced Ferdinand to purchase a device for the prayer room of the coffee shop and invite Ms. Reluctant to use it as often as she liked.

Ms. Reluctant greatly improved physically, mentally, and spiritually, which led to positive behavior. Her gratitude was demonstrated by fully forgiving Ferdinand for the past. Together, they helped several others who had been emotionally, physically, or spiritually wounded, by sharing their personal testimonies and their helpful resources.

Grace thanked God for giving her the tools to facilitate behavioral, spiritual, and physical improvement.

During her 2017 ascent up dream mountain, Grace began hearing rumors that A+ Sports was on their way down.

In the fall of 2017, Grace attended a retirement party, hosted at A+ Sports, in honor of Rick, the industry legend described earlier in the Cabela's initiation story. Rick had worked for A+ for over 40 years and Grace was honored to celebrate his victory in the building that she once considered home with the people she had called family.

Her best friend, Swooperwoman, was there and together, they took an unexpected tour of the new A+ Sports. The facility had been modified and expanded to the extent that it felt completely foreign to Grace. While astonished by the state-of-the-art façade Grace saw, her gut instinct told her the rumors were true. Her beloved A+ Sports was dying.

In early May 2018, A+ Sport's filed for bankruptcy. Grace's heart was broken.

She never imagined a time when A+ Sports would run out of business.

Happily, it was only a couple of weeks later when Grace was at a party celebrating the phenomenal success of Commander Bad Axe. A visionary, the Commander insisted that Ruger manufacture the American Ranch Rifle in .450 Bushmaster. His prediction of that model's success was correct, and he was recognized as Ruger's Retailer of the Year for outstanding performance.

The speaker for the Commander's event was Mr. Lipsey, owner of a national distributor of firearms located in Baton Rouge, and before they filed bankruptcy, a competitor to A+ Sports. Grace had heard only marvelous stories about Mr. Lipsey and she felt privileged to have the chance to meet him.

Approximately 500 people attended this celebration, including retailers who had previously won this prestigious award. One of those retailers, was a soft-spoken southern gentleman from Mississippi named Guy Goldgunz. A pilot with his own plane, Guy had picked up a fellow Ruger retailer in Alabama and they had flown to the Commander's event.

As the celebration neared its end, Guy approached Grace and asked if he could speak with her in private. They made their way to an adjoining room to escape the noise of the crowd and sat at a round table. Once seated, Guy quietly said "I think I need your services."

Guy shared: "Once upon a time, I envisioned my business living on through my two daughters. In 2011, that vision was shattered when my youngest daughter took her own life. It appears my other daughter isn't interested in taking over."

Instantly, Grace knew that God had orchestrated this connection. In her mind Grace saw herself alongside Guy's daughter, encouraging her to take the reins just like Winnie had done with her many years before. She told Guy "Don't give up. With my help, I believe your daughter will make your vision a reality."

On the lengthy drive home, Grace called Moppsie and prophesied "I believe God has delivered my next client and my gut tells me that I'll soon be flying to Mississippi in a private plane."

In the perfect seventh month of 2018, Guy Goldgunz became Grace's next client. As a bonus, Guy decided to fly to Grace's hometown to pick her up. Grace asked Moppsie to drive her to the small regional airport so she could meet Guy in person and watch them fly away.

The funny thing was that, when the Commander had originally called to invite her, Grace turned him down because it took place during the week. She felt that she needed to be working on finding clients—not going to a celebration. Fortunately, as soon as they hung up, she was ashamed of how she had just treated her long-time friend, client, number one promoter and sometimes guardian angel.

She immediately dialed him back, apologized, then negotiated. "I'll attend under one condition; you need to require something of me so I can make a valuable contribution." The commander responded, "Okay, would you happen to have a projector that you could bring?"

Just a couple of weeks prior and without any known need, Grace had purchased a projector because of the sign that caught her attention. The projector was $700 on clearance. She laughed as it was becoming clear that God had run ahead of her and placed that perfect sign in her path as a projection of His plans for her.

"Yes, I have a brand-new projector, so yes, I'll be there to help."

Thinking only about how she could be valuable to the Commander, it never occurred to her that there would be potential clients at the event.

What Grace didn't anticipate was all the connections that awaited them that day.

When they entered the airport, the ceiling immediately caught Grace's attention. On the panels were pictures of local pilots. She couldn't believe it, as she was looking up, staring back at her was a picture of Golden Boy.

Seeing Golden Boy's smiling face triggered Grace's memory. She recalled the email he had sent, informing her that he had purchased a plane and that he and Dr. Russia were now the best of friends and flying together. "I have you to thank for that," he shared. Wow, what a transformation that was—triggering rival enemies to become best buds.

Then she mentally replayed their last phone call that had been filled with laughter and failed persuasion.

Golden Boy: Grace, how about you go flying with me and Dr. Russia?

Grace: There's no way I'm getting in that plane with the two of you because... surely, we would die. While truly happy for them, her words expressed her sincere belief.

Lastly, she relived the range of emotion she felt seven years earlier. Shock, as she glared at Golden Boy's face on the front page of a newspaper under the heading: "Plane crash claims..." and relief, as she read: "He looked peaceful, but he was already gone" from an eye-witness.

Grace's attention was broken by a man's voice.

"Grace, is that you?"

Looking at his face, his name or how she knew him she could not place. "Hi" she awkwardly replied, "how do we know each other?"

"We rode dirt-bikes together. How could you forget?" he replied with a smile. Then, they reminisced about those days and their mutual connection, Sir Lyman, as they took the very brief tour of the airport offices and hanger.

"Your pilot is about to arrive" he said, as he, Moppsie and Grace walked outside to greet Guy. As soon as he got close enough, Moppsie gave Guy a great big hug. It was as if she couldn't contain herself. Observing the enthusiastic, rapid fire, southern-twanged conversation filled with yes ma'am's and no ma'am's that was taking place between Guy and Moppsie, Grace noticed that Guy's eyes were sparkling and he appeared much more gregarious then when she had originally met him. *Yep, Guy's a golden glower!* Grace thought.

Moppsie turned to Grace and said "Do you hear this? Here's a man whose Mama raised him with respect—a true southern gentleman!" Then Moppsie turned back to Guy and the admiration fest continued.

It was as if Moppsie and Guy were smitten with each other in a mother-son relationship way. While Grace was used to people loving her mom's vivacious nature, the aura around Moppsie and Guy's first meeting was like watching fireworks. As soon as they were in the air, Guy commented "I've never felt a connection like I just did with your mom." This must be God inspired.

At that moment, as she was looking down, Grace noticed Charming Taz and Sweetie's house. "Do you see that beautiful abode?" Grace asked Guy. "I am pretty sure that's my ex-husband's house. I've never seen it before; however, my gut tells me that's it. I'm happy they've done so well!" Guy made no comment.

Grace continued, "While we are on the subject of ex's, let me add that I had three romantic relationships while employed at A+ Sports. The last one may or may not have led to my demise. I'm sharing this now in case you would like to do a loop-de-loop and drop me back off."

"Only three? That may be a record!" Guy retorted with a southern smirk.

Grace must have looked confused because he voluntarily added "In our industry, I'm guessing twenty would be a good average."

"That is sad." Was the only thing Grace could think to say.

She told him that she had learned great lessons from her bad behavior, had repeatedly repented to her savior, and constantly prayed to avoid falling into temptation.

At that, Guy asked her if she had heard of Emmaus. "The story from Luke or the current day experience? I'm familiar with both." Grace acknowledged.

"The Emmaus experience changed my life. I was flying 180 degrees upside down, convinced that I was right side up. I went into the experience thinking I knew it all and justifying every aspect of my behavior and came out humbled and transformed." Grace understood exactly what Guy meant.

"By the way, did you have any reservations about getting in a private plane with an almost complete stranger?" Guy asked.

"None what-so-ever because I felt the Holy Spirit's presence at the second you said 'I think I need your help;' which is pretty amazing since...," she filled him in on the Golden Boy story.

"Do you have any doubts that I can help you?" Grace said.

"After talking with Commander Bad Axe, I'm convinced you have the knowledge and ability. I want you to change my daughter's mind about taking over the business, but I'm struggling to believe that is possible. After you meet her, you'll see what I mean." Guy shared.

"Is this struggle to believe coming from the same Guy whose email signature to me was his favorite verse: 'I can do all things through Christ which strengthens me. Philippians 4:13'"? Grace didactically asked.

They both knew the answer was yes, so Grace decided to throw a little gas toward Guy's Holy Spirit ember.

"Guy, how can you look out the window of this plane that you are blessed to fly, at the clouds and the beauty that surrounds us, and not have 100% peace that we are in Heavenly hands? You know that for God, transforming lives and minds is easier than pulling the lightest trigger we could ever find. He would not have put me in this seat if I couldn't get the results He wants."

At the end of that statement, it dawned on Grace that she didn't know the details of Guy's youngest daughter's departure. She didn't want to pry; however, she was concerned that her ignorance may cause Guy unintentional grief.

Gently, she asked if he could share the story.

He did and it helped Grace comprehend how it would be easy for Guy to doubt that his legacy would be carried on. The rest of the flight was delightful and inspiring.

When they arrived at his store, Grace observed that every square inch of it was dedicated to displaying or storing inventory. Even the store's bathroom served dual-purpose as a supply closet. As a successful business owner of stores in two towns, Guy had strong relationships all around.

Guy anticipated Grace's need for a large space for group training, and smaller spaces for private one-on-one meetings.

Early the next morning, Grace drove to The Mission to meet with half of Guy's staff. During their planning phone call, Guy told Grace "You'll likely be at Mossy Oak's office when you need space." A few days later, Guy called back to say the meeting location had changed. "You'll be meeting at a place called The Mission." He said, to which she replied, "Yes, of course I will—that makes perfect sense." Guy went on to explain the rich family-business history and details behind The Mission and Grace knew that was exactly where she was meant to go.

As she turned onto the premises, she grinned from ear to ear as the first sign she saw read "Hell Fighters." The sign immediately triggered her mouth to softly sing a lyric from David Crowder's song "In the House." Then she remembered the day, years before, when David Crowder had sat down right next to her, at a round table, in the community center of her beloved church. "That was amazing!" she said to herself.

As she walked through The Mission's entrance, a second sign caught her eye. This one read "Everyone has a story, welcome to ours." Grace's heart leaped with joy as that was a phrase very similar to the one that had been in her head for years. God flashed a vision of the book she would write honoring Him, and her mouth was triggered to softly say: "God gives everyone a story, welcome to mine."

As Guy's staff was assessed, their day was blessed. Grace's process revealed only one mild concern.

On day two, Grace drove to a bank, located directly across the street from Guy's Gun Shop, where she was scheduled to meet with the second half of Guy's staff. As planned, she arrived before the bank opened. Her heart was warmed by the bank president's southern hospitality. As he opened the door to her, his first words were: "Welcome home!" Right at home was how she felt as he escorted her to the second floor and gave her access to abundant space and privacy.

She was in the middle of her third employee session and had just finished sharing her Jennifer Lopez story, accompanied by the picture that proved it was real, when she got a strange urge to look out the window and toward Guy's parking lot.

For a split second, she couldn't believe her eyes, then she burst into laughter as she said to the employee "come look at this." What they saw was Commander Bad Axe's very well branded truck. To the employee she explained: "That truck with the out-of-state license plate belongs to the man in this picture, and the purpose of me sharing that picture and story was to illustrate how God delivers surprises when you're least expecting them."

Understandably, the employee wasn't nearly as impressed as Grace was.

She finished the session then called the Commander. "How's Mississippi?" she asked, trying not to laugh. "How do you know

I'm in Mississippi? He replied. "Because I'm staring at your truck." She shared. He seemed just as surprised as she was that they were in the same place at the same time and that it totally wasn't their plan.

Over lunch, the Commander beamed as he explained to an employee traveling with him, that Guy and Grace had connected at his Ruger event.

The Commander said to Guy: "You and Grace have a lot in common. She told me that God brings the right people together at just the right time, for His purpose, and here we sit."

After lunch, Grace returned to the bank. The remaining employee sessions went smooth like butter and Grace sensed meeting Guy's daughter Gigi, at the end of the day, would be as sweet as honey. Her senses were correct and Grace was goo-goo over Gigi from the instant they met. Gigi got a kick out of Grace, too. Among other things, learning that only 10 percent of family businesses are projected to make it to the third generation made a valuable impact on Gigi and motivated her decision to stay in her family business. Gigi had two sons. During her first visit, Guy made sure Grace understood that his grandsons were the apples of his eye and that their salvation was the number one mission in his life. Grace knew loving Gigi was the best way she could help Guy and his grandsons.

By the time their meeting ended, Gigi told Grace her arrival had to be a God thing.

During their second private meeting, Grace shared her long-running dream to write a unique book about being a girl in the gun business. Gigi expressed her love for art, and then described what she saw, in her mind, as the cover to such a book.

Chills ran through Grace as she listened to what Gigi described; as it perfectly matched the vision that had been in Grace's mind for over ten years.

With no biological children, Grace was convinced that God had placed Gigi in her life to provide a mission for the book. As another gritty, determined girl growing up in the gun business, Gigi could certainly relate. She showered Grace with kindness and love and encouraged her to pave the way!

Guy agreed to fully immerse Grace into his business. She worked alongside Gigi to implement operational improvements and create a succession plan. Grace began traveling to Mississippi, every month, with a promised stay of seven to fourteen days each visit. By the third visit, Guy and Grace agreed that flying commercially would be the best idea from an investment perspective.

On the flight Grace took from Atlanta to Mississippi in October of 2018, God placed a published author in the seat next to her. During small talk, Grace learned that this man was originally from the area where Guy's store was located. He was on his way there to give a speech. Further discussion revealed that he was also a professor of writing, literature, and publishing.

After several minutes, Grace worked up the courage to say, "I have a dream of writing a book." In a kind professor tone, the author asked "what's stopping you?" Taking a page out of her own training manual, Grace replied, "The same thing that stops every dream—fear."

He inquired about the theme. She explained her background and without hesitation he said "oh, so you're going to write a memoir." At that second, something leaped in Grace's spirit—the professor put a simple label on it.

Mr. Author spoke with professorial authority: "Grace, I've read thousands of books, I read all the time, and I can tell you that you have to publish your story because there's nothing like it out there." Grace was astonished.

As they disembarked at the Golden Triangle Regional Airport, Mr. Author continued to encourage her. When they reached the tarmac, he handed Grace his business card and said, "if you need any help, contact me." Grace thanked him as she whispered to herself, "God's opening golden gates of blessings."

In addition to selling guns, Guy and Gigi were successful in the pawn business.

Properly assessing the value of the items to be pawned is a critical component to sustaining success in the pawn industry. Value is another of Grace's favorite subjects to discuss during training sessions. Most of Grace's clients find her "Time Value of Money Exercise" exceptionally challenging. And, when it comes time to evaluate how much one position should be compensated versus another, identifying what an employee's value to the organization is worth, or what charge should be applied to certain services; most business owners would rather Grace pull their hair than make them put those evaluations in writing.

Even with the right tools and expert guidance, determining value remains a difficult task many people prefer to avoid. Whether evaluating inventory levels and technology needs (things) or important resources for getting things done (people, time, and money) or a full business evaluation ("How much is my baby worth?"), Grace finds most clients prefer the common time wasters of failure to delegate, procrastination, and postponing the unpleasant over simply getting the appraisals done.

To drive more customers and value to his business, Guy told Grace he wanted to increase his social media presence; however, he and Gigi needed help doing so. By this time, Grace was much more familiar with the area and realized there were several colleges nearby. Grace arranged a meeting with a local college advisor who then connected her with the college's marketing professors.

On a day the store was closed to the public, Guy and Gigi invited a professor and her class to their store for an educational field trip. In exchange the students would share ideas on how they would use social media to market the business.

Right before the students arrived, Gigi handed Grace a wrapped present as she said "Grace, I know receiving gifts isn't your thing, but this jumped out at me and I just had to give it to you." While unwrapping the gift, Grace's eyes filled with tears as she looked at a brown leather-bound journal. It was embossed with these words: "FOR I KNOW THE PLANS I HAVE FOR YOU," DECLARES THE LORD, "PLANS TO PROSPER YOU AND NOT TO HARM YOU, PLANS TO GIVE YOU HOPE AND A FUTURE." Jeremiah 29:11. As Grace hugged her, Gigi joyfully proclaimed, "This is for your book writing."

The students were engaged during the visit; listening as Guy taught them useful tips for their financial futures and sharing the rich history of how pawn shops came to be. Toward the end of the visit, Grace watched as a confused look came over the professor's face when Guy handed her his business card, on which was a logo of a plane.

Inquisitively she asked "are you a pilot?" "Yes!" Guy replied.

Lovingly she said: "My daddy was a pilot—he died in a plane doing the thing he loved most."

"Was your dad's name Richard?" Guy asked.

"Yes, did you know him?"

Guy replied, "What a small world! Not only did I know him, I believe I bought his plane." Hearing this gave Grace chills.

Grace listened and watched the rest of their exchange with delight and the words "this connection was meant to be." Grace had helped bring them together; however, it was crystal clear, to her, that God was orchestrating a bigger, more valuable plan, to their future.

Not long after this meeting, Guy and Gigi selected a local female-owned, frog-logoed company that was recommended by the Professor to fulfill their marketing needs long-term.

While in the shower of her Mississippi home, Grace asked God to reveal why she was plagued by frogs of "tomorrow" when it came to writing her story. The answer she received was, *Because you're afraid that your past sin will rob me of My glory.*

"Yes, that's it!" She shouted, then asked, "How can I promote Your glory and the grace You gave me without causing harm?" Immediately she saw "Gracie Rae Faith" on the cover of her book. "Ahhh, I see, like biblical Jacob, Abram, and Sarai—You're changing my name." Grace praised.

In January 2020, during their contract value review, Guy, Gigi, and Grace determined they were roughly half-way through implementing the succession plan she'd designed for them. Gigi was excited and willing to extend Grace's contract for 18 more months.

Although Guy admitted to receiving enormous value and progress, he still struggled to believe that Gigi would accept the keys to his kingdom. Experiencing this scenario before with Bo and King George, Grace understood the real struggle was letting go of those keys.

Guy and Grace made a deal. She would return to Mississippi in February and together, they would create a long-term contract to begin in March.

On February 9th, they were working out the details when Grace got a text that King George's heart had stopped—he was gone. Grace's heart was broken. "Go home for George, we'll finish the details when you come back in March," Guy compassionately urged. He understood how much she loved all her clients, especially George.

Eerie best described Grace's view of the airport as she headed home. Not one to watch the news, seeing large masses of people wearing masks grabbed her attention. After educating herself, she prayed for global healing. She never imagined a time when her monthly travels would be denied by disease.

While the 2020 pandemic temporarily stopped Grace from flying to Mississippi to work side-by-side with Gigi, it also eliminated any excuses to accomplishing her book-writing dream.

Grace returned to Bob's office. Upon hearing she planned to pursue her next dream, Bob offered her writing space in his office and editing services from his delightful wife Debbie. Grace is convinced that God provided the generosity and support of Bob and Debbie to ensure her endeavor would take flight.

With ample time on her schedule, Grace reached out to Chris Candoit, a former A+ Sports co-worker, to see how his business was going. A talented computer network engineer, Chris made Grace's life better and she wanted to repay the favor. "Now would be a great time for us to brainstorm about business" Grace offered.

He accepted and Grace introduced him to her behavioral assessment process; in which he found value.

While together, they reminisced about A+ Sports and the fun times. She told Chris about the book she'd started and he encouraged her to "get that book done."

Having no idea how to get a book published, Grace prayed for guidance. Later that day, she heard an internal voice whisper "call David." "That's it" she exclaimed out loud—to herself. David was the man she had met eight years earlier at the Christian radio station. She obeyed and learned that David's daughter had published a book. Indeed, David delivered the referral she sought which freed her to take the next step in her journey.

She possessed years of planners that contained in-depth details along with certificates, receipts, and pictures organized chronologically which helped jump start the process, yet it took over a year of defining, designing, aligning, and refining thousands of words before Grace completed a rough first draft. As she filled the pages, Debbie made daily edits and encouraged her to keep going. At the end of each day, Grace read what she had written to Moppsie who also cheered her on.

Time passed quickly. One day, as she watched the snow fall, it dawned on Grace that almost a year had passed since she'd physically been in Mississippi, which made her miss Gigi even more. Grace sent Gigi a video of the snow. Gigi's reply: "I want it to snow here in the Golden Triangle."

On January 11, 2021, Gigi got her wish.

To Guy, that day may have felt he was in the Bermuda Triangle because his southern business came to a screeching halt due to ice, snow and freezing temperatures. To his daughter, the snow was her answer to three days of prayer. At 7:57 a.m., Grace received a special breaking news video from a bundled up Gigi playing the role of weather girl reporting live. Gigi panned the snow-covered forest behind her, and expressed her unwavering faith in God, as the beautiful snow fell all around her. She added that the Golden Triangle was getting more snow than the counties above and below her.

Later that day, Grace got goosebumps when she viewed the images attached to another text from Gigi. On her art wall, Gigi had drawn a depiction of the snowy tree-lined road she was emotionally moved by earlier that morning. Eerie because at that exact same time, yet 700 hundred miles away, Grace was depicting Frank's snowy tree-lined story in words yet, the pictures painted were nearly identical.

Grace welcomed spring and the call she received from Rick Robinhood. Now a few years into his retirement, Rick called Grace to see how her book was progressing. Grateful, she invited him for coffee. "I'd like your blessing for our Cabela's story." Grace shared.

On a beautiful day in May, they met at a coffee shop in Grace's hometown. Grace first inquired about Rick's progress on the romance novels he dreamt of writing. "Well, I've put that aside for now. Instead, I bought an old Rolls-Royce and I'm having a ball driving it around," he shared.

"Wow, interesting. My client Guy Goldgunz owns an old, gold Rolls-Royce." Grace connected.

After an hour or so of catching up, Rick read Grace's pages. She silently watched as his facial expressions changed from smiling to laughter to concentrating and back to laughter. When finished, he looked directly at her and adamantly exclaimed: "Girl, you've got to get this book out!"

Then Rick appeared to have an epiphany. "What are you thinking?" Grace inquired

"The NASGW (National Association of Sporting Goods Wholesalers) is going to be held in Columbus, Ohio this year. You need to get this book published ASAP, so you can have a copy in hand to take to the show. When all the people you know realize you've written a book—they'll all want a copy," Rick insisted.

Falling back in her chair, Grace tried speaking: "Wow, I had no idea... I don't know if I can... I'm not even sure what the next step is..." Politely interrupting, Rick said: "Grace, stop! The draft is done, figure out how to get it in print and take it to the show. No excuses—you have nothing to fear, just go!"

She listened, then negotiated. "Okay, I'll do it under one condition, you have to go to the NASGW show with me." As the words came out of her mouth, she thought "great relationships stand the test of time." In her mind, she was already picturing them at the show, like old times.

Only this time Rick's response was "no!"

Grace couldn't believe her ears.

"Why wouldn't you go? You know everybody and they all love you, please go with me, I need you." She begged.

"No, I'm not going." Rick said firmly.

Grace was in shock; she didn't understand Rick's why.

To relieve her grief, Rick shared a story that was extremely brief: "After over 40 years of service, my end at A+ Sports was completely different from what I had ever imagined. I won't go to the show because when people see me, they only focus on the negative. I just can't take it."

Grace didn't need any more details. She accepted Rick's "no." They moved on to lunch at a different place and spoke only of happy times.

Thinking of all the times she had taught: "begin with the end in mind," it was her turn to walk that talk. Rick gave her a due date of October 2021.

Grace's next step was getting her draft to a professional editor. Her editor required a commitment date of July 14th for manuscript submittal. This helped Grace push past paralysis from too much analysis.

July 14, 2021, a.k.a. 7-14-21, was a magical day; however, it didn't start out that way. Realizing this date had multiples of seven caused Grace to spring out of bed. "God, today is the perfect day for releasing our first draft!" she praised.

As she was showering and praying some more, the bathroom light began to flash. That's odd, she thought. After quickly drying off, Grace went downstairs where Moppsie was working out. "Did you notice the lights flickering?" she asked. Moppsie had not noticed any problems and told Grace she didn't think there was anything to be concerned about.

Grace wanted to believe Moppsie, but her gut told her there was a problem. "Lord, we don't have time for this today, we've got to get our book out!" she expressed.

As she picked up her cell phone to find an emergency electrician, a text came in at 7:59 a.m. from Chris Candoit which read: "Good morning! My #1 customer would like for you to give her a call. I told her about how you've been helping me and she's interested in your assessment process."

Thrilled for the referral, Grace promised to call Emergency Plumbing that day. She thanked God out loud and Chris by text. Then laughing she added: "Now, do you happen to have any clients that are *emergency electricians*?"

She found an electrician and made an appointment for later that day. In the meantime, Grace went to Bob's office and submitted her manuscript per her commitment.

That evening, Grace learned the electrical issue was real. A new panel was later installed by the nephew of her first love, Remi, who insisted she let him help her.

During the install, she told him about her book and that his dad and uncle were in it. His reply: "I want a copy." To encourage her, he refused to cash her check explaining: "your check will serve as my book mark—so get that book done!"

The call to Chris's #1 customer was a success. Grace felt an instant connection to Princess Peach. Her dad started Emergency Plumbing in 1977 which was also the year Gigi was born. In 2008, Princess, along with her two brothers, Mario and Luigi, executed a succession plan. Their second-generation business was strong and growing.

On Saturday, July 31st, Grace envisioned how her first meeting, scheduled for 8:00 a.m. on Thursday, August 5th with Princess, would go. Suddenly, a pang of fear hit her along with an immediate need to hear Gigi's voice. Although a bit busy at work, Gigi answered Grace's call.

Sensitive to Gigi's time, Grace rapidly explained the reason for her call. "Gigi, I think I've found my next client and it feels like

I'm abandoning you," and tears uncontrollably streamed down Grace's face.

Sweetly, Gigi replied, "Auntie Grace, don't feel that way because as soon as the pandemic is over, you'll be back in Mississippi." Relieved, Grace thanked Gigi and disconnected.

Her edited manuscript was expected to arrive back on Friday, August 6, 2021; however, the editor delivered it two days early. Seven pages filled with editorial comments and critiques accompanied the manuscript.

At exactly 7:00 that evening, while on the phone with Moppsie, a second call came in from Mississippi. The cell number of a Goldgunz employee appeared and immediately Grace sensed there was trouble. She disconnected with Moppsie to take the call and instead of answering "hello," Grace instinctively asked, "what's wrong"?

A very shaken voice on the other end of the line answered, "Ms. Grace... Mr. Guy and Gigi's youngest son are gone. They perished in a plane crash."

Their time on earth had very unexpectedly run out.

Grace welcomed the calls she received from people needing to share their grief. Although it was a sleepless night, she prayed for a glimpse of future joy.

The next morning, August 5th, Grace met with Princess Peach as planned. The Princess welcomed Grace into a small conference room. Before she sat down, Grace said "this may seem a strange request; however, would you happen to have a box of Kleenex?" Princess obliged. As calmly and with as few details as possible, Grace explained what had happened the day before. She also shared her interesting words to Gigi that previous Saturday, ending the story with: "So, I'm pretty sure we are meant to be together."

Realizing how precious Princess' time was, Grace offered to return on Sunday, August 8th, to sample a solo assessment process. Princess accepted and gave Grace a hug instead of a handshake.

Next up was Princess Peach's assessment results reveal, which they tentatively scheduled for Thursday, August 12th, at 5:00 p.m. The time was tentative because Guy and his grandson's funeral arrangements had been delayed.

Gigi's faith in God and love for Jesus was illuminated during this unimaginably traumatic time. In trying to discern when she should go to Mississippi, Grace got this clarity from Gigi: "I'm going to need you when the outpouring evaporates. Until then, please help Princess."

Due to Gigi's assurance, when Grace learned the joint funerals were scheduled for August 12th, she viewed it as a blessing that she had Princess Peach's results to focus on.

Grace arrived to the plumbing business a little early in order to prepare. Princess walked into the small conference room right on time; however, she looked sad. Before Grace could ask, Princess said "now it's my turn to share what just happened with you. Today, we lost our number one plumber." She continued with a beautiful story about Neal who was the first plumber to join the company after she and her brothers bought the business from their dad. "In the beginning, we told him, we can't afford to pay you, yet he kept coming to work anyway." Then laughing through her sadness, she added "but we did pay him!"

In her heart, Grace believed God had put she and Princess together on that day, at that time, so they could lift each other up.

In the most perfect doses, Gigi, Princess and many others continued to ask Grace "how is the book coming along?" Not wanting to disappoint, Grace gave them any glimmer of hope she could, explaining she believed God was still guiding her.

In February 2022, Rick Robinhood left an uplifting voicemail for Grace. "I'm checking in to see where my copy of that book is." Grace could hear the smile in his voice. His last words were, "I'll call you back in a few days." After retrieving his message, Grace was going to call him right back; yet thought, *He said he'll call me back and he will.*

At the end of July 2022, realizing it had been almost a year since Guy's departure, Grace prayed then forced herself to open the editor's critique and start making the suggested changes. It was a day of good progress that was short lived.

Then, in December 2022, Grace went to Swooperwoman's house to enjoy time together and bake cookies. Near the end of the visit, Swooperwoman realized that she had forgotten to tell Grace that Rick had been ill and was possibly at the end of his life.

Early the next morning, Grace texted a former A+ Sports colleague who was also close to Rick to get more details on his condition. The text she got back read: "Rick passed away this morning." She was heartbroken and extremely regretful about not calling him back months before. She scolded herself, thinking, *how many times have you reminded people to not procrastinate because tomorrow may evaporate?*

On their social media page, Henry Repeating Arms, who manufacturers the Golden Boy series of rifles, had paid a beautiful and well-deserved tribute to Rick along with posting a picture of him with his Rolls-Royce. Looking at the post, she positively projected what she believed and shifted her mindset from day-dreading to daydreaming.

Grace pictured Rick, Gigi's boy, and Guy Goldgunz together in a glowing gold convertible, driving down a street made of gold. They were joyfully waving to Grace's beloved Poppsie, Nanny, both Georges, Remington, and Golden Boy as they paraded through Heaven.

As she was about to walk out the door, The Commander called her to make sure that she was aware of Rick's recent transformation. She couldn't believe she'd forgotten they knew each other.

Grace arrived at the funeral home early. The first thing she saw was Rick's Rolls-Royce parked under the funeral home canopy. She smiled. The first person she saw was Becky, one of her favorite A+ hires from years before. Seeing Becky triggered the time when she had yelled "Grace, did you know Grace was the name of my favorite heifer?" across the A+ Sport's salesfloor. That picture connected Grace to delightful times spent with Deed's Dairy Equipment.

Once inside, she gazed at an abundance of happy photos, proof that Rick knew how to enjoy life while loving God, his family, hunting, and many people.

Grace hadn't given any thought to who else might be there to celebrate his life. When Wildman and three of her former A+ Sports co-managers walked in; she felt joy. A female that had been on Rick's team sat next to Becky. She shared: "Rick called me after your meeting at the coffee shop. He was so excited about your book; he couldn't wait to tell me all about it."

Emotionally moved, Grace looked toward the front of the room where she could see Rick's mortal vessel resting, yet, she felt his spirit alive and well swirling the room. She heard his voice whispering, *you're right Grace, I'm right here and I'm still willing to help.*

There was a person, or two, in the room that Grace was very surprised to see. She guessed it was no longer a surprise to Rick as she imagined he now had a bird's-eye view of who and what he was leaving behind.

Grace gave the pastor an A+ in uplifting the audience. The pastor shared that he and Rick had connected over bird hunting. He admitted he was jealous that Rick had been given so many opportunities to hunt all over the world.

A young man who had worked with Rick gave a moving speech. Grace thought she heard him say "while on a horseback ride, Rick told me: 'son, you've got to ride your own horse.'" Grace took that as Rick's spirit validation to her because it agreed with Moppsie's continual wisdom about reaching Heaven.

After the young man finished, the pastor praised him, then noted, "You expressed some *fowl* words that I'm not allowed to say." The audience laughed.

The pastor joyfully asked for volunteers to say something about Rick; explaining that he knew it may be difficult to do, even perhaps awkward. There was silence.

"To help you, please understand that this silence is awkward for me too, so I'm going to give you a little more time to share a story about Rick." He added.

In her mind, Grace was raising her hand... yet, it wasn't going up. She was seated roughly three-quarters of the way to the back of the room.

The pastor stressed: "Time is running out. I know it takes courage, but this is your last chance to share a story about Rick before we leave."

Grace looked at Becky who was enthusiastically mouthing "Stand up." So, Grace stood up.

"Yes, thank you for volunteering!" she heard the pastor say.

She thought she would be able to speak clearly; however, as she opened her mouth, tears and a broken voice erupted. She fought the vision of the day she ran off the A+ Sports stage and out the door—toward the end of her marriage.

Unlike that day, she hadn't prepared a speech or considered this moment would happen. Like that day, she did the only thing she knew, she embraced her Holy spirit and spoke from her heart. That Holy-Spirit driven eulogy for Rick went something like this: "Perhaps you've heard of a little retailer called Cabela's. Years ago, their executives told me: 'Grace, to continue our relationship, you need to visit us in Sydney, Nebraska.' I invited Rick because he was well-known and highly respected, plus, I trusted him to have my back." At this, several people seated in front of her turned around which triggered her to turn around and hand gesture toward the men seated behind her.

"Now, I could have asked one of these three handsome men to go as they were my fellow managers." She continued as she looked directly into their eyes. "Or, I could have asked President Wildman to go. He was always happy to help me." Grace noticed her voice was sounding stronger and less shaken. She felt like Rick was beside her, cheering her on: "keep going!"

Joy had taken over and she quickly finished the rest of the highlights of the story including the last day she saw Rick when he told her: "Girl, you've got to get this book out, just go!"

Then, looking toward his quiet remains resting peacefully, her emotions hit again. Through sudden tears she expressed: "Rick I'm so sad to see you go, but so happy to have known you and where you've gone." Grace sat down.

The pastor thanked her and then asked for others to follow Grace's lead. Wildman stood. He said something to the effect of: "It's just like Grace to have the courage to go first. I can't let her be the only one to share. Rick only had one speed." The person next to Wildman added, "slow."

"That's right! He was slow and steady and our company's compass that always pointed North." Wildman continued.

The celebration ended and Grace couldn't wait to escape. She apologized to Becky, saying, "I'm sneaking out the side door, I've just got to go." But, when she got out into the hallway, she realized she wanted to say a proper good-bye to her former A+ Sports colleagues who were still there.

Awkwardly, she stood in the vestibule and waited.

A beautiful young lady walked toward Grace, extending her hand as she approached. "Thank you so much for your words. May I hug you?" said the young lady. Grace welcomed the embrace while being pleasantly stunned.

A second female came next showing similar sentiments.

Then a third... and the fourth; a more mature female who gushed with gratitude for what Grace had shared about Rick. Grace had no idea who those girls were or how they were connected to Rick and she didn't need to. In her book, they were angels, sent to deliver a message of hope, reassurance, and truth from those who had gone before her.

A perfect seven days later, which was Christmas Eve, Grace awoke to an amazing gift. A text, time stamped 5:04 a.m., from a young man named Nick whom she had met at Bob's office in 2016 while she was preparing to speak at the Shot Show. Grace found it interesting that right before they met, Nick had interviewed at A+ Sports. Wildman had given Nick the tour because they were connected through Hillsdale College. Nick's Mom had published a children's book and his dad loved guns. Their connections were abundant. Grace hadn't seen Nick since June 12, 2020, however, his text made perfect sense.

The text read:

> Grace, I was awoken in the night and felt the Lord ask me to pray for you. I saw a vision where your foot was stuck by a stone but angels were being sent on assignment to free your foot so you might move forward. Angelic assistance come now for Grace! Let every stumbling block and heavy weight be removed NOW by the Lord's angel armies! Spirit of delay be broken in the name of Jesus; we say it's time for the fullness of His goodness to be released!

> For He will command His angel concerning you to guard you in all your ways. On their hands they will bear you up lest you strike your foot against a stone. You will tread on the lion and the adder; the young lion

> and the serpent you will trample underfoot.
> Psalm 91:11-13 ESV

Grace knew she wouldn't be stuck much longer.

On February 26, 2023, Grace attended her home church. That day, the alter call was to those who felt alone or stuck in accomplishing God's plan for their life. That triggered Grace to go to the altar.

"If we can't find a woman to pray for you, are you comfortable with a man?" the prayer director asked. Grace nodded "of course" as she laughed.

Immediately, a man put his hand on her shoulder and began speaking to her. "Grace, God says He sees you and the work you are doing with your hands—keep going! God says He is your father and He is proud of you. I'm not sure if you have heard that a lot in your life, but God says to make sure you hear His Words, He loves you and He is proud of you. You are not a disappointment; you are His child and you are on the right path. Soon, you will have greater peace than ever before."

As time marches on and these final phrases are written, with God, Guns and A Girl, we hope you are smitten.

The author thought God clever when He gave her Grace to complete her endeavor.

Through tears from joy and loving laughter, this story ends happily ever after.

Takeaways: Refine

Did you ever have one of those electric racetracks? You use a controller to accelerate your little cars around a track until the parts wear out and it doesn't work anymore. At first, it's a challenge to use the controller in such a way that you keep the car on the track, but once you figure that part out, you realize that there's nothing more to do. You just race in an oval until you decide someone is a winner.

It's around that point that someone figures out that it's more fun to try to crash the cars. You go too fast around a curve so you spin out or fly off the track, or you try to derail your car in front of your brother's so his crashes, too.

Where am I going with this? The fun stuff isn't in finding a rut and staying there. It's in exploring the edges of the ruts and going off course. It's in experiencing greater speeds and learning what you can and can't do.

If you're obsessed with getting it right the first time or, frankly, getting it right ever, then you will find your growth plan frustrating. It simply may never be foolproof. But you can learn to have fun along the way and enjoy the ride.

As Grace refined a bulletproof plan for her life, she found many things to celebrate along the way:

- ☐ Abundance
- ☐ Her calling
- ☐ Saving the day
- ☐ Transformations
- ☐ Resources
- ☐ Heaven
- ☐ Life itself

Don't be afraid to create a plan that you eventually change completely. You're learning, and each new plan will get you closer to the life you want, because each new plan will teach you that life isn't about arriving but about who you will become along the way.

Chapter Forty-Six

With God It Never Ends!

"But he who endures to the end shall be saved."
—Matthew 24:13 (NKJV)

Life eternal, that's what it was all about for Grace!

Grace believes that if you truly want a better life, God will trigger transformation and Jesus is the key!

While she didn't have to go through a major conversion, it didn't mean her life was void of trials and tribulations. Those trials and tribulations made her stronger and explained why she held onto Jesus for one more day.

In the Name of Jesus, Grace commanded her enemies to flee.

With childlike Faith, inviting Jesus into her heart and believing the best was yet to come, Grace's dreams are coming true.

Grace wished the same for everyone and especially you!

About the Author

Gracie Rae Faith is the pen of Carla, a girl whose determination landed her at the top of the sales leader board, within the good-ole-boy firearms industry, before she was thirty. She graduated Summa Cum Laude in business management/organizational leadership while rising to an executive position on the corporate ladder. Along the way, her passion for behavioral science was ignited which led to her becoming a trusted agent of transformation.

After many years of successfully leading strategic development and growth initiatives, an unexpected separation triggered her to pursue and achieve her dreams of becoming an author, coach, educator, speaker, and founder of Clear Cut Strategies; a consultancy dedicated to replacing chaos with results.

When she's not working, she may be found teaching, volunteering, or spending quality time with God and the people she loves the most.

CLEAR CUT STRATEGIES
Replacing Chaos with Results

A Powerful Strategy.

FOCUS

- ORGANIZATION
- RELATIONSHIPS
- ENGAGEMENT
- COMMUNICATION

RESULTS

PEOPLE: Our benchmarks save you time and money. Together, we'll select, train, engage, and retain the right people.

PURPOSE: Our plan clarifies your vision, mission, core values, and succession to ignite team passion.

PROCESS: Our alignment process streamlines operational procedures for efficiency and structured growth.

PROFIT: Unknown return is *replaced* with clear measurements of your key metrics.

PERFORMANCE: Conflict and stress are *replaced* with clear organizational expectations.

PRODUCTIVITY: Barriers to growth are *replaced* with strategies for saving time and selecting the right technology.

clearcutstrategies.com

www.ingramcontent.com/pod-product-compliance
Lightning Source LLC
LaVergne TN
LVHW041744060526
838201LV00046B/904